CITIZEN 16 +
GCSE LAW AND YOU

CITIZEN 16 +
GCSE LAW AND YOU

Brenda Mothersole
Lecturer in Law in further education
Citizens Advice Bureau worker

MACMILLAN

© Brenda Mothersole 1986, 1991

All rights reserved. No reproduction, copy or transmission of this publication may be made without written permission.

No paragraph of this publication may be reproduced, copied or transmitted save with written permission or in accordance with the provisions of the Copyright, Designs and Patents Act 1988 or under the terms of any licence permitting limited copying issued by the Copyright Licensing Agency, 33–4 Alfred Place, London WC1E 7DP.

Any person who does any unauthorised act in relation to this publication may be liable to criminal prosecution and civil claims for damages.

First published 1986
Second GCSE edition 1991

Published by
MACMILLAN EDUCATION LTD
Houndmills, Basingstoke, Hampshire RG21 2XS
and London
Companies and representatives
throughout the world

Printed in Hong Kong

British Library Cataloguing in Publication Data
Mothersole, Brenda
Citizen 16+ : GCSE law and you. – 2nd GCSE ed.
1. Great Britain. Law
I. Title
344.2
ISBN 0–333–49490–3

To

Alan, Hugh, Alison and Deyo

Contents

List of Figures and Tables   ix
Preface   xi
Acknowledgements   xiii

1 Society and the Law   1
Introduction: why do we have law?; Defining the law; The making of law; Some general principles of law

2 Coming of Age   16
General knowledge quiz; Answers to the quiz; Exercises

3 Shopping: The Law of Buying and Selling   31
The law and the consumer; How the law operates; The trader and the law; A wise shopper's guide; Assignments and exercises

4 Going to Work   66
A contract and main terms and conditions of employment; Young trainees and health and safety at work; The role of trade unions; Exercises; Role play assignments; Suggested visits

5 No Job   108
A scenario: at the Citizens Advice Bureau; State benefits; Work experience schemes; Written and role play exercises

6 Somewhere to Live   127
Rented accommodation; Nowhere to live; Buying a home of your own; Exercises; Assignments

7 Family Law Quiz   155
Quiz; Answers and additional information; Exercises and assignments

8	**Citizenship and Civil Liberties** Citizenship; Civil liberties; Police powers and public order; Exercises and assignments; Suggested outings	174
9	**Crime and Punishment** Elements of a crime; Criminal liability; Problem-solving exercises on crimes; Specific crimes; General defences; Criminal punishments; Victims of crime; Exercises and assignments	212
10	**Ways of Seeking a Remedy** Out-of-court solutions; Legal and quasi-legal services; The courts; Legal personnel; Legal remedies I Seeking a solution out of court II Going to court: the courts; The civil action; The county court; The magistrates' court (civil); The High Court of Justice; Court of Appeal (Civil Division); The criminal courts and their procedures; The magistrates' court; The Crown Court; Court of Appeal (Criminal Division); The House of Lords; The Coroner's Court; Tribunals; The Courts of Europe; Exercises; Essays; Assignments	234

Glossary	*273*
Useful Addresses	*276*
Suggested Reading	*281*
Table of Cases	*284*
Table of Statutes	*285*
Index	*288*

List of Figures and Tables

Figures

1.1	An example of a Bill before it becomes an Act of Parliament	7
1.2	Acts of Parliament, other legislation and reports are published by the government through Her Majesty's Stationery Office	8
3.1	What kind of shopper are you?	31
3.2	The reverse side of a standard form contract – the 'small print'	53
3.3	Examples of the range of leaflets for consumers published by the Office of Fair Trading	61
4.1	Starting work	66
4.2	An extract from the Department of Employment leaflet *Written statement of main terms and conditions of employment*	70
4.3	An example of a self-certification form for claiming statutory sick pay from your employer	88
4.4	Health and safety at work – an extract from a leaflet for young workers, produced by the Health and Safety Executive	94
4.5	An example of an accident report form	104
4.6	Applying for an industrial tribunal	106
5.1	Looking for work	108
5.2	Seeking advice from the Citizens Advice Bureau	109
5.3	The National Insurance Numbercard	110
5.4	Useful leaflets for those leaving school, published yearly by the DSS	118
6.1	Leaving home	127
6.2	Home improvements – an Office of Fair Trading leaflet	141
6.3	A squat in south London	144
6.4	Buying a flat	147
7.1	A British family today	155
8.1	A passport for subjects of the European Community	174
8.2	The influence that citizens can have on law-making	179
8.3	The police meet the public	196

8.4	The detention clock	200
9.1	A view of Leicester prison	212
10.1	Seeking advice from local agencies	235
10.2	Two separate ways of training lawyers	243
10.3	The structure of the courts in England and Wales	247
10.4	A county court	249
10.5	The county court plan – (a) the main court (b) the arbitration proceedings	252
10.6	Steps to an action in the county court	253
10.7	Plan of a typical magistrates' court	257
10.8	The Crown Court trial	261
10.9	Steps in a criminal action	262
10.10	Plan of an industrial tribunal	268
10.11	Decisions made by the European Community can affect the law in the UK	269

Tables

4.1	Differences between unfair and wrongful dismissal	75
5.1	A guide to social security	120
5.2	Places where help can be obtained	123
6.1	Tenancies since the Housing Act 1988 came into force	135
7.1	The law of succession when a person dies intestate	172
9.1	Some traffic offences and their penalties	224
10.1	First steps to solving problems out of court	236
10.2	The Legal Aid Scheme	245

Preface

It is the intention of this revised edition of *Citizen 16+* to meet, in a lively and practical way, the innovatory learning requirements of the 'law in context' programmes of the various GCSE Examining Boards. The text is equally suitable for work-experience courses such as CPVE (Certificate in Pre-Vocational Education), TVEI (Technical and Vocational Education Initiative) and similar syllabuses taught in schools and colleges of further education. Students of 'A' level Law and students on distant learning programmes may also find the text a useful supplement to their studies. This text particularly provides for young people a general guide to the law as it affects them in their daily lives, and demonstrates some of the legal pitfalls which they are likely to encounter. Moreover, it aims to develop their communication and social skills in certain appropriate areas of the law.

Drawing on my combined experience as a law lecturer in further education and as a trained worker in a Citizens Advice Bureau, I have attempted to write a book which is a departure from the conventional law textbook to assist both students of most ability levels and teachers who are legally trained and untrained. I have presented the law as it might apply in real-life situations and, at the same time, have incorporated various learning approaches, skills and techniques. The chapters relating to the consumer, the workplace, housing and civil liberties, are so arranged that they take the natural sequence of events – concentrating initially on the problems themselves, presented as case-study cameos, followed by a question-and-answer analysis of relevant legal issues and then by a straight explanation of the law and legal principles. Two other chapters take the form of a quiz accompanied by informative answers, another chapter the form of a CAB interview, and the chapter on crime and punishment is designed to incorporate the technique of problem-solving. The final chapter focuses on ways of seeking an appropriate remedy, first, without recourse to the courts and then through the civil and criminal court systems. Each chapter includes a set of appropriate exercises and assignments for the student to work through and suggestions in respect of GCSE coursework, available leaflet material, guest speakers and class visits.

I wish to acknowledge the help and advice of others: Dave Wadsworth and Margaret Greaves, for their comments on parts of the book; to those law lecturers I have met at various conferences who have offered constructive comments on the first edition of *Citizen 16+*; to my husband, Geoffrey, for patiently correcting my typing errors, and to the National Association of Citizens Advice Bureaux for making the writing of the interviews possible. To the best of my ability and belief the law stated here is correct up to April 1990. Names mentioned in the case-studies are fictitious and resemblance to any person or private organisation is purely coincidental.

Brenda Mothersole

Acknowledgements

The author and publishers wish to thank the following who have kindly given permission for the use of copyright material: Consumers' Association for material from the August 1988 issue of *Which*; London East Anglian Group for a question from a past examination paper; The Controller of Her Majesty's Stationery Office for leaflets, *Mind How You Go, Leaving School, Going to College or University, A Shoppers Guide to the Furniture Safety Labels,* European Community Passport, National Insurance Number Card, Form 1T1 and Leaflet PL 700, Crown copyright.

The Lord Chancellor's Department for the County Court Form.

The Office of Fair Trading for the montage of various OFT leaflets.

The author and publishers wish to thank the following for the use of photographs: Gina Glove, The Photo Co-op p. 155; Sally Lancaster, The Photo Co-op p. 196; Abel Lagos, The Photo Co-op p. 212.

Every effort has been made to trace all the copyright holders but if any have been inadvertently overlooked the publishers will be pleased to make the necessary arrangement at the first opportunity.

1 Society and the Law

Introduction: why do we have law?

We often declare that Britain is 'a free country' and that we, its citizens, are 'free to do as we like'. Yet everyone of us is governed by an enormous number of rules and laws in the course of our daily lives. Anyone who joins a sports club or becomes a student at the local college is expected to comply with the rules and regulations of that organisation. Rules of this kind are *internal rules* and rarely apply to anyone who is not connected with the organisation. As we travel to the club, the college or our place of work, we are governed by a much wider set of rules which apply to the public at large. Rules of this kind are referred to as *'law'*. The law requires certain conduct from us: to stop at a red traffic light; to attend school up to the age of 16; to pay the correct fare on the bus; to pay our rent on time; and not to assault a stranger. Whenever we go shopping, go to work, draw money out of the bank, collect our social security benefit, engage in a business or drive a car, the law lays down a set of guidelines and restrictions and expects everyone to comply with them. So how can we say we are 'free' when we readily accept these rules which limit our freedom? In other words, why do societies have law?

Assignment 1.1

Either working as a group or on your own, carefully consider the following situation. On a spare sheet of paper, answer the questions given below:

Imagine that you and the other members of your class or group are on a spacecraft trip and that the craft gets into difficulties. It loses all contact with earth and is forced to crash on a hitherto unknown planet. There is no hope of return. On the planet, however, you find many natural resources such as spring water and a variety of plant and animal life.

 (i) List in order the priorities of the group.
 (ii) What action do you think you would take to bring about these priorities?
 (iii) What further strategies, if any, do you think would be necessary?

After deciding your answers, compare them with the specimen answer on the next page.

Specimen answer to Assignment 1.1

(i)
| food and water; shelter; protection from (i) outside harm, and (ii) deviant members within the group. |

Basic needs for human survival

(ii)
| organise the members of the group, according to their skills and experience; provide everyone with food; allot them a piece of land on which to build a shelter, and take measures to protect and care for the people in the group. Some interchange of skills, bartering and 'trading' of materials may result. |

Effective organisation and control in response to basic needs.

(iii)
| the appointment of a leader and also some assistants to govern and co-ordinate the activities of organisation, and to decide what should be done. This would make it necessary to lay down certain rules and guidelines. |

A government to make decisions and to make and administer laws. Headed by a leader.

This simple exercise serves to illustrate the basic survival structure of all societies, be they primitive tribes, or advanced civilisations such as our own. The structure may look like this:

A tribal society	**Great Britain**
Chief (or Head) of the tribe	Monarch (Nominal Head) Prime Minister
↑	↑
Elders (decision-makers; administrators; arbitrators)	Houses of Parliament Cabinet, Lords and Commons, Judiciary
↓	↓
Members of the tribe	Citizens of the country

Society and the Law

So why do societies have rules or law and leaders? The answer is, if a group or society is to survive and to live and work harmoniously together, some form of social order and control is necessary. The more advanced the civilisation is and the greater its population, the more numerous and more complex will its rules of law and government become.

Societies will vary considerably in the type of government and leader they have, and this will determine the system of law they adopt.

A society where the leader and the government are elected and the power given to the people, in so far as they can change the government or influence what it does, is a **Democracy**. Where there is no freely elected government and the leader rules with absolute authority, this is a **Dictatorship**. But whatever the system is, both kinds of society create laws, enforce them and have a system of penalties for those who do not comply with them. A society without government and without rules is unlikely to survive, and can be reduced to a state of anarchy. All governed states must operate a **rule of law** which ideally recognises equal justice for all and operates a court system which gives a fair trial to alleged offenders and separates its judiciary from its government.

Group discussion

1. What would our imaginary planet society be like without any attempt to organise the people and their behaviour?
   Reference to William Golding's novel *Lord of the Flies* could be made at this point.
2. What kind of responsibilities do you think people should have towards each other?
3. What kind of rules would you make to bring these responsibilities about?
4. Consider other kinds of 'rules' the society would observe such as moral, religious, scientific and social rules.

Exercise

After the discussion try to define what we mean by **Law**. Compare your definition with the one given in the next section.

Defining the law

When defining what we mean by 'law', it is helpful first to identify the **aims** of law and then to see how these aims are applied:

The aims

- To protect the people from their enemies.
- To protect individuals from evil and criminal elements in society.
- To bring offenders to trial and punish them, and deter others.
- To settle disputes and grievances between individual citizens.
- To bring about an orderly and peaceful society so that everyone may live, work and play without undue interference.
- To take the responsibility for providing the basic needs of our present day society, such as food, health and medicine, housing, education, and social and welfare services.
- To control the resources and their distribution within and outside the country.

How the aims of law are applied

- By imposition of a set of rules which govern behaviour and protect the people.
- By enforcing the rules by sanctions (i.e. punishments and remedies).
- By the general consent of the people.

Definition of the law

Law is a set of rules governing human behaviour, which are recognised, set down, and applied by the state in the administration of justice.

Because the rules and the situations in which they are applied in a complex civilisation are many and varied, the law is classified into definable areas (see diagram on facing page).

The making of law

Before we proceed further, it is necessary to know how the laws that govern us are made. The law in England and Wales has developed in two distinct ways – first, by the common law system of judicial precedent, sometimes referred to as 'judge-made law', and second, by the laws made by Parliament.

Society and the Law

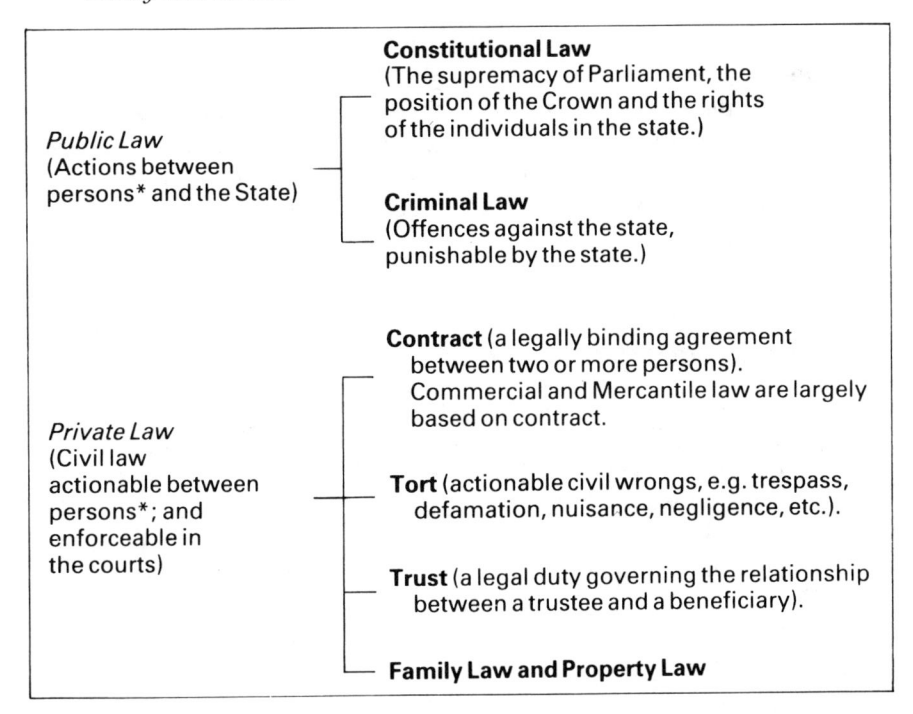

```
Public Law                  ┌─ Constitutional Law
(Actions between            │  (The supremacy of Parliament, the
persons* and the State) ────┤  position of the Crown and the rights
                            │  of the individuals in the state.)
                            │
                            └─ Criminal Law
                               (Offences against the state,
                               punishable by the state.)


                            ┌─ Contract (a legally binding agreement
                            │    between two or more persons).
                            │    Commercial and Mercantile law are largely
                            │    based on contract.
Private Law                 │
(Civil law                  ├─ Tort (actionable civil wrongs, e.g. trespass,
actionable between          │    defamation, nuisance, negligence, etc.).
persons*; and           ────┤
enforceable in              │
the courts)                 ├─ Trust (a legal duty governing the relationship
                            │    between a trustee and a beneficiary).
                            │
                            └─ Family Law and Property Law
```

A classification of the law of England and Wales

> * 'persons' – this word is used to describe not only individual citizens but also individual businesses, corporations, management committees, and any other collective organisations which in law are referred to as 'artificial' or 'juristic' persons.
>
> In our relations with Europe we observe *Community Law*, which will be dealt with in detail in Chapter 10, under 'The Courts of Europe'.

Common law system of judicial precedent

This system of law-making was established in the time of the Norman Conquest of 1066. Before William the Conqueror arrived the laws and courts varied from area to area, and the Norman kings, relying on many of the former laws and customs, set about making a centralised system of government and one uniform set of laws. From this developed our present-day system of **judicial precedent** (or **case-law**), in which judges refer to decisions made in previous court cases in which the facts are similar to the case they have before them. Once the law has been established in terms of certain decided cases, we say that a *binding precedent* has been created and this must be followed by the courts in later cases. The idea is to create a historical uniformity and certainty of justice, but at the same time to create a law which is flexible enough to meet changing social and moral conditions.

Parliamentary-made law

This covers both Acts of Parliament and delegated legislation.
- *Acts of Parliament* have to meet the approval of both the House of Commons and the House of Lords, and the proposed Act – referred to as a 'Bill' before it receives the Queen's Consent – has to go through three readings in which it can be discussed and amended in both Houses. The Stages of the reading of a Bill in the House of Commons are as follows:

1. **First Reading**   This is an informal introduction of the Bill.

2. **Second Reading**   Members of the House debate the general principles of the bill to decide whether it should proceed for further detailed consideration.

This stage is followed by a detailed examination of all the clauses in the Bill usually by a 'standing' or 'select' committee. The committees consist of members of the House appointed on the basis of the political parties' numerical strength. Sometimes all the MPs undertake the task as a Committee of the Whole House. At this stage amendments can be moved (i.e. put forward for adoption or rejection).

The Report Stage follows the Committee stage. This is when the House considers the amended Bill. More amendments may be added.

3. **Third Reading**   At this stage the amended Bill is debated in order to approve it. If it is approved it is sent to the House of Lords to make recommendations and amendments which the Commons or the Government may accept, reject or negotiate.

The House of Lords has no powers to overthrow a Bill. The idea is that Parliament (as elected by the people of the land) is the supreme law-maker, and the statute (Act of Parliament) is superior over all other sources of law. This is referred to as the 'Sovereignty of Parliament'. Judges are then required to interpret the statutes and further case-law evolves from this. Today decisions from the

Auctions (Bidding Agreements) Act 1927 (Amendment) Bill

EXPLANATORY MEMORANDUM

Clause 1(1) enables the mischief aimed at by the Auctions (Bidding Agreements) Act 1927 to be prosecuted as a conspiracy as an alternative to the summary offence provided for in that Act.

Clause 1(2) is designed for the removal of doubt and to ensure that evidence normally admissible in conspiracy may be adduced in proof of such a charge.

Clause 2 is designed to clarify the fact that prosecution and conviction are not necessary to render fraudulent a sale resulting from an agreement made illegal by this Bill.

Clause 3 requires a copy of this Bill as enacted to be exhibited, additional to the copy of the Auctions (Bidding Agreements) Act 1927 required to be displayed thereunder.

[Bill 35]   44/3

Figure 1.1   An example of a Bill before it becomes an Act of Parliament

European Court of Justice can influence our parliamentary law-making.

- *Delegated legislation* Parliament does not have enough time to make all the necessary law; it therefore gives ministers, government departments and other bodies such as local authorities the power to make laws, rules and regulations which are binding on the courts. Generally Parliament lays down the framework of the law and the authorities with delegated powers fill in the gaps. However, these authorities must work within the powers given to them, it is unlawful to go beyond the delegated powers. Statutes regulating Road Traffic, Health and Safety at Work and Social Security Benefit laws are some examples of delegated legislation. Other forms of delegated legislation are statutory instruments made by Ministers in Government departments and byelaws made by local authorities.

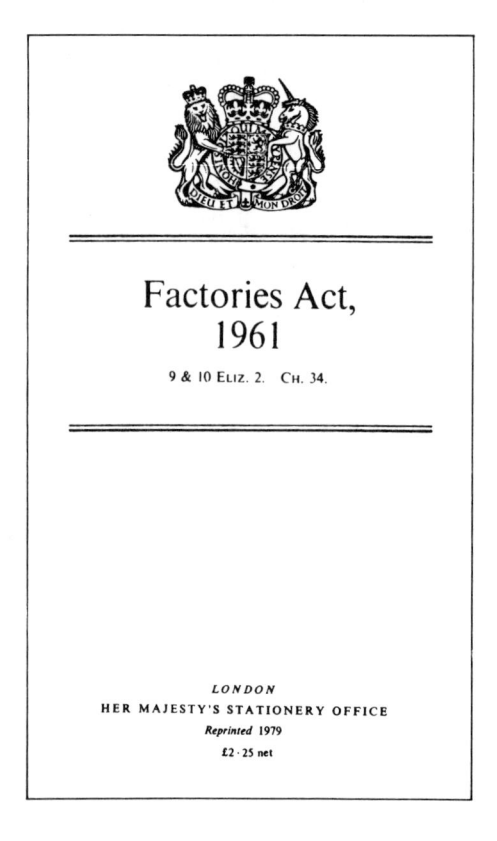

Figure 1.2 Acts of Parliament, other legislation and reports are published by the government through Her Majesty's Stationery Office

Law in a democratic society will only work effectively when it is generally accepted and respected by the people. The law must coincide with the people's idea of justice. For example, if Parliament introduced a law decreeing that 'all men and women should live apart on Sundays' no one would be likely to obey it. Such a law would be regarded as silly, undesirable and impractical to carry out. On the other hand, a law saying 'all users of the highway should drive on the left' makes sense. We can see the rationale behind a law which aims to prevent many fatal accidents on our roads, and most of us willingly accept this restriction of our individual liberty in the greater interest of making society a safer place. In many respects we accept legal restrictions on our individual freedoms, but in return we expect certain legal safeguards of our individual rights or privileges. Also, in Britain, we assume a number of 'human rights' such as the freedom from race and sex discrimination.

Some general principles of law

Below is an outline of certain basic principles of law, many of which will be contained in case studies in subsequent chapters:

Contracts

A contract is a legal agreement which binds two or more parties to certain obligations which become enforceable in the courts. There are two classes of contract:

1. *Specialty contracts, or contracts made by deed.* All such contracts, e.g. a house conveyance deed, are said to be 'under seal' – a thin red seal is attached to the document – and must be 'signed, sealed and delivered'.
2. *Simple contracts.* Most contracts fall into this category, and they may be expressed verbally, in writing or by the conduct of the parties.

Four essential elements must exist:
- a valid and firm offer by one party to another;
- a valid and firm acceptance by the other party, or parties;
- valuable consideration – where one party gives a promise in exchange for a promise, i.e. money for some goods or a service;
- an intention to create legal relations, i.e. a business rather than a social or domestic agreement.

The capacity to form a contract must also exist:
- **minors** (people under 18) have limited capacity (see pp. 34, 82);

- **persons suffering from a mental disorder**, or **drunkards**, who could not understand the contract at the time of forming it and the other party knew this, have no capacity.
- **corporations** – these are referred to as 'artificial persons' for the purpose of court action. They may be:
  (a) a body incorporated by Royal Charter (e.g. Royal Society for the Protection of Animals);
  (b) a body formed by a special Act of Parliament (e.g. electricity, gas or water boards); or
  (c) companies registered under the Companies Act 1985.

The capacity of Corporations is defined in terms of certain powers and actions given to them under the Royal Charter, by Statute, or in the memoranda of registered companies.

Certain matters affect the validity of a contract.

- **A misrepresentation** This is a false statement of fact made by one party which attracts another person to enter into a contract with him or her. The contract may be set aside (i.e. voidable) by the wronged person. A misrepresentation may be fraudulent, negligent or innocent. (See Case 4, Chapter 3.)
- **A mistake** Normally, a mistake in a contract does not affect its validity, especially when the mistake can be corrected. The courts may recognise that where there is a mistake of the existence, or identity, of the subject matter, then the contract is invalid (i.e. void). Where there is a mistake over the identity of one of the parties, the law only makes the contract void when the identity is fundamental to the formation of the contract. The general rule is: you contract with the person in front of you even if he happens to be a con-man.
- **Duress and undue influence** The law requires that all parties to a contract enter into the agreement willingly. **Duress** is the act of one party of actual or threatened violence to, or restraint of, the other party. The duress may also be economic pressure. **Undue influence** is where one party, such as a close relative, solicitor, bank manager or someone in a position of trust, takes unfair advantage of the other party by means of persuasive pressure.
- **Illegal contracts and contracts against public policy** The courts will not recognise: contracts which agree to criminal acts, sexual immorality, and which force people to marry against their will; contracts which threaten national security and are prejudicial to good foreign relations; and contracts which Parliament has made unlawful, such as cheating the Inland Revenue, defeating the bankruptcy laws, and exercising trade restrictive practices which prevent fair competition and are not in the public interest.

Sometimes terms of a contract may be seen to be unfair or unreasonable and the court may decide that a party may not be bound by such terms. This is explained more fully under the **Unfair Contract Terms Act 1977** (see Chapter 3).

A contract can be terminated by:
- agreement between the contracting parties;
- a breach by one party leaving the other free of his obligations and able to sue the defaulting party for compensation or some other remedy; it is possible to receive compensation for the partial performance of a contract.
- by frustration – where something prevents the continuing performance of the contract which is outside the control of the contracting parties, e.g. a war or disaster.

Torts

A tort is a civil wrong done by one party to another. There are various torts such as trespass, defamation (i.e. libel and slander), negligence and nuisance. Each tort has developed its own set of principles and defences which either permit or do not permit the injured party to sue the other, the *tortfeasor* or *tortfeasors*, for compensation. Sometimes an injunction or court order is a more appropriate remedy.

The law on trespass Trespass is probably the oldest form of tortious liability, dating back to the times when civil and criminal law had not been recognised as separate. **Trespass to land** has always been a civil wrong, or tort, but some forms of trespass are a criminal offence under the Public Order Act 1986. The tort of trespass to land is committed by one who either intentionally or negligently enters the land of another who is in possession of the land. Trespass must be a direct action so it also includes someone who comes on to the land lawfully but refuses to go when required by the occupier to do so, or when someone dumps rubbish on another's land. 'Land' includes buildings, rooms in the buildings, plants, vegetables, and anything attached to the land. It also extends to things under the land such as a cave, a hole or a mine, and to the air space above the land – no action can lie in respect of civil aviation where the plane is flying over a property on its normal scheduled flight but it can lie in respect of an aircraft which has an advertising banner attached to its tail or to a crane which swings over a neighbouring property.

The Public Order Act 1986 makes it a criminal offence for two or more persons to enter land as trespassers in certain circumstances (see under *Freedom of Movement* Chapter 8).
Child trespassers The normal rules of trespass apply, but an extra duty of care is applied to young children in circumstances where they

are likely to come on to the land, either lawfully or as trespassers. An occupier of premises must be prepared for the fact that children are less careful than adults and that they cannot be expected to observe warning signs as an adult can. The occupier must provide adequate fencing to keep them away from hidden dangers, such as poisonous berries, fires and electric railway lines (*British Railways Board v. Herrington (1972)* and the Occupiers Liability Act 1984).

Defences The person in possession of the land can either ask the trespasser to leave, use reasonable force to eject him from the property, or seek a court injunction to get him to leave. If a trespasser damages the property this could be a criminal offence.

- **Trespass to goods** (chattels) is the intentional interference to goods in the possession of another – owner, agent, or bailee, such as shifting them to another place, selling or destroying them. Under common law rules the wronged person may regain his or her goods with the minimum of necessary force, and may peacefully enter upon the land of the person who took them. The **Torts (Interference with Goods) Act 1977** enables anyone whose goods have been the subject of any 'wrongful interference' to claim back the goods and also any compensation for damage to the goods. Alternatively the defendant may entirely recompense the owner with a sum for the value of the goods if they are not recoverable. However, if the defendant has improved the value of the goods while they have been in his or her possession, then he or she may have the value of the improvement taken into account. Trespass to goods becomes a crime when the intention to deprive another of his or her goods becomes both permanent and dishonest.

- **Trespass to the person** takes the form of assault, battery or false imprisonment:
  Assault is an act which causes another person to apprehend immediate and unlawful personal violence. 'Mere words' are not enough. The behaviour must be *menacing* and need not physically harm the other person.
  Battery is applying force of hostile intent, however slight, to another against his or her will: e.g. punching someone in the eye, throwing water over him or her, spitting at him or her, removing chair from under him or her, engaging in excessively rough horse-play.
  False imprisonment – the infliction of bodily restraint of another without lawful justification. The mere holding of an arm by the police is sufficient, and threat of imprisonment is enough.

Neither is it necessary for the person to know that he or she is being imprisoned. There can be no false imprisonment where it is possible to move away from the situation.

The wronged person may reasonably defend him/herself, other people or his/her property. Judges and the police must not unlawfully detain or physically hold a person. Reasonable punishment of children is permitted and a surgeon can operate on a person with that person's consent. An innocent accident is unlikely to be construed as a tort.

- **Nuisance** Nuisances are of three kinds: public, private (see p. 152) and duties created by statute, such as the Public Health Act and statutes which control pollution.
- **Rylands v. Fletcher** is a tort created in the case of *Rylands v. Fletcher* (1868) for a unique situation where an occupier brings on to his land and collects and keeps there something 'unnatural' to the use of the land, e.g. an artificial reservoir of water, tropical snakes, oil or similar substances. The tort only arises where the unnatural thing escapes into neighbouring land and causes damage there. It is a tort of **strict liability** (i.e. it is not necessary to prove blame to bring an action). The tort does not apply to 'Acts of God' such as excessive flooding after a very heavy storm, or if the escape was caused by someone other than the occupier of the land.
- **Defamation** (libel and slander) is the publication of a statement which tends to lower a person in the estimation of right thinking members of society. The defendant must show that the statement was false and was published to a third person. (For further details and Defences, see Chapter 8.)

Negligence   Negligence is probably the most commonly used tort, and is given detailed coverage in Chapters 3 and 4. In general terms, the person who sues, the plaintiff, must show that the other party was to blame for some injury or damage caused to him or her, i.e. that a duty of care was owed to him or her, that there was a breach of that duty by the defendant and that the harm or injury suffered was the result of the breach. For example, a motorist owes a duty of care not to injure other road-users. If he or she breaches that duty by carelessly knocking down a pedestrian and injuring him or her, then the pedestrian could sue the motorist for compensation for his/her injuries in negligence. There must always be a foreseeable link between harm that was caused and the cause of the wrong, i.e. the damage must not be *too remote* from the original wrong.

General defences in tort

A person sued in tort may wish to deny the action taken against him or her by raising a defence. There are two kinds of defence to an action in tort, *specific defences*, which apply to one particular tort – these have been mentioned under the different torts above – and *general defences*, which may apply to most torts:

- **Volenti non fit injuria (volens) or consent**
  A tort cannot be upheld where the person who has suffered a wrong, expressly or implicitly, either agrees to some intentional act of harm done to him or her such as when a dentist pulls out his/her tooth or a surgeon removes his/her appendix, or agrees to run the risk of accidental harm such as participating in a rough sport or being a spectator at a dangerous sporting occasion such as a car race. In order to show a defence of *volens* a defendant must show not only that s/he knew of the risk but that s/he freely consented to run the risk. In a case where a quarryman knew a dangerous crane to swing stones was being used above where he was working was injured, the House of Lords held that he did not consent to the injury done to him because he was bound by his obligation to work; it was the employer who was to blame for not doing anything to make the crane safe. In rescue cases, where a person may risk life and limb to save another person, the general rule is that where the plaintiff can show he or she acted out of a sense of social or moral duty then s/he did not consent to run the risk.
- **Mistake** Generally a mistake of either law or fact does not provide a defence. Exceptions to the general rule are: in malicious prosecution, where someone has commenced the prosecution of a person in the mistaken belief that he or she was guilty; in false imprisonment, where a policeman mistakenly believes on reasonable grounds that he is lawfully entitled to arrest a person without a warrant, and, under the **Defamation Act 1952,** a publisher who did not intend to make a false statement against a certain person may make an offer to publish a suitable correction and an apology of amends.
- **Inevitable accident** Some harm to another may occur without a negligent act and which could not ordinarily have been prevented, such as where a pellet from a sportsman's shotgun bounced off a tree and hit an onlooker (*Stanley v. Powell (1891)*).
- **Act of God** This is where some unexpected natural force or circumstance outside human intervention or prevention, such as flooding or a hurricane, causes damage.

- **Statutory authority** An Act of Parliament may authorise an alleged wrong, such as running a railway or a motorway through a plaintiff's land, causing a nuisance.

Crime

Crimes are unlawful acts against the state, resulting in the accused person being put on trial to establish his/her guilt or innocence. The accused is presumed innocent until guilt beyond all reasonable doubt is proven. Then, s/he will be punished by the state according to the seriousness of the crime. The general principles and defences to a crime are dealt with in Chapter 9 (*Crime and Punishment*).

Civil liberties

In English law there is no written constitution or Bill of Human Rights, yet the law of the land still upholds certain rights to individual freedoms – of expression, movement, association and assembly. See Chapter 8 (Citizenship and Civil Liberties).

Throughout this book the emphasis is on the part that law plays in the lives of young adults as they begin to pay their way, to shop, to work, to find somewhere to live and generally to take on their full role as citizens. Also, the question of crime and punishment is explained and finally, in Chapter 10, the various ways of seeking a remedy, both in and out of the civil and criminal courts sytems, are described.

2 Coming of Age

In this chapter we are concentrating on the general legal rights and obligations, or liberties and limitations, of young people. The **Family Law Reform Act 1969** lowered the age of majority from 21 to 18 and it is said that at 18 'we come of age'. This is the age when the adolescent assumes many of the full responsibilities of adult citizenship. However, not all rights and responsibilities are conferred on the individual at the crucial age of 18 – some take effect at 16 and even earlier, while a few do not take effect until 21 is reached. Some of your rights you will already know; for example, you know that you are entitled to free compulsory education until you are 16 and that you can't take a car out on the road until you are 17. But what else do you know about your legal rights and responsibilities? Try the quiz below and test your knowledge.

General knowledge quiz

Grouped under specific headings below is a list of many of the rights and responsibilities which affect children and young people living in England and Wales. Either test yourself or organise a classroom quiz team game. The correct answers, with additional items of useful information can be found on pp. 18–30.

Money and property

At which age can you:
1. Withdraw money from a National Savings Bank?
2. Hold a Giro account?
3. Apply for social security benefits?
4. Apply for a mortgage and be a full legal owner of a house and land?
5. Be housed by the local council?
6. Be a tenant of private rented accommodation?

Personal

7. Choose your own doctor?
8. Agree to, or withhold consent to, a medical operation without your parent's consent?
9. Be convicted of a sexual or unnatural offence (males)?

Coming of Age

10. Consent to having sexual intercourse (females)?
11. Leave home?
12. Change your name?
13. Apply for a passport on your own responsibility?

At work

14. Be employed for a few hours a week?
15. Work full-time?
16. Join a trade union?
17. Qualify for a redundancy payment?

Shopping

18. Buy cigarettes or tobacco?
19. Buy alcoholic drinks at a bar?
20. Buy fireworks?
21. Be sold or hired a crossbow?
22. Buy a pet animal?
23. Enter into a hire purchase agreement?

Licences and restrictions

24. Hold a licence to drive certain tractors and ride a motor-cycle?
25. Hold a licence to drive a lorry or a bus?
26. Hold a private air pilot's licence?
27. Hold a firearm certificate?
28. Hold a licence to sell intoxicating liquor?
29. Enter a betting shop?

At the courts

30. Sit on a jury?
31. Be a witness in court?
32. Sue and be sued in the civil courts?
33. Quality for legal aid?
34. Be capable of a criminal offence?
35. Be held fully responsible for a crime?
36. Be the subject of a probation order?

Civic rights

37. Vote?
38. Be a candidate in a parliamentary election?
39. Join the police force?
40. Join the armed forces without parental consent?

Now check your answers.

Answers to the quiz

Question No.	Correct age	Additional information

Money and property

		Savings
1	7	It is possible to withdraw money from a National Savings Bank and a Trustee Savings Bank account at the age of 7. Building Societies generally do not stipulate an age: their criterion is that the child must be able to sign his or her name.
2	15	Giro accounts at Post Offices, which are equivalent to current accounts with banks, can be held by anyone of 15 or over, but s/he has to have a guarantor. Anyone can have an account with a bank or building society or hold Premium Bonds in their name from birth where a parent, guardian or friend has given it on their behalf. Young people under 18 can draw on a deposit account at the discretion of their parents and the bank manager, though, strictly speaking, a cheque signed by someone under 18 is not enforceable.
		Benefits
3	18	Social security benefits are available to anyone over the age of 18 who is not working full-time and who does not have enough money to live on. There are a few exceptional cases who may claim at 16. (More on this in Chapter 5.)
		Housing
4	18	The purchase of a house or land requires the formation of a contract referred to in law as a 'deed of conveyance', and minors cannot generally be sued if they breach their obligations under a contract. The law takes the view that anyone under 18 is unlikely to have sufficient money to meet large

Coming of Age

Question No.	Correct age	Additional information

payments and therefore is a 'liability risk'. For the same reason a minor cannot apply for a mortgage because there is very little the organisation lending the money could do if the minor refuses to pay the instalments. An adult, however, may act as a trustee or guarantor if a young person wants to buy, sell or mortgage a house.

Few people over 18 have the means to purchase a house or flat outright, and have to borrow the money. Between them, the building societies, banks, insurance companies and, in some cases, local councils, offer a wide variety of mortgage loan schemes for the purchase of property. It is always wise to shop around to see what kind of terms are on offer and to seek expert advice. Most loan organisations will lend money only on the basis of the applicant being able to afford the monthly repayments. Some schemes, designed for first time buyers, may forgo the initial deposit of 10 per cent of the purchase price.

Local council housing

5 — 16 or 18 — Children have the right to live in the parental home until they are 18. Some local authorities have a policy for housing anyone between the ages of 16 and 18. Some places put young people on the waiting list at 16, in other places, the person has to be 18, or even 21. To be housed by the council, there is also a residential qualification requirement: most councils will only accept applicants who have lived in the area for a stipulated number of years – the number varies from council to council. However, there is an acute shortage of houses, and it is unlikely that young people will be housed within the first few years of being on the list. The only way to find out is to contact your local Housing Department.

Question No.	Correct age	Additional information
6	16	**Rented accommodation** Bedsits, flats and houses from a landlord are generally hard to find and they can often be shabby and sometimes in a poor state of repair. Such accommodation can be expensive. Also there are often 'extras' such as rates, heating and electricity to pay for. (See Chapter 6 for more on housing.)

Personal

7	16	**Medical care** At 16 young people can choose their own doctor and dentist. They can consent to, or withold consent for, any medical, surgical or dental care.
8	16	In case of an operation some hospitals will only operate on a person between 16 and 18 with the consent of the parent or guardian of that person. All operations performed in hospitals require a signature of consent, either of the patient of 16 or over or of the next-of-kin. A 16-year-old can enter a mental hospital as a voluntary patient and can also appeal to a Mental Health Tribunal to be discharged. No one under 18 is allowed to give away a body organ or tissue for transplants, nor donate blood without his or her parent's consent. However, parental permission is not necessary for contraceptive advice from the age of 16.
9	14	**Sex** Boys under 14 cannot be found guilty of rape, or of assault with intent to rape, but they can be found guilty of common assault against a girl. Males cannot engage in homosexual acts until they are 21 and then the act can legally be conducted only between consenting adults in a private place. Persistently importuning in a public place is illegal.

Question No.	Correct age	Additional information
10	16	A girl may consent to intercourse at 16. It is an offence for a man to have intercourse with a girl under 16 unless he can show he believed the girl to be over 16.
11	16	**Leaving home** Children have the right to live in the parental home until they are 18, but at 16, young people can leave home with their parent's permission. Within their means parents are under an obligation to feed, clothe and provide properly for their children up to 18. They must also see that they receive compulsory education, are not neglected by starvation or improper punishment, and receive proper medical care and attention when necessary. When parents fail to do what is 'reasonable', then the children can be taken into care by the Social Services Department of the local authority. If a child in its mid- or late teens wants to leave home, the courts will rarely intervene to stop the child, provided s/he has reached what the courts decide as 'the age of discretion' (approximately 14 for boys and 16 for girls). Where the child is thought to be in some kind of moral danger, then the child may be taken into 'care and protection', but generally speaking, the child who has reached the age of discretion, has found a job and is leading a steady life is unlikely to be troubled by the law.
12	18	**Change of name** You may wish to change your name either because you dislike it or for some other personal reason. At 18 you may change your SURNAME but not your forename or Christian name. The change of a forename is only possible on adoption or within a year of birth. The change of a surname may be done in three different ways.

Question No.	Correct age	Additional information
		(a) *By making your new name as widely known as possible* to anyone who is likely to use it, e.g. the bank, Inland Revenue, insurance companies, doctor, friends and acquaintances. One effective way is to put an announcement in your local newspaper and then keep a copy as a record of the change. Sometimes a note signed by a respected member of the community such as a solicitor, a JP, a doctor or clergyman may suffice. The advertisement and the note would have to confirm the change from the old name to the new. But these methods and a common usage of the new name may not always satisfy the bank and may present difficulties when you apply for a passport. So you may be advised to try one of the two more official methods of formalising a change.

(b) *By statutory declaration.* This is an official way of formalising a change of name and one that is generally acceptable for most purposes. You would have to go to a solicitor and make a sworn statement. The solicitor will charge a modest fee for preparing it.

(c) *By deed poll.* This is the most formal and reliable method. You would have to go to a solicitor who will draw up a deed which you will be required to sign in your old and new names in front of a witness. The deed is then stamped by the Inland Revenue and a duty stamp fee is paid. This service will cost approximately double that for a statutory declaration.

A married woman can use either her maiden or married name.

Forenames or Christian names cannot be changed legally, neither can your name on your birth certificate be changed. This means that any documentary evidence of a |

Question No.	Correct age	Additional information
		change of name should be put with your birth certificate. Be prepared to produce both for evidence of your identity.
13	18	**Passports** Until you are 18 you will need written consent of a parent or guardian when making an application for a passport. All young people can be included on a parent's passport until they are 16 except when they have applied for their own passport. Children under 5 will not normally be issued with a passport. British Visitor's Passports, which are available from post offices and are only valid for one year, can be obtained for children over 8. Passports normally have a ten-year duration.

At work

14	13	**The employment of children** **The Children Act 1972** generally prohibits the employment of children below the age of 13. Children between 13 and school-leaving age may not be employed for more than two hours on school-days or Sundays, and then they must be employed only between 7a.m. and 7p.m. and not until after school hours on school-days. But, as many a young person knows, many local education authorities allow one hour's work before school for any child who wishes to do a newspaper delivery round or act as an errand-boy or girl. The exception to the prohibition of the employment of children under the age of 13 is where a local education authority agrees to lower the age-limit to allow children to work with their parents in light agricultural or horticultural work. Children between the ages of 13 and 16 must not do any work which involves heavy lifting or carrying heavy

Question No.	Correct age	Additional information
		loads, or which would be likely to cause them an injury. They may not work in a mine.
15	16	At 16 you can be fully employed and you will be required to pay National Insurance contributions, and also income tax if your income rises above the standard allowances laid down by Parliament. (See Chapter 4.) **Part VI** of the **Factories Act 1961** regulates the times of factory employment of those under 18. No one between the ages of 16 and 18 may work longer than 48 hours a week and be employed for more than 5 hours without a rest or meal break of half an hour. Under-18s who deliver, load or collect goods or run errands may work only 13 hours a day (including breaks). Under-18s are also forbidden to work in certain jobs which might be hazardous to their health, and they may not work in a bar (this does not include restaurants where alcoholic drinks are served). At any age *your* earnings belong to *you*.
16	16	**Joining a trade union** You are entitled to join a trade union which looks after the interests of the workforce at your place of work. A few unions allow people under 16 to join.
17	20	**Redundancy** Entitlement to redundancy pay requires a minimum of two years' continuous employment. The years of employment before your 18th birthday are disregarded. However, you can claim to have been unfairly dismissed. (See Chapter 4.)

Shopping

18	16	**Cigarettes** It is illegal to sell cigarettes, tobacco or cigarette papers to anyone apparently under

Question No.	Correct age	Additional information
		the age of 16 whether they are for his/her own use or not. It is not an offence for a person under 16 to smoke, but it is considered unwise for health reasons.
		Alcohol
19	18	It is an offence to sell alcohol to someone under 18. Young people under 14 are not allowed in bars or licensed premises during drinking hours, but those over 14 and under 18 can enter a bar as long as they do not drink alcohol there. At 16 young people can have beer, cider, porter or perry with a meal in a part of the premises usually set aside for the service of meals. Between 5 and 16 young people can drink alcohol as long as they are on private premises. It is an offence to give intoxicating liquor to a child under 5 either in private or in public unless it is prescribed by a medical practitioner.
		Dangerous items
20	16	It is an offence to sell fireworks to anyone under 16.
21	17	The sale of crossbows is severely restricted. No one under 17 may be sold or may hire a crossbow.
		Pet animals
22	12	It is an offence to sell a pet animal to anyone apparently under the age of 12.
		Consumer credit
23	18	A hire-purchase or consumer credit agreement is a contract and the restricted liability of persons under 18 applies, that is, minors under the law can only be bound by contracts for their training, education and necessary goods such as food, clothing, and accommodation. It follows therefore that if someone under 18 wishes to buy something

Question No.	Correct age	Additional information
		on credit, a responsible adult may have to stand guarantor or surety for the minor.

Licences and restrictions

		Driving licences
24	16	You may hold a licence to ride a motor-bike, drive certain tractors and also an invalid carriage at 16. At 17 you may hold a licence to drive any vehicle which is not a certain type of heavy goods vehicle. This usually means you may drive a car.
25	21	You may hold a licence for *any* mechanically propelled vehicle including heavy goods vehicles such as a lorry or a bus.
26	17	At 17 a young person may hold a private air pilots' licence, and at 16 s/he may fly a glider. However, no one under 18 may hold a commercial air pilots' licence.
		Firearms
27	14	The law relating to the possession and use of firearms is complex, as various conditions apply according to the type of firearm, the age of the user, whether its use is being supervised and whether the firearm is carried securely in a fastened case or cover. If you are under 14 you may not possess, purchase or acquire any firearm or ammunition, nor may anyone give or lend you any unless you are a member of an approved club. No one under 17 is allowed to use an airgun in a public place. Young people of 14 and under 17 may own or be lent an air weapon but may not buy or hire any firearms. If under 15 they may handle a shotgun under adult supervision but may not be given one. Young people of 17 and over may buy or hire firearms and apply for a firearm certificate. The police have powers to issue certificates.

Coming of Age 27

Question No.	Correct age	Additional information
28	21	**Intoxicating liquor** A licence to sell intoxicating liquor can only be obtained by a person over 21. The application has to be made to the magistrates' court. Anyone of 18 and over can work in a bar serving drinks.
29	18	**Betting and gaming** Young people of 17 and under are not allowed in betting shops, except when they are employed as postal clerks. Neither are they allowed to gamble in public houses, bingo halls or gaming clubs, although they may be present at a bingo hall.

At the courts

30	18	**Jury service** Anyone between the ages of 18 and 65 may be called to sit on a jury in either the criminal Crown Court or in a coroner's court (which decides the causes – innocent or criminal – of a person's death). On rare occasions you could be called to a civil court jury. Certain groups of people cannot serve (see Chapter 10).
31	14	**Being a witness** A young person may only be accepted as a witness if the court thinks that s/he is able to understand the questions put to him or her and is able to tell the truth. It depends on the nature of the case. In civil cases the accepted average age is 13–14. In some Crown Court trials where child abuse is alleged, it is possible for under 14s to give evidence through a video link.
32	Any age	**Civil actions** To this question the answer is not clear-cut. No one under 18 can sue in his or her own name, but this does not prevent the minor from suing in the courts. Anyone under 18

Question No.	Correct age	Additional information
		who wishes to enforce or protect his/her rights in a civil court may bring the action through a 'next friend'. This must be a responsible person, such as a parent, guardian, relative or close friend. A child of *any age* may be sued for a civil wrong other than a breach of contract. These civil wrongs which are called torts are such acts as trespass, causing a disturbance and negligence. But the child has to be considered old enough to realise the consequences of his act. Where a child is sued for a breach of contract, the action is only enforceable in contracts for training, education and necessaries (according to the child's station in life).
33	16	**Legal Aid** A young person can apply for 'Legal Aid' at 16. Normally Legal Aid is financial help which is only available to people with low earnings and savings for advice and representation in court. In civil proceedings, the parents or guardian of children under age can apply on their behalf. In criminal and care proceedings legal aid is available to children. Since 1989 legal aid has been made available for the under 16s for child abuse cases (see Chapter 10).
34	10	**Criminal actions** A child under 10 cannot be charged with a criminal offence, but a child of 8 or over suspected of a criminal offence can be the subject of care proceedings. Between the ages of 10 and 13, young people can be charged with a criminal offence but it must be proved that they knew the actions were wrong. Young offenders may appear before the magistrates at the juvenile court or may receive a caution.

Coming of Age 29

Question No.	Correct age	Additional information
35	14	At 14 or over a person is assumed to have reached the age at which he knows the difference between right and wrong, but generally any young person under 17 will be dealt with in private in the juvenile court. However, someone charged together with an adult will be tried in the magistrates' court, and children on charges of murder and certain other grave crimes can be tried in the Crown Court.
36	17	If the offender is male he can be sent to prison if convicted of a serious crime (see Chapter 9).

Civic rights

37	18	**The vote** At 18 you can vote in local and parliamentary elections provided that your name is listed on the electoral register. The electoral register is available for viewing at public libraries, town halls or civic centres, and at Citizens Advice Bureaux.
38	21	**Be an MP** It is assumed that by the time a person reaches 21, s/he has had sufficient experience and knowledge of people and of the community to take on this kind of responsibility.
39	18	**Join the police force** You may join the police force at 18 but you may become a cadet before that at 16.
40	18	**Join the armed forces** You may join the armed forces without your parents' consent at 18. With your parents' consent you may join earlier at 16 for boys and 17 for girls.

Exercises

In addition to the quiz, you may like to try the following exercises:

1. For class discussion or coursework:
   Select any instances of age limits and liberties that you consider are inconsistent and say why. (For example, a boy of 14 can hold a licence to possess an air rifle but it would be an offence for a shopkeeper to sell him fireworks while under the age of 16.)
2. A formal debate:
   Title: The Motion of this House is that the age of Majority should be lowered to the age of 16.

   You may also find it useful to refer to the sections on *minors' contracts* and *family law*.

3 Shopping: The Law of Buying and Selling

What kind of shopper are you? Do you take what is offered without questioning your rights as a consumer and never bother to complain when things go wrong? Or do you look carefully at what you are buying to make sure that the goods you want are the right size or colour or are durable enough to last you a long time, or are exactly right for your particular purpose? Moreover, when the kind of buying you are doing is on a business footing and may require your signature, or when you are buying something on credit, do you carefully scrutinise the small print before putting pen to paper? And how far are you aware of your rights when you take your watch or car to be repaired? Wise shopping means being aware of the various ways in which you, as a consumer, may be protected by law. Conversely, if you are the trader, shopkeeper or salesperson, would you know the

Figure 3.1 What kind of shopper are you?

31

extent of your customer's rights and your own legal responsibilities? Indeed, the customer need not always be right; there are times when you can assert your own rights as a dealer. Sometimes individual rights and obligations are clear and a remedy is readily available. At other times, the law may appear to work against you and you may find you are the 'loser', or that you are bound to a certain obligation you didn't intend to happen. It is a wise precaution to know something about the law both as a consumer, and as a dealer.

Legal protection

Since the late nineteenth century when there was extensive industrial expansion and a vast growth in trading and consumer buying, Parliament had been introducing laws which have increasingly given protection to the consumer against unfair bargaining practices. The last century saw an increased number of commercial disputes which brought with them new complexities in the common law of contract. Businessmen began to create terms in their contracts which would work in their own interests but which also became binding on those with whom they had business relations. This meant that the weaker party to the contract would get the worst of the bargain. So, in order to protect the individual trader and consumer, Parliament introduced the very important **Sale of Goods Act 1893**, which governed every sale of goods and was designed to assume certain terms of legal obligation for both the buyer and the seller. Today we rely on its descendant, the **Sale of Goods Act 1979**, which incorporates the amendment of the former 1893 Act, the **Supply of Goods (Implied Terms) Act 1973**. The **implied terms** now contained in the 1979 Act are of considerable importance to the consumer against faulty goods and should be known by everyone who shops or trades. Parliament has also introduced numerous other statutes which encompass all aspects of trading and consumer buying, many of which will be discussed below.

The law and the consumer

Whenever you buy something from a shop or retailer, or have a service done or something repaired, or enter into an insurance or credit agreement, you enter into a legally binding agreement, or **contract**, with the shopkeeper, dealer, insurance company or finance company.

Look at the following situations. Can you say which of these is a legally binding contract?
- Beryl saw a swimsuit in the window of Rubina's shop. She went in and bought it.

Shopping

- Martyn took his watch to Ivor's shop and Ivor agreed to repair it.
- Boris signed a hire-purchase agreement for Jack to install some new office furniture.
- Janet insured herself as a driver of a motor vehicle.
- Jack bought a tin of beans, some potatoes and a packet of soap powder at his local supermarket.

The answer is that **all** these transactions are legally binding agreements. In each instance a contract has been formed. In fact, when Jack shopped at the supermarket he made a separate contract for each item he bought, so by purchasing three items, he made three separate contracts.

When buying goods the formation of the contract is the **offer by the customer** to purchase the goods, and **the dealer accepting the offer** by agreeing to sell the goods. When you pay for the goods, you show **consideration** by exchanging money for the goods, i.e. you promise the dealer a certain sum of money, the cost of the goods, and in return he promises you the supply of the goods of your choice. An **intention to create legal relations** is assumed as this is a 'business' transaction, and not a social or domestic arrangement, regulated by the conditions and terms laid down by legislation such as the Sale of Goods Act. The consumer contract is rarely expressed in writing; it is more likely to be expressed verbally or by the implied conduct of the parties, such as the acts of handing over the goods and taking the money. The receipt which you are given is the documentary evidence that the transaction of the contract took place at that particular shop on a particular day, so it is always a good idea to keep your receipts in a safe place for a period of time after the purchase.

Certain consumer contracts such as **hire-purchase** or **credit agreements** do have to be in writing and some contracts are printed on what are called 'standard forms'.

Standard form contracts are contracts which are printed forms on which the conditions and terms are already stated. They are being used increasingly by businesses and in certain industries such as building, insurance, furniture stores and the motor trade, and also by the Gas and Electricity Boards. They have become very popular with groups of dealers who belong to a trade association such as car dealers and double-glazing firms. Standard form contracts are used to save time in repetitive types of transaction.

Sometimes when you buy a large item, such as a TV set, or a washing machine, you may be supplied with a **guarantee**, which may include a set of obligations for the **manufacturer** of the goods. A guarantee must never take away your statutory rights under the Sale of Goods Act 1979.

The Sale of Goods Act 1979

The Act provides that the contracts of sale are made in the course of business with private individuals, and that the seller must own or possess the goods and have the right to sell them. The buyer must pay a reasonable price for the goods – this will depend on the circumstances of each particular case. The duties under the Act are owed by the shop or dealer and cannot be fobbed off on to the manufacturer. The Act makes **implied terms** of the contract of sale:

1. that the goods supplied under the contract correspond to the description (Section 13);
2. that the goods supplied under the contract are of merchantable quality (Section 14[2]) i.e. they should have been sold in that condition;
3. that the goods supplied under the contract are fit for their purpose (Section 14 [3]);
4. that if goods are bought after seeing a sample (e.g. of material, floor covering etc.) then the bulk must correspond with the sample when delivered (Section 15).

Any fault with the goods must be present **at the time of sale**. It is no good returning goods because you have changed your mind; or when the fault was apparent or pointed out to you at the time of sale; or if you have damaged or interfered with the commodity once you have taken it away from the shop or dealer. Also, **the test of reasonableness in the circumstances can be applied**: for instance, an expensive pair of shoes would be expected to wear longer than a cheap pair, therefore it would be reasonable to expect redress after a longer period of time for the better quality shoes.

Consumer contracts and minors

Young people under the age of 18 are denied full contractual capacity. The reason for this is twofold – to protect the interests of the minor, and also to protect the interests of those likely to become parties to their contracts. Minors rarely have sufficient means to meet their contractual commitments and therefore could easily get into debt or conversely be exposed to exploitation by disreputable dealers. This however does not mean that a minor is never liable for his contracts. He may be liable for contracts considered to be either 'necessaries' or 'beneficial contracts of service' (see also Chapter 4 – employment and educational contracts).

Contracts for 'necessaries' are contracts on which a minor can be sued at common law for goods which are suitable for his station in life and actual requirements. This would include items such as food, drink, clothing, medicine, lodging, etc. 'Necessaries' are measured according to the status and life-style of the minor. In *Nash v. Inman* (1908) where a Cambridge student bought on credit eleven fancy waistcoats from a Savile Row tailor and failed to pay for them, the court held that there was no contract and the tailor had no claim to the money owing to him because the minor already had sufficient clothes and the waistcoats were not 'necessaries'. In *Peters v. Fleming* (1840) the court decided that it was not unreasonable for a wealthy infant undergraduate to be liable for the purchase of a gold watch and chain.

The Sale of Goods Act 1979 S.3(3) provides that a minor shall be obliged to pay a reasonable price for necessaries. The Act says 'necessaries' means 'goods suitable to the condition in life of the minor . . . and to his actual requirements at the time of sale and delivery'. It is unclear whether this means that an infant can only be sued on a contract for necessary goods where they have been delivered.

The Minors' Contracts Act 1987 replaces the former *Infant Relief Act 1874*. In line with common law it prevents a minor from being sued for breach of contract unless the contract was for: necessaries, a beneficial contract of service, or voidable contracts which allow the minor to escape liability for future obligations. It allows a minor to sue a defaulting party. Where the minor has an adult guarantor, the guarantor must meet the minor's obligations.

Once a minor has reached 18, the Act allows him or her to make good a previous agreement on which he or she has defaulted or to create a new contract on the same terms as the previously unenforceable contract. Any property acquired by the minor, even if not fraudulently, under an unenforceable contract can be recovered by the person to whom it is owed where it is just and equitable to do so.

How the law operates

The way in which much of the law and consumer protection legislation operates will be illustrated in the case studies given below. The cases are each followed by a question-and-answer analysis and information on the relevant law.

CASE 1:

Invitation to treat – offer and acceptance – purchases bought in a sale

Reg and Peg were out shopping in the town shopping precinct. Reg saw a jacket in the window of Immaculate Man priced at £60. It was clearly a bargain at the price and Reg hurried into the shop to buy it. The sales assistant told Reg that the price tag of £60 on the jacket was a mistake and that the jacket's true price was £80. Reg was angry and told the sales assistant he was within his rights to have the jacket at the displayed price. The manager was called over and he explained to Reg that the jacket in the window was merely part of the window display and that he had the right to decide whether he sold it or not. Disappointed, Reg decided instead to buy some trousers he saw in a sale, but by this time he was in too much of a hurry to join Peg so he decided not to waste time trying them on. They were clearly marked his usual size. However, when he arrived home and tried them on he decided he did not like the trousers as they were too tight, 'I shall take them back and exchange them tomorrow,' he told Peg, 'Marks and Spencers took back a pair I bought there the other day.' But Peg expressed her doubts: 'You may not be able to because you bought them in a sale,' she said.

Was the manager of Immaculate Man within his rights to refuse to sell Reg the jacket at the displayed price?

Unfortunately for Reg, the manager was within his rights when he refused the sale of the jacket even though there had been a mistake over the price. He was also correct when he said that he is under no obligation to sell any items that are on display in his window. The common law protects the shopkeeper from genuine mistakes by defining displays as 'an invitation to treat' – that is, displays are merely an enticement to persuade the shopper to make an offer to buy. This takes place at the 'bargaining' stage of the transaction, and therefore the manager of Immaculate Man is free to reject Reg's offer to purchase the jacket, regardless of whether Reg was willing to pay £80 or £60 for it. Had he accepted Reg's offer to purchase then a contract of sale would have been formed and this would have been binding on both parties.

'An invitation treat' This arises out of the common law ruling in the case of *Fisher v. Bell (1961)* when a distinction was made between an offer and 'an invitation to treat'. The facts were that a shopkeeper displayed a flick knife in his window which caused him to be prosecuted for the criminal offence of offering for sale a flick knife, contrary to the

Shopping 37

Restriction of Offensive Weapons Act 1959. Held: That no offence had been committed since the display of an article in a window in the law of contract is merely 'an invitation to treat' and not an offer of sale. Likewise in supermarkets, the display of various foodstuffs and household commodities is 'an invitation to treat'. The offer to buy is made when you place your goods before the cashier at the till, and it is accepted when the cashier takes your money. (*Pharmaceutical Society of Great Britain v. Boots Cash Chemists (Southern) Ltd (1953)*)

Is Reg right when he says the shop will have to change the trousers which he finds do not fit him?

This is turning out to be Reg's unlucky day. The law permits no remedy for merely changing one's mind. The law of contract provides a remedy only where there has been a breach of contract – that is, when the goods were faulty, or misrepresented in some way at the time of sale. Reg should have tried on the trousers at the shop when he bought them. In terms of the law he has changed his mind, there is no breach of the contract, therefore he cannot expect an exchange or a refund of his money. It is true that chain stores such as Marks and Spencer do allow refunds and exchanges when people change their minds about their choice of purchase or when a garment which they have purchased at the shop does not fit, but this is part of that company's own policy to keep the customer's good will and has nothing to do with the law. Such stores may also lack changing and consider it would be unfair not to change items that are not to the customer's liking when they are obliged to try them on at home.

Is Peg right when she suggests that goods bought in a sale cannot be changed?

This is a common mistake. Any items sold in a sale are subject to the same law as items not sold in a sale. If Reg's trousers had had a faulty seam or were shop-soiled and these faults had not been apparent or had not been pointed out to Reg at the time of sale, he would have been entitled to a refund or a replacement. The implied terms of the Sale of Goods Act would have applied.

CASE 2:

The Sale of Goods Act and the 'implied terms' – the Food Act – the Consumer Protection Act – manufacturer's liability in the tort of negligence

When Peg left Reg at Immaculate Man, she made her way to Dregs Department Store where she had seen a green drinking-mug in the chinaware department. It was the exact replica of one which she had been given and she thought she would like to have a matching pair. When Peg explained what she wanted the assistant told her there was a green mug already wrapped in its box and Peg bought it. She then remembered that her friend, Usha, was coming to tea that afternoon so she bought a box of expensive chocolate cakes from the food store in the basement. On her way out of the shop, Peg found herself in the Do-It-Yourself Department. She saw there a record assembly unit, just the kind for which she had been looking for some time. The instructions on the box advised the use of Hold-Tight Adhesive for the assembly of the kit. However, the shop assistant said he had sold out of Hold-Tight Adhesive and recommended another brand, Gum-Up, as a suitable alternative. But Peg's apparently successful shopping spree was to end in disaster. On arriving home she discovered she had been sold a blue drinking mug and not the green one for which she had specifically asked, and, after putting together the record assembly unit, she found that it collapsed under the weight of the records; the adhesive she had been sold had not been strong enough to hold the sections of the unit together. When Usha arrived for tea, she told her about her unlucky purchases. While Usha was eating one of the chocolate cakes she noticed some green mould on the cream filling inside, and, as the girls looked closer, they saw a dead cockroach embedded in the cake itself. 'I should take all your purchases back to Dregs Department Store,' Usha said to Peg, 'I'm not sure what the legal position is about the glue for the assembly unit, but I am sure you should return the mug and the cakes. I read something about it in a leaflet I got from the Citizens Advice Bureau.' The next day Usha's mother telephoned to say that Usha had been ill and was being treated in hospital for food-poisoning. She thought it was the result of eating the mouldy cakes.

Will Peg be able to change the blue mug for a green one?

As Peg had specifically asked for a green mug, she can safely rely on one of the implied terms of the **Sale of Goods Act 1979**, which provides that if **goods do not comply with their description** you can take them back to the shop and demand your money back. Alternatively, Peg could ask to exchange the blue mug for a green mug if one is available.

Can Peg get her money back for the mouldy and contaminated cakes?

Peg has a number of courses of action open to her here. She can rely on the implied term of the **Sale of Goods Act 1979** which says that the seller must not sell goods which are **not of merchantable quality**, i.e. are not of the quality or suitability a buyer would commonly expect, taking into account the cost and other relevant circumstances. This would apply to all consumer goods, not just foodstuffs. Clearly no reasonable person would expect cakes which were meant to be eaten to be covered in mould, so Peg could take the cakes back to the shop and demand her money back. However the law takes a serious view of matters which affect the general health and safety of the public, and Peg may be better advised to take the cakes to her local **Trading Standards Office** at the Town Hall, as anyone who sells contaminated food, whether he knows it to be contaminated or not, is committing a criminal offence, and that person can be prosecuted under the **Food Act 1984**. This may mean, however, that Peg cannot get her money back unless she takes separate action against Dregs Department Store and sues the company for compensation under the **Sale of Goods Act 1979**. Also under the various Public Health rules, the manufacturer of foodstuffs must comply with certain standards of hygiene. For this reason, Peg could also return the adulterated cakes to the manufacturer who will no doubt recompense her handsomely if this avoids his being prosecuted, although this may not necessarily eliminate that possibility. Also, the rights of Usha – who apparently was made ill through eating the adulterated cakes – must be considered. Usha may be able to rely on the **Consumer Protection Act 1987** which makes manufacturers strictly liable to consumers if they suffer injury or are made ill by consuming their products. This means that Usha could sue the manufacturer without having to prove that the company was negligent. The product has to have had undergone a process such as baking, which Peg's cakes had. However, Usha may find she falls outside the ambit of the Act if the total cost of the damage which she has suffered comes to less than £275. If this is the case, then a claim cannot be made under the Act. The idea of this limit is to prevent trivial claims. Then Usha may have to turn to the common law for a remedy. If she can show that the manufacturer of cakes was negligent by allowing the cockroach to be embedded in the cake and that her illness was caused as a result of the neglect, then it is likely she could successfully sue the manufacturer for compensation in the **tort of negligence**.

Would Peg have a remedy under the Sale of Goods Act for the unsuitable adhesive sold to her by the assistant in Dregs Department Store?

Peg's chance of a remedy for the unsuitable adhesive depends upon one significant factor which is: should she have relied on the advice of the shop assistant? Another implied term of the **Sale of Goods Act** is that the goods sold by the retailer must be **reasonably fit for the purpose**. Certainly the adhesive recommended to Peg was not fit for the purpose of sticking together the sections of the record assembly unit. But she has to ask, should the person on whose advice she relied be expected to give skilled or expert advice on this matter? If the assistant had been properly trained or experienced in DIY matters and appeared an authority on the adhesive he gave, then Peg could expect her money back. If, however, the assistant had clearly been inexperienced, for example had been a student working a Saturday morning job, then the dealer would have been within his right to refuse her the money.

The Sale of Goods Act 1979 The provisions of the Act are described in the introduction to this chapter (see p. 34).

Credit Notes Some retailers will offer you a credit note in place of a refund. You are not obliged to accept a credit note for faulty goods; but if you do so, you may find it difficult to get your money back later if you don't find anything else you want in the shop, as you would no longer have the original article to prove it was faulty. A credit note may be worth having when you merely change your mind and have no right to a refund.

The Food Act 1984 This Act is intended to protect the purchaser against the sale of food which is not of the nature, substance or quality one would reasonably expect. It is a **criminal offence** to sell food which is not fit for human consumption, and the seller of such food is **strictly liable**, i.e. it is irrelevant whether he knew or did not know that the food was not fit, and he can be prosecuted for the offence. Complaints are usually made to the local trading standards officer who will investigate the complaint and prosecute where necessary.

The liability of the manufacturer
The Consumer Protection Act 1987 is in two parts.
Part I makes the manufacturer, or producer, of a defective product strictly liable for damage caused by the product. 'Strictly liable' means that the person who has suffered the damage does not have to establish negligence. The 'product' means any goods, or their components, which have been processed in some way, e.g. tinned, frozen or cooked foods, or which are factory-made, e.g. car tyres, electrical goods and all kinds of other commodities. It also applies to electricity. Agricultural produce and game do not come within the scope of the Act. A 'defect' is where 'the safety of a product is not such as persons generally are entitled to expect' (S.3(1)) and takes into account the purposes for which the product has been marketed and the kind of storage it has received. 'Damage' covers death, personal injury or loss or damage to property (but not damage to the product itself). Where the damage is less than £275, then a claim cannot be made under the Act. A person making a claim can either be the person who suffers the damage or, in the event of his or her death, a relative or dependent. Under the Act the complaint has a three-year limitation period from the time of the harm becoming

apparent. A right of action ceases after ten years after the date the product was put into circulation.

Part II replaces previous consumer safety legislation and creates a new offence of supplying consumer goods which fail the general safety standards defined by the Act (see Case 5 below).

The Act does not allow manufacturers or producers, by notice or any other form of communication, to limit or exclude themselves from their legal responsibility to those who consume or use their products.

The tort of negligence   Generally there is no statutory redress for the consumer against the manufacturer. The consumer has no contract with him. However, the manufacturer owes a common-law duty of care to those who consume or use his goods not to make them negligently. This means that private action can be taken against him in the **tort of negligence.** In order to do this the onus is on you, as the injured person, to show to the court that the manufacturer was to blame, and the harm done to you was actually caused by his negligence, not to take proper and reasonable care.

The authority for a manufacturer's liability lies in the case of **Donoghue v. Stevenson (1932).** The facts are that a friend bought a bottle of ginger beer for Mrs Donoghue to drink in a cafe. Having drunk half the contents, Mrs Donoghue poured out the remainder in a glass and noticed the remains of a decomposed snail in the bottle. This caused her nervous shock and gastro-enteritis. She could not sue the retailer because she had no contract with him. She therefore sued the manufacturer for negligence. *Held* the manufacturer was liable. By carelessly producing contaminated food he ought to have foreseen that he would expose a member of the public to a clear risk of harm.

The neighbour principle and its general application

The case established the famous common-law **neighbour principle** that 'you must take reasonable care to avoid acts or omissions which you can foresee would be likely to injure your neighbour'. 'Neighbour' is defined as 'person(s) who is/are so closely affected by my act that I ought reasonably to have them in contemplation as being so affected'.

Since the case of *Donoghue v. Stevenson* the principle has been extended to cover more people than just manufacturers. Nowadays, under the same principle, you can sue professional people such as bankers, surveyors, doctors, solicitors, where they may have offered misleading advice carelessly, or may not have performed their professional duties and expertise according to their particular skills and training, or you can sue employers whose carelessness causes you to be injured at work, or other people who may harm you such as other road-users because of their lack of care. You have to show that there was a duty of care owed to you, that there was a breach of that duty and that you suffered harm or injury as a result of the breach. You then could sue in the **civil courts** for compensation.

CASE 3:

Answering an advertisement – shopping by post – unsolicited goods

Brian saw an advertisement in *Sunday Magazine* inviting members of the public to join the Rowdee Record Club. The advertisement read:

> **THREE RECORDS FOR THE PRICE OF ONE WHEN YOU JOIN THE ROWDEE RECORD CLUB. MAKE YOUR CHOICE FROM OUR ADVERTISED LIST.**
> ***ONLY* £14.00 including p. & p.**
> Fill in the slip below and send it to us. If not satisfied there is no further obligation. Just return the records to us within 10 days and we will refund your money. If absolutely delighted, you will be sent three records every month for a mere £22 payable on receipt.

Brian saw that some of the records on offer were playing his favourite music so he filled in the form and sent Rowdee Record Club a cheque for £14.00, but on receiving the records he found them to be of poor quality and the next day he returned them with the return slip of the invoice. Two weeks later he was very surprised and annoyed when he received a further consignment of three records and an invoice for £22. Brian returned the records with a letter explaining the mistake, but a month later he received yet another batch of three records and a written demand for £44. Brian was both angry and exasperated. He wondered whether he ought to go to his local Citizens Advice Bureau, or whether there was any other course of action he could seek.

Shopping

Did Brian enter into a legally binding contract when he answered the advertisement?

The general rule is that an **advertisement is not an offer but an 'invitation to treat'**. However there are situations, such as Brian's, where the advertiser binds himself to a conditional promise to anyone who performs the condition, so, when Brian answered the advertisement he accepted an offer made by the Rowdee Record Club and the parties were bound to the conditions and terms made in the advertisement. One condition of the contract was that if Brian was not satisfied with the records he could have his money returned. Once he returned the records in good condition there was no longer a contract and no further obligation on either party.

The advertisement Generally an advertisement, whether it be displayed in a newspaper, magazine, brochure, catalogue, in a public place or on TV, is **'an invitation to treat'** – that is, an enticement to you to make an offer to buy the goods on display. However, **where the advertiser makes specific conditions which he intends to be binding upon him, then the advertisement becomes 'an offer made to the whole world', and when a member of the public responds and accepts the offer a contract is formed** and both parties are bound by what was said in the advertisement. In the case of *Carlill v. Carbolic Smoke Ball Co. (1893)* a lady saw an advertisement for a medical preparation called the Carbolic Smoke Ball with an offer to pay £100 to any person who contracted influenza after using the ball three times a day for two weeks. She used the ball as advertised and suffered an attack of influenza during the course of treatment. The company failed to follow up their offer by saying it was merely an advertising 'puff', and Mrs Carlill sued for breach of contract. *Held:* that the advertisement was an offer to the whole world and that a valid contract was formed at the point of its being accepted by someone. Acceptance was by conduct.

Is Brian committed to pay for the records he has not asked for?

As Brian's contract had come to an end when he returned the trial records, he is under no further obligation to the record club. By continuing to send further consignments of the records and demanding money from Brian, the Rowdee Record Club are acting in breach of the **Unsolicited Goods and Services Act 1971**, so the further two consignments of records that Brian has not asked for are 'unsolicited goods'. This means that Brian is under no obligation to send the £44 demanded of him. In fact the law allows him to keep the records if they have not been collected by the record club after six months.

Unsolicited Goods and Services Act 1971 This Act makes it an offence for traders to demand payment for goods such as records, books and Christmas cards, which people have not ordered. If the receiver of the goods does not want to keep them, he can:
(i) Do nothing. If he has not agreed either to keep or return them, the goods become the recipient's property after six months, and he can use or dispose of them as if they had been a gift;
(ii) Cut short the six-months period by writing to the sender giving his name and address and stating that the goods were unsolicited. If the sender fails to collect them within thirty days they become the property of the recipient. The sender must be given 'reasonable access' to collect the goods. Anyone who demands payment for unsolicited goods can be fined.

How can Brian get back the money he paid for the first offer of records?

Brian did consider going to his local Citizens Advice Bureau, which is always a good idea if you find yourself in this kind of difficulty. However most publications such as national newspapers, magazines and periodicals belong to a trade association who between them have set up a **Mail Order Protection Scheme**, whereby readers can be reimbursed by the publication if they have sent money for goods and cannot get it refunded. So Brian's first step should be to write to the Advertisement Manager of the *Sunday Magazine* giving him full details of his case, and ask to be reimbursed.

CASE 4:

The private sale – misrepresentation – the supply of goods and services

Mary wanted to buy a car to take her to Scotland where she had booked an hotel for her annual holiday. She saw an advertisement for a private sale of a second-hand car which read:

> **Ford Escort,** 1983, good condition will go 1000 miles without servicing. MOT £1950.
> Tel. Midtown 64582.

She telephoned the number and arranged with Mr Black, the owner of the advertised car, to go to his house that evening to inspect the car. When she saw the car, she took it for a short drive, liked it and bought it. Two days later, when the car had been driven only 10 miles, it broke down and Mary had to have it towed to the Brakespoke Garage, where the mechanic inspected it and told her the car needed

Shopping

a new engine. He promised Mary that he would have the car working properly before her holiday in three weeks' time and estimated the supply of the engine and cost of repairs at about £280. Four days before her holiday, Mary called at the garage to collect the car. The mechanic told her that they had found several other things wrong with the car and to get it into a roadworthy condition the cost of the repairs had come to £500. Mary protested that this was nearly double the amount of the estimate and said that she was only prepared to pay the estimated cost of £280. The proprietor of the garage said unless she paid the full amount they would not allow her to have the car. Mary was very upset because this meant that she would have to forgo her holiday. It's all Mr Black's fault for selling me a faulty car, she thought angrily. I wonder if it is possible to take the car back to him and get my money back?

Can Mary get her money back from Mr Black for selling her a defective car?

Unfortunately Mary has no redress under the **Sale of Goods Act 1979** because the rights of merchantability and fitness for purpose do not apply to private sales. She has to rely on the common law of contract, which means it is up to the parties to make their own terms, so that anything which was said and agreed **at the time of sale** becomes the conditions and terms of the contract, and since Mary and Mr Black negotiated a simple purchase of the car as Mary saw it, she would normally not be in a legal position to sue Mr Black. However, all is not lost for Mary, as she may be able to rely on the **Misrepresentation Act 1967** if she can show that **she was induced to enter into the deal by a false representation** made by Mr Black in his advertisement. In the advertisement, Mr Black clearly stipulated that the car 'will go 1000 miles without servicing'. If Mary has a copy of the advertisement this would provide her with the necessary evidence to sue Mr Black for misrepresentation in the County Court and claim damages from him not only for the £1950 she paid for the car, but also for the extra cost of putting the car in the condition he claimed it to be at the time of sale plus any extra costs she incurred because of the misrepresentation.

The private sale For all private sales, the common law of contract normally applies, which means that the parties are free to create their own terms, the general rule of contract – 'let the buyer beware' (*caveat emptor*) – applies. When buying something like a second-hand car from a private seller, it is advisable to get a competent expert such as an AA or RAC examiner, or a trained mechanic, to inspect the car before purchasing it. Also, it is possible to make your own conditions of sale, such as getting the seller to agree to putting something right or having the car back if something goes wrong with it during the first week. If the seller refuses to co-operate, then it is likely he has something to hide and you would be advised to look elsewhere.

The Misrepresentation Act 1967

A 'representation' is a statement of **fact** made for the purpose of **inducing someone to enter into a contract.** If this statement is false or misleading it is called a '*mis*representation'.

The Misrepresentation Act 1967 enables a buyer of goods, whether they be second-hand goods or new, to cancel or sue for compensation for any loss suffered because of the misrepresentation the seller has made. The false statement must have **induced** the buyer to enter into the contract and must be a statement of **fact**, not opinion. The Act may also apply to misleading statements made in holiday brochures and various kinds of prospectus.

Was the garage owner within his rights to keep Mary's car when she refused to pay the full amount for the repairs?

The garage proprietor had no right to keep the car unreasonably but many proprietors engage in this practice if they do not get the money they feel is owing to them for the work they have done. However Mary is within her rights to contest a bill which is double the estimated cost. An **estimate is not a quotation**, which means that the amount charged does not have to be the exact sum that was estimated, nonetheless it should be reasonably close to it. If the proprietor of Brakespoke Garage had genuinely discovered that extra extensive repairs were needed to Mary's car, he should have contacted her to get her confirmation that he should do them so that she would have had the opportunity of accepting or rejecting the new terms of the repair agreement. As it is, Mary can rely on the **Supply of Goods and Services Act 1982** which provides that services, such as car repairs, should be a 'reasonable cost' where no price has been fixed (i.e. an estimate, not a quotation), but if the proprietor will not reduce his charge and continues to keep her car, the only course of action open to Mary is to pay the full cost, ask for an itemised bill of the supply and labour costs, and sign it putting the words 'signed under protest' under her name making sure that both she and the proprietor have a copy. Then she could get an independent inspection of the car, and if necessary, sue the proprietor for the extra charge and for the cost of the inspection, making use of the small claims court (see Chapter 10). If the proprietor belongs to the **trade association**, the Motor Agents' Association, she can ask them to intervene on her behalf. This makes court action unnecessary and is cheaper.

Shopping

Estimates and quotations Many people are unaware of the difference. An **estimate** is a rough calculation of what the job is likely to cost and the person supplying the service can't be held to it – although the estimate should be reasonably close to the final bill. If you are given a **quotation**, the cost should be carefully itemised, and the supplier should stick precisely to the figure, unless you had agreed to further work along the way. When you need your car, your roof, your washing machine repaired, or central heating, kitchen units or double-glazing installed in your home, it is wise to get three estimates or quotations and to accept the one that you think offers the best value for money.

The Supply of Goods and Services Act 1982 This Act is designed to give to customers who hire items, buy them in part-exchange, or have them supplied as part of a service, the same protection that is given to customers who purchase goods by the **Sale of Goods Act**, so that any goods supplied as part of a service, bought in a part exchange transaction, or hired must be:

- of merchantable quality (fit for their normal purpose);
- fit for any particular purpose you have made known to the supplier;
- as described.

Where a firm does not meet these requirements, it has breached the contract it has with you. This means that if you hire a video camera or a garden mower and they break down, or you buy a gas cooker or a washing machine in part exchange for your old one or you obtain an item in exchange for trading stamps, and the commodity doesn't function properly, you can claim against the firm or supplier. In the case of hiring goods you must not have damaged the item in any way through your own neglect or carelessness. It also enables you to claim against a garage which supplied and fits an engine or gearbox which turns out to be faulty. **The Act also requires services to be performed with reasonable skill and care, within a reasonable time and at a reasonable cost** where no price has been fixed in advance. For example, the repairer of such items as shoes, clocks, TV and radio sets and cars,must not leave the goods unrepaired for months without a valid reason, e.g. not being able to get the correct spare parts for an old radio or a vintage car.

The withholding of goods Certain classes of people such as repairers, innkeepers and common carriers, are entitled to hold on to goods until their proper charges have been met (i.e. they are entitled to a 'lien'). These come within the **Supply of Goods and Services Act** in that their prices must be 'reasonable' unless previously agreed. In cases where the repairer whose charges are unreasonable or whose work has been poor, refuses to release the goods and an agreement can't be reached, it is probably best to pay under protest (as illustrated in Mary's case above) and to recover damages for the excess cost of the repair under the small claims procedure (under £500) at the county court. To sue for the return of the goods would cost a lot more because the small claims procedure only applies to money claims.

The trader and the law

Anyone who is engaged, or is likely to become engaged, in trading should be aware of how the law protects both the consumer and the trader. Clearly all that is contained in the foregoing section of this chapter on the consumer contract will be of importance to the trader. Conversely, this section, while still of interest to the consumer puts a special emphasis on the role of the trader or retailer.

CASE 5:

False trading – warranties – standard form contracts – exclusion clauses and unfair terms – Codes of Practice

Max ran a business, Electrical Improvements Ltd, and traded in electrical appliances. To 'make a bit on the side', he would trade-in old washing machines, spin-driers and vacuum cleaners for new ones, then fit them with new parts and re-sell them as 'reconditioned'. When Sarah came into his shop to buy a reconditioned front-loading washing-machine, he told her the machine was 'as new' and pointed to a ticket he had stuck on the side which read:

> 3 YEAR OLD AUTOMATIC
> Fast Spin   1000 r.p.m.
> One year warranty – free
> parts and replacements
> Only £120

Sarah was delighted and Max produced a standard form contract for her to sign. On the reverse side of the form the conditions of sale were printed in a pale-coloured ink. Sarah did not spend time reading them as she was anxious to catch a bus, and she quickly paid Max by cheque. Max was pleased with the sale as he had made quite a bit on it. He had 'patched-up' a five-year-old machine whose spin speed was in fact only 800 r.p.m. He delivered the machine the next day to Sarah's house but when unloading it from his van he dropped it, jarring it badly. Two days later, a harassed-looking Sarah returned to his shop with one arm in a

Shopping 49

sling and waving her copy of the standard form contract at him with her free hand. She complained that the machine had not been drying the washing properly and when she had switched it on that morning there had been an explosive flash causing severe burns to her arm. It meant she would have to be off work for at least two weeks. She insisted that Max collect the machine and put it right under the one-year warranty. Max refused. 'You should read the small print, lady,' he said. Looking at the faded print on the standard form, Sarah read:

The company shall not be liable for loss of life or personal injury suffered by the customer however caused.

and underneath that:

No parts and repairs can be supplied under the warranty of this agreement where the said appliance has been damaged through the fault of the purchaser or a third party, or damaged as a result of being faultily fitted to a faulty electrical socket or such other attachment.

Sarah was disgusted. 'Surely this does not mean I have no rights at all,' she exclaimed, 'I don't think that the machine you sold me was as new as you led me to believe. I also don't think the law can be so unfair. There must at least be some code of practice to protect people like me from people like you.' 'Take it or leave it, lady,' replied Max, 'that's the way it is.'

Is there any law that can protect Sarah from Max's unfair practice of lying about the age and description of his reconditioned appliances?

Sarah can simply report the matter to the local trading standards officer in the area in which the purchase took place, which would be the area in which Max does his business. Then the trading standards officer will make his own investigation. If he finds that Max has falsely described the age of the machine and the speed of its spin, then he has special powers to prosecute Max in the magistrates' court. Any dealer who applies a false description to goods he supplies is committing a criminal offence under the **Trade Descriptions Act**. Sarah could also make a claim against Max in the civil court for misrepresenting the goods he sold to her (see section on Misrepresentation).

The retailer and false trading   **The Trade Descriptions Act 1968** makes it a criminal offence for a trader, or retailer, to describe inaccurately, or falsely, the goods he is selling, or the services he is offering. The Act applies to all kinds of consumer sales and services and may be made in a variety of ways. Some examples are:

(a) A label on a tin or packet of food must not describe the contents or the ingredients inaccurately.
(b) A label on a garment which claims the garment is 'pre-shrunk', 'washable', 'drip-dry', 'fast-colour' must be what it says.
(c) Advertisements and brochures must not make claims that are untrue. A holiday camp site which claims it is 'near the sea' must be within easy walking distance and not an hour's car drive away.
(d) Selling or attempting to sell a motor vehicle on which the mileometer or odometer gives the incorrect mileage.
(e) It is no longer an offence to reprice food and drink already on the shelves. Traders may reprice goods already on display by sticking a second price label on the goods which may cover up a previous price label. However, where the same article is marked or advertised with more than one price the lowest price applies, but only where the trader accepts the customer's offer to produce the goods. Then the 'invitation to treat' principle still applies (see Case 1 above). Neither can a trader make a price reduction and show this unless the higher price has been charged for twenty-eight consecutive days within the last six months.

The Consumer Protection Act 1987, Part II makes it a criminal offence if manufacturers and producers supply goods which fail general safety standards laid down by the Act in respect of the composition, design and labelling of goods. Under the Act prohibition notices may be served to prevent the supply of defective or harmful goods, and warning notices issued where goods have already been sold to a trader to warn consumers about an unsafe product, and to suspend the supply of goods where a general safety requirement has been ignored. The kinds of product commonly covered by the regulations are children's nightclothes which must be as fire-proof as possible and must be clearly labelled; prams and pushchairs must have safe brakes and harness attachments and not be able to collapse easily; and cars or electrical goods which develop a faulty component must be recalled.

There are other statutes such as the Food Act 1984 (see above), and the Weights and Measures Act, 1963.

Weights and measures If any goods are sold underweight or an item measures less than shown in its description, the trader can be prosecuted under the **Weights and Measures Act 1963.** The Act makes it a criminal offence to sell less than the quantity claimed. Items must be labelled with the correct quantity and weight. Scales and other measuring equipment of traders must be accurate in line with trading standards guidelines. There does not have to be any fraudulent intention. It is not illegal to sell food which has passed its expiry date, that is, when it has passed the date on the 'sell by' or 'eat by' label, provided that it is still of good quality and fit for human consumption, but it is illegal to remove or tamper with the date markings.

Shopping

Is the warranty and its set of exclusion clauses printed on the standard form contract as legally worthless as Max implies?

The warranty that Max has given Sarah with the automatic washing machine is an agreement between the buyer and the seller which lays down certain conditions regarding this particular sale. In this instance Max has promised free repairs and free replacement of parts should certain mechanical faults arise over a period of a year from the date of purchase. A warranty *cannot* restrict Sarah's rights under the Sale of Goods Act 1979 which stipulates that goods must be of 'merchantable quality' and 'fit for their purpose', provided she can show the machine was defective at the time of purchase, and not because of her own negligence. The warranty issued by Max may not be as worthless as Max has given Sarah to believe. It is true that Sarah should have read the small print before signing the standard form contract, but she should check the validity of Max's exclusion clauses by referring to the **Unfair Contract Terms Act 1977**. This Act protects consumers from unfair exclusion clauses or clauses which limit liability unfairly. The Act makes it impossible for Max to exclude his liability caused by his negligent conduct (of carelessly renovating and selling a faulty machine) which he could foresee would be likely **to cause death or personal injury** to the person who bought it. The other clause, restricting the repairs and replacement of parts, would normally be seen to be **'fair and reasonable in the circumstances'** in so far as Max may exclude his liability for any damage done to the machine by Sarah or some other person, or which was the result of any faulty electrical connection or wiring in her house. In this case the fault appears to rest with Max, first by supplying a defective machine and second, by negligently dropping it and thereby contributing to the damage, and he should therefore meet his obligations under the conditions of the warranty. Sarah should ascertain whether Max, being in the business of electrical goods and servicing, is a member of the **Radio, Electrical and Television Retailers' Association (RETRA),** a trade association which operates a **Code of Practice**, covering the sale, servicing and repair of domestic appliances, and which also runs a customers' conciliation service for settling out-of-court disputes between aggrieved customers and its trader members. However, it is very unlikely that someone like Max, who sets out to cheat his customers and to evade his responsibilities generally, is a member of a trade association. If this is the case, then Sarah would not be able to make use of the customers' conciliation service which the association offers. The most obvious course of action for her is to get an independent expert's report on the machine which would provide her with evidence for a claim, and then take a civil action against Max in the county court, claiming not only for the cost of putting the faulty machine right, or even of purchasing a replacement machine, but also for the cost of the independent report, loss of wages, hospital fares and any other expenses she had to meet as a direct result of Max's conduct.

Warranties A warranty may run collaterally with the **Sale of Goods Act.** It is an agreement with regard to goods which are the subject of the sale. It cannot take away the customer's statutory rights.

Standard form contracts and the small print **Standard form contracts** are increasingly being used by businesses in certain industries such as building, insurance, furniture, motor and road haulage, and by statutory bodies, such as the Gas, Water and Electricity Boards. These contracts are printed forms on which the conditions and terms are already stated. Other specific details relating to the customer's requirements such as quantity, quality, make, colour and price may be filled in by the dealer or official and the customer is asked to sign that he agrees to the terms. Although these contracts are used for repetitive types of transaction and are time-saving, they are criticised for putting the customer in a 'take it or leave it' situation. The terms of the contract are not negotiable before the contract is made and this is contrary to the common-law idea that contracting parties should voluntarily agree their own conditions and the terms to which they are binding themselves. The standard form contract creates an inequality of bargaining power for the parties, the customer being in the weaker position. Many standard form contracts and other forms of written contract state their terms and conditions in small print, often pale in colour and generally on the reverse side of the form. This makes it difficult to read and it is a brave person who keeps the dealer and possibly other customers waiting while he insists on reading all the small print before signing the agreement. On the other hand for the customer to say he did not have the opportunity to read the small print before signing his name will not untie him from the agreement.

Customers should always try to read the small print before signing their names to anything. If there are conditions or exclusion clauses you are not prepared to agree to, you can cross them out on both your copy and on the copy you return to the trader and initial the deletion, and tell the trader what you have done. If he does not accept your amended terms then you may have to face the possibility of either trading with him on his terms or trading with someone else. Unfortunately where the other party is part of a monopoly, such as the Gas, Water or Electricity Boards, then you have no choice.

Deliveries to your home – in cases where you receive goods delivered to your home and you do not have the opportunity to examine them, add after your signature the words 'received unexamined'.

Shopping 53

ABC DOUBLE GLAZING LIMITED
TERMS AND CONDITIONS

1. THE DELIVERY of goods ordered is conditioned on labour, materials and transport being available. No responsibility is accepted if the order remains wholly or partly unexecuted or there is non-delivery or delay due to any cause beyond the Company's control.

2. THE COMPANY agrees to sell to the Purchaser and to install at the address mentioned overleaf, the Double Glazing as shown in the Specification, complete and in good working order. The Purchaser agrees to pay in manner hereinafter mentioned for the Double Glazing specified.

3. THE PURCHASER agrees to permit access to the installation address to the Company, its servants and workmen at a time mutually agreed in writing to complete the installation subject to such time being varied under the provisions of Clause 1 hereof.

4. THIS DOCUMENT when accepted by or on behalf of the Company is a complete record of the items of the Agreement and no variation of this Agreement or any term therefore shall be relied upon unless such variation shall be in writing and signed by a Director of the Company. No omission by the Company whether by way of indulgence or failure or delay to enforce promptly the Company's rights hereunder shall be construed as a waiver of the Company's rights.

5. PAYMENT is due immediately upon completion of the work. The Company's Installers are authorised to accept cash and/or cheque on behalf of the Company. Cheques are to be made payable to ABC Windows Limited.

6. THERE SHALL be payable on the signing of this Agreement a minimum deposit of 25% which shall be forfeited to the Company on account of damages in the event of the Purchasers' breach of contract.

7. THE COMPANY does not guarantee against any imperfection or variation inherent in the glass-making process nor does it accept responsibility for optical phenomena occasionally seen as interference colour bands known as 'Brewsters Fringe'.

8. THE COMPANY will in its absolute discretion carry out such work as it considers proper to reduce condensation, but without warranty that such condensation (if any) will be reduced. IN NO WAY WILL THE COMPANY GUARANTEE BY ITSELF OR ITS REPRESENTATIVES THAT CONDENSATION CAN BE ELIMINATED OR REDUCED.

Figure 3.2 The reverse side of a standard form contract – the 'small print'

Unfair Contract Terms Act 1977 Up to 1977 exclusion-of-liability clauses were valid where a service was being provided, so long as the clause was brought to your attention before or when you entered into the contract. This caused a considerable amount of public concern, for example when companies such as car-ferry operators contracted out of all responsibility for damage to cars in transit, or when tour or holiday-camp operators refused to take responsibility for the safety of the clients when they used their facilities such as swimming pools.

The Unfair Contract Terms Act 1977 now makes it impossible for **a trader to restrict or limit liability, or contract out of his liability, for death or personal injury which results from negligence or breach of**

duty. The Act also states that in cases of **other loss or damage (e.g. property), the exclusion clause will only be valid in so far as it is fair and reasonable 'having regard to all the circumstances' of the case.** Any 'unfair' clauses found in contracts should be reported to your local Trading Standards Office.

When the circumstances of the case are unclear, it is left to the court to decide what is 'fair and reasonable'. For example, in 1981 Dixons Photographic who displayed an exclusion clause disclaiming liability for loss of a customer's films or photographs, lost a Mr Woodman's wedding photographs which he had left at the shop to be processed. Dixons offered to supply Mr Woodman with a roll of film as compensation. The county court held that this was not 'fair and reasonable' in the circumstances as the loss of the wedding photographs was greater than the value of a roll of film and that Dixons should compensate Mr Woodman for the cost of the distress to him. (Reported in *The Times*, June 1981.)

Some kinds of clauses are more likely to be successfully challenged in the courts than others. Certain clauses relating to lifts and ferries still appear to have no legal force.

Codes of Practice   Under the **Fair Trading Act 1973** the Director General of Fair Trading has a duty to encourage trade associations to draw up Codes of Practice for their member firms. These voluntary codes are designed to improve traders' standards of service to customers, although they do not give any extra rights in law. Traders covered by a Code usually display the symbol (if there is one) of their trade association on their premises or in their brochures. So try to shop where you see any of the symbols. You can get full and up-to-date details and leaflets about Codes in existence, and what safeguards they offer you, from your local authority Trading Standards (or Consumer Protection) Department, Citizens Advice Bureau, or Consumer Advice Centre, if there is one in your area.

CASE 6:

Doorstep salesman – deposits – consumer credit – repossession

Mr Carrot of Draft Double Glazing Ltd called at Jan's house and she agreed that he should return that evening when her husband, Jim, was in, to demonstrate the double-glazing units. Mr Carrot was highly persuasive with his salesman's techniques and persuaded Jim into signing a hire-purchase contract agreeing to pay a deposit of £200 and the remaining instalments, totalling £2000 to be paid over the next twelve months. Mr Carrot promised he would get a copy of the agreement to Jim within a few days. After Mr Carrot had gone Jan

Shopping

and Jim gradually realised to their dismay that they really could not afford the repayments. 'But we have signed the contract', said Jan, 'I think that means we are bound by it and that we shall lose our deposit of £200. I remember when my brother, Jamie, signed a contract to pay cash for some furniture and backed out, he had to forfeit his deposit, and when Janet became unemployed and couldn't keep up her payments on her new car, the finance company came and repossessed it. Oh dear, we might find ourselves on the 'black list' of debtors.'

Is Jim legally bound to the hire-purchase agreement?

Normally the parties to a written contract are bound by the terms and conditions of the agreement at the point of signing their name. However, Jim and Jan are lucky because Jim has signed a hire-purchase agreement at home and the **Consumer Credit Act 1974 allows a five-day 'cooling-off' period for any cancellation of an agreement signed off the supplier's premises after a face-to-face talk**. This only applies where the credit is more than £50 and less than £15 000. Jim will be able to serve a notice of cancellation **in writing** within five days from the day he receives his copy of the agreement from Mr Carrot.

Does this mean that Jim, like Jan's brother Jamie, will have to forfeit his deposit?

Jim will not lose his deposit and should get the £200 that he paid returned. The reason why Jim is entitled to a return of his deposit and Jamie was not is that Jim's purchase is a hire-purchase transaction, and provided he withdraws from the agreement during the 'cooling-off' period, he can get his deposit back. On the other hand, if Jamie paid cash for his furniture, he was most likely paying a deposit with a promise to pay the remainder of the money on receiving the goods, and if after paying the deposit he changed his mind about the purchase then he would have had to forfeit his deposit. Generally, the deposit should be a reasonable percentage of the full price paid for the goods or service, a general approximation is between 10 and 20 per cent of the full price, but this is only a guideline and **not** a legal requirement, unless specifically stated in the contract.

Consumer credit transactions These take the form of **credit sales** and **hire purchase** (HP) transactions. In both schemes the consumer has the use of the goods on paying the deposit and while paying the remainder of the money by instalments over an agreed period of time. The difference is that with a **credit sale** the goods became the property of the consumer on paying the deposit and with a **hire-purchase** agreement, they become the consumer's property on payment of the final instalment, the goods remaining the property of the

dealer or finance company until then. In the majority of HP agreements a finance company is used. The system operates as follows:
  (i) The finance company buys the goods from the vendor.
  (ii) The consumer borrows the money from the finance company, and is required to pay back the borrowed sum plus interest to them over a stipulated period of time.
  (iii) The ownership of (or **'title to'**) the goods passes on to the finance company until the last instalment is paid. This means that if the trader, or vendor, does not supply the goods, both he and the finance company can be liable, and if you are not successful in suing the vendor, you can then sue the finance company.

Deposits   A true deposit is a payment in advance which the trader insists upon as a condition of doing business with the buyer. If the contract is cancelled by the buyer the payment may be forfeited to the trader. The exception to this is within the five-day 'cooling-off' period for HP transactions conducted away from the company's premises, such as the customer's home, place of work or someone else's home or in the street. Sometimes a deposit is confused with a **part-payment**, which is where goods are actually purchased and a part of the price is payable before delivery. In the event of the sale being cancelled by the purchaser, the seller would not automatically be entitled to keep the money deposited, but would be entitled to retain 'damages' sufficient to cover his loss on breach of the contract. This usually amounts to the part-payment made.

The Consumer Credit Act 1974   Under the **Consumer Credit Act a system of licensing was introduced for all traders offering credit**, such as banks, building societies, finance houses, shops, TV rental firms and insurance companies. Licences are granted by the Office of Fair Trading and it is a criminal offence to trade without one. The idea of granting licences is to stop disreputable firms from lending money. The Act only covers agreements where the amount of credit given does not exceed £15 000 and the receiver is a private individual, sole trader or a partnership. The Act has three basic aims:
  (i) to redress bargaining inequality in consumer credit transactions;
  (ii) to control malpractices;
  (iii) to regulate remedies for default.
The Director General of Fair Trading is the watchdog and overall controller of the Act.

The Act lays down certain strict rules:
- **All credit transactions**. The agreement **must be in writing** and it must contain all essential information such as the names and addresses of the parties, the agreed instalments, the time of payment, any applicable rights to terminate the agreement and to

Shopping

pay the debt off early and to receive a rebate on an early settlement. The customer must be given the total charge for the credit as well as the annual percentage charge, so that he knows exactly how much he has to pay altogether. Under the Act **the customer is entitled to receive a copy** of the unsigned agreement and a further copy of the agreement once it has been signed.

- **Hire-purchase agreements**. The debtor (the customer) has the right to terminate the agreement by giving the creditor (usually the finance company) written notice. The debtor must pay off the outstanding arrears, or return the goods and pay half the hire-purchase price of the goods if he has not yet paid this much for them. Also, if the goods are not in good condition the debtor may be required to pay an additional sum of compensation to the owner.

Defective goods Although you are 'hiring' goods under an HP agreement; whilst you are paying off the instalments you are entitled to rely on the **Supply of Goods (Implied Terms) Act 1973** if the goods prove to be defective and you may request a remedy, and either the vendor or the finance company can be held liable. **The Consumer Credit Act 1974** also covers other types of credit transactions, such as loans of money from banks, building societies, insurance companies, money-lenders (but the risk is high), pawnbrokers, credit-card schemes, and consumer-credit schemes, such as those with the grocer, milkman, garage or department store.

Non-credit agreements made at home Since July 1988 there have been new rights for anyone who agrees to buy goods or services from an 'unsolicited' trader and pays for them by cash or cheque but not by credit. The right only covers transactions:

- for more than £35 (including VAT);
- which takes place at home, at work or at someone else's home, such as a Tupperware party;
- where the trader's initial contact was not made at the express request of the customer.

In such situations, the customer has a 'cooling-off' period of seven days in which to change his or her mind. The customer must then return any goods s/he has bought or pay for any items s/he has used. The trader is under an obligation to provide the customer with a written notice explaining the right to cancel, and, if the customer decides to cancel, the trader must return the customer's deposit or commitment fee. These rights do not cover agreements relating to land; food, drink and newspapers supplied by roundsmen, and goods bought from a mail order catalogue. They do not apply where the customer buys goods or services at the trader's business premises.

Jan says that when Janet had failed to meet some of the instalments of her hire-purchase agreement, she had the car she was buying 'repossessed'. What does this mean?

In hire-purchase agreements, where the customer cannot or does not pay the instalments according to the agreement, the creditor, usually the finance company, can **repossess** the goods. This can only be done where the debtor has paid **less than one third of the total price**. When Janet could no longer keep up her payments, she must have paid less than one third of the total price of the car, so that the finance company came and took it back. Janet probably made the mistake – which many people make when they can no longer keep up the hire-purchase payments – of not informing the finance company of her changed circumstances. If she had done this the finance company may have come to some temporary agreement with her over the payments until her financial situation improved. This, of course, would depend on how long Janet was expecting to be without the means to pay. But such a move might have prevented her from being put on the 'black list', or recorded as a bad payer by the credit agencies.

Repossession As goods under a hire-purchase agreement belong to the creditor until the last instalment is paid, he or she remains the legal owner and is entitled to take back the goods where the debtor has paid less than one third of the total price. (The total price must always be stated on the agreement.) The creditor (the person to whom the money is owed) is required to serve a 'default notice' to give the debtor an opportunity to pay. Once the debtor has paid more than one third of the total price, the goods become 'protected' which means that the creditor cannot repossess them, but can sue the debtor for the amount unpaid plus his or her costs. This cannot apply to credit sales where the creditor is no longer the owner of the goods and can only sue for unpaid money.

The 'black list' of debtors and refusal of credit There are a number of credit reference agencies who keep a record of bad payers. They accumulate lists of people who have defaulted on hire-purchase agreements and also search the Registry of County Court Judgements, which records all the judgements of £10 or more which have remained unpaid for twenty-eight days. These lists are frequently referred to as the **'black list'** and you may be refused credit if your name is on them.
If you are refused credit you may write to the credit reference agency (name and address from the person refusing you credit) and ask them to send you a copy of any file on which your name appears. They should reply within seven working days either to tell you that they have no information on you or to send you the copy of the file. You can then write

Shopping

to the agency asking them to correct the false information, and the agency should confirm the correction with you. If you cannot get the correction accepted, you should write to the Office of Fair Trading giving full details of the agency and the errors against you.

A wise shopper's guide

Here is some useful advice for the shopper followed by some appropriate assignments and exercises for you to try.

- Spell out what you want to buy. Be sure of the size, colour, quantity, quality, etc., of the commodity **before** you buy. If you are unable to examine any item at the time of purchase, accept it only on the condition that you want time to examine it more closely when you get home, and get the dealer to agree to exchange it if it is not to your satisfaction or requirements, but be sure to return the item **immediately** undamaged and unsoiled.
- Look out for notices and small print before you buy. If you have to sign on delivery write 'Goods not examined' on the delivery note.
- Keep receipts so that if you take something back to the shop you have a clear record of the purchase. Some receipts, especially those printed out by the till, are often very faint, so it is a sensible safeguard to write on them what you bought, the date and the name of the shop. This can save a lot of complicated explanation if you have to return a purchase.
- Return faulty goods, or goods that don't fit the description as soon as you possibly can. The sooner you reject them the greater the chance of getting all your money back. If you leave it for any length of time the dealer can deduct a small amount of the refund to allow for 'fair wear and tear'.
- Never buy anything from a door-to-door salesman unless you are sure the firm is a reputable one. These salesmen are trained in psychological techniques and can be very persuasive indeed. And don't sign the same day if buying at home – allow time to think the matter over and to shop around to compare other prices before you agree to the deal.
- If you are having a job or service done, especially at home, establish whether the price you are given is a **quotation** or an **estimate**. Don't be rushed, shop around and get a firm quotation in writing from at least two firms. Make sure that the contract is in writing and includes a firm price. Beware of making large payments in advance. Always query any price increase on estimates and ask why they were not included in the original one. Try to delay final payments until you are quite satisfied with the completed job.

- Beware of the con-man. If strangers come to your door offering to re-lay your drive or prune your trees and ask for 'cash only', they are clearly 'tax-dodgers'. They may also be 'cowboys' and not skilled in doing the job they offer. Be suspicious and don't accept their service unless they can show you some positive proof of identification and a proper business address. If a stranger who comes to your door asks for money in advance of doing a job, NEVER agree. The chances are you will never see the man nor your money again, and, without any means of tracing him, you will be unable to sue him in the courts.
- Look for special labelling. Some clothes and furniture may have fire warning labels. The Office of Fair Trading has published some excellent leaflets on these.
- Look out for Codes of Practice. These are operated by Trade Associations and Public Utilities and can give you rights additional to those you have in law. They cover such things as dry cleaning, funerals, cars, electrical equipment, photographic purchases and services, and also holidays and insurance. The Office of Fair Trading publishes a range of colourful leaflets explaining basic consumer law, the codes of practice and how to go about making a complaint.
- NEVER allow yourself to get into debt by overspending on credit and charge cards.

Assignments and exercises

1. Self-assessment test.
   Advise the following consumers of their legal rights, if any, stating the kind of action and advice they should seek.
   (a) Paula bought a dress in the summer sales at Dregs Department Store and the dress came unstitched at the seams after the first wash.
   (b) Frank told the shop-assistant at the D-I-Y shop that he wanted a weatherproof paint for the exterior of his house. The assistant advised the brand Anyplace. Two months later the paint began to bubble and peel.
   (c) Penny bought a pair of shoes, then decided she did not like them as they pinched her big toe.
   (d) Michael purchased a loaf of bread from the supermarket and broke his tooth on a piece of metal embedded in the loaf.
   (e) Elizabeth purchased a reconditioned tumble drier displaying a label which read, 'A two-year-old model'. This had induced her to buy it. Later she discovered that the model went out of production four years ago.

Shopping

Figure 3.3 Examples of the range of leaflets for consumers published by the Office of Fair Trading

(f) Henry booked a holiday for himself and his elderly mother at Bestbay Hotel. The hotel brochure had stated that the hotel had a lift and that all the bedrooms had a shower. When they arrived, they found there was no lift and that only a few of the rooms had a shower.

(g) Armajit saw some radio cassettes marked down at £1 each in the Music Market catalogue. When she went to buy some, the dealer told her the real price was £2 and refused to sell them at the catalogue price saying this was a printing error.

(h) Clive received in the post some Christmas cards and gift tags from a well-known charity, requesting from him the sum of £4.50 to pay for them. Clive had not requested them.

(i) Sally hired a hover-mower for the weekend from Machine Hire. She thought the hire charge of £100 was excessive but took it. She did not bother to read the instructions and the machine developed a fault, ran out of control and injured her foot. The manager of Machine Hire disclaimed any responsibility.

(j) Bert, a grocer, tampered with his shop scales so that the produce he sold was under the weight for the price. He also regularly changed the 'sell by' dates on some of his packaged food.

(k) Abdul signed a hire-purchase agreement for a home computer in the shop Moderntechno. The hire-purchase price was £700 and he paid a deposit of £100. Two days later he saw the same model in Videoware marked at the reduced price of £600. He wondered if he could undo the agreement with Moderntechno.

(l) A decorator, who knocked on Joyce's door touting for work, agreed to paint her room for £520 cash. After he had completed the job he demanded an extra £180, making a total cost of £700.

2. Make a consumer library or catalogue.
   (a) As a class or group collect as many of the wide range of consumer leaflets issued by the Office of Fair Trading as you can. The leaflets are available from Town Halls, Civic Centres, Citizens Advice Bureaux, Consumer Advice Centres, and some libraries. A classification of the information can be done either on cards or on a computer.
   (b) Individually, choose a leaflet from your library or catalogue and *either* explain to the group or class the information it contains, *or* write a summary of the contents.

3. Making a complaint
   (a) *Role-play* The relevancy of consumer law can readily be illustrated by reference to the buying experiences of members

Shopping

of the class or group. Either by using these experiences or by reference to some of the appropriate situations outlined in the self-assessment test, simulate a shop in which a customer or several customers bring back goods to be exchanged. This could be done in groups. Students should make close reference to the consumer law and to procedures already outlined, but they should also be free to invent minor details and circumstances. In some cases the shopkeeper may comply with the law, in others the customer may be wrong, and in one instance he may refuse to co-operate when he clearly should have provided a refund, repair or replacement of the goods in question.

(b) *A letter of complaint* Write a letter of complaint to the Managing Director of the head office following up this particular instance. When writing a letter of complaint:

- List the vital facts. These should include, date of purchase, where purchased, name, make and other details of the item and how much it cost.
- State the facts and the events as they happened, including the shopkeeper's refusal to deal with the matter, as simply, clearly and logically as possible. Avoid abusive or emotive language.
- Politely request a remedy to put the matter right as soon as possible. Sometimes it helps to request a reply within fourteen days of the receipt of the letter.
- The first letter should never threaten legal action. Give the firm a chance to put the matter right first. Most firms are genuinely anxious to handle customers' complaints as fairly as they can and they will respond willingly to a polite and rationally written letter.
- If a second letter of reminder is required keep this polite as well but be a little firmer with your request. A third letter may be the one in which you suggest seeking a legal remedy in the courts. ALWAYS KEEP YOUR LETTERS ACCURATE, BRIEF AND CLEAR.

(c) *Taking the matter further* Despite several letters and phone calls to the firm, you have still received no satisfactory reply to your complaint. *Discuss* in groups or as a class, the next steps to take. Ask yourselves:

- Is there a trade association who may help? (Refer to your index system.)
- If a trade association cannot be used, what are the alternatives?
- What is the cost of taking action? Will it be worth it?

Guest speaker Sometimes organisations such as the Citizens Advice Bureau and Consumer Councils may be prepared to send a guest speaker to talk on consumer problems and to assist with this kind of discussion.

4. *The Standard Form Contract* Students should be asked to bring in copies of such contracts and be ready to discuss their merits and demerits. Exclusion clauses can be of particular interest; it can be asked, in which situations might they be 'fair' or 'unfair'?

5. You have been asked by your local paper to write an article of no more than 500 words on the various aspects of trading standards that should be observed when working in a shop.

6. Study this extract and then answer the questions which follow:

John had used his local garage's car wash for years without any problems. But on his last visit, the revolving brush tore off one of his headlamp wipers and slightly damaged the paintwork... John knew he had positioned the car correctly. He reported the damage to the assistant on duty, and was told that the manager wasn't there. Eventually John received an estimate for the repair which came to £124.12. He checked at the garage to see whether there were any notices by the car wash disclaiming responsibility. There weren't, so he wrote to the manager with all the details – but received no reply. Unsure of his rights John then contacted *Which? Personal Service* for advice. We said that in order to recover the cost of repairs from the garage, he would have to show that they'd failed to act with reasonable care when providing the car wash service.

(*Which?*, August 1988)

(a) Why did John return to the garage to see whether there were any disclaimer notices?
(b) Explain what is meant by 'an estimate' and say what is its legal effect.
(c) What other actions, other than negligence, are available to John?
(d) Explain why it is important that John would have to show that the garage 'failed to act with reasonable care'?
(e) If John decided to sue the garage, at which court would he take action?

7. *A coursework suggestion* Select an actual case of consumer law which particularly interests you. The case can be one you saw decided in court, one which was broadcast on a TV consumer programme, like *Watchdog* (BBC 1) or one you saw in a newspaper or the magazine *Which?* Or you may prefer to find a decided case in a law textbook or law report. Once you have selected your case, identify and discuss:

(a) The relevant areas of law, statute or common law, which might assist to resolve the problem, and the legal issues these may raise. For example, are there any gaps or flaws in the law?
(b) How to take action, in and out of court, to resolve the problem (see Chapter 10).

(c) The legal process. Is it simple, inexpensive and quick, or none of these?

4 Going to Work

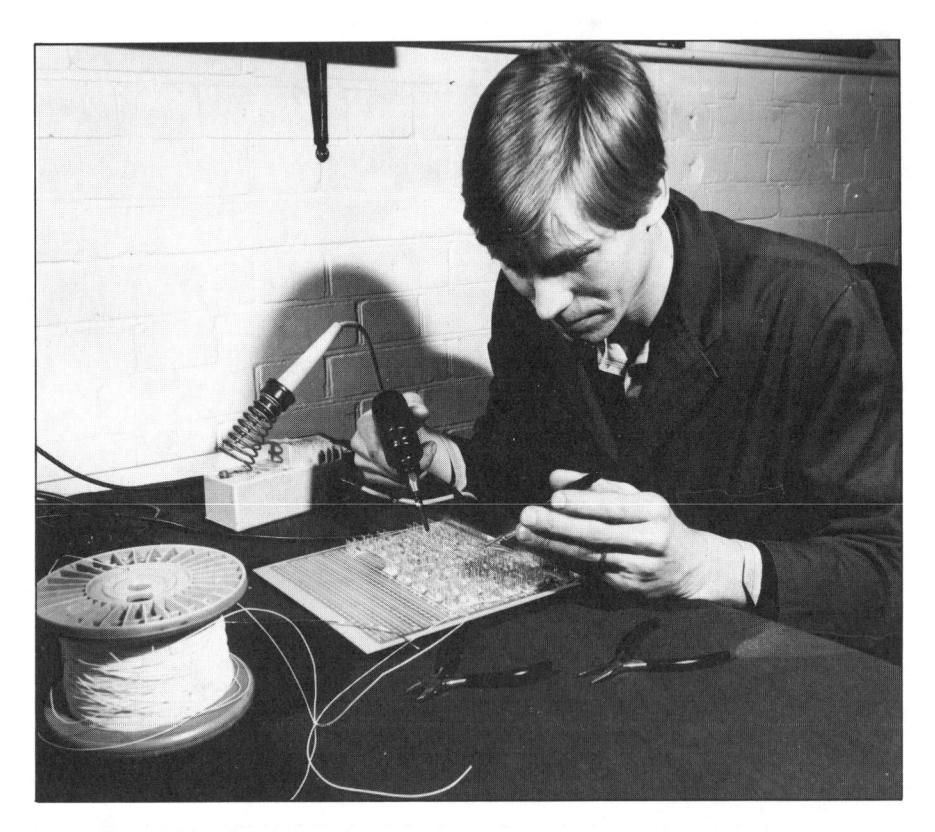

Figure 4.1 Starting work

On leaving school or college you expect to find yourself a job. The first day at work is a daunting experience for most people: not only are the surroundings strange but also the language connected with the work invariably has an unfamiliar jargon of its own. In time, as you get to know the other employees and learn the job, these things become as commonplace to you as to the rest of the employees. But not even long-term employees are always sure of the legal rights and obligations placed on both them and the employer.

A contract and main terms and conditions of employment

Here are some examples of a contract of employment:
- Harry turned up at Bob's building site. Bob offered to take him on for six months for £105 a week. Harry agreed (**verbal agreement**).
- Jane was interviewed by Dennis for a job in a bank. Dennis offered her the job and asked her to sign a document on which were stated the terms of employment (**written agreement**).
- Kevin asked Molly if she would like to become a partner in his retail business. Molly agreed and turned up the next day and began working with him (**acceptance by conduct**).

Ideally, the terms and conditions of employment should be stated in a written contract, but this is not always done. You may receive a written **Statement of Main Terms and Conditions of Employment**, which unlike a properly drawn-up contract does not have to be signed by the parties. Or you may receive nothing in writing at all, but **what was said and agreed on at the time you were offered the job is as legally binding upon both you and your employer as if there had been a written contract or statement.** The trouble with these 'verbal agreements' is that they provide no concrete evidence when a dispute arises over what the agreed terms were. So, after each interview for a job, make a note of any promises and conditions which were agreed between you and the employer and then confirm them in writing (and keep a copy of your letter) if he offers you the job and does not confirm them himself.

How does the law define a contract of employment?

The legal relationship between employer and employee is one of contract based on common-law principles. This means that one party (the employer) has **made an offer** (of a job) and that the other party (the employee) **has accepted that offer** together with all the terms and conditions that went with the offer. **This legal agreement is the contract.** The agreement, as we have already seen, can be expressed either in writing or verbally, but there must have been **an intention to create a legal relationship** (there must be a clause to the contrary if no legal relationship was intended). The agreement must also be supported by what is termed in law as **'consideration'**, i.e. that which is actually given or accepted in return for a promise (the employer pays you a wage or salary for the work you have promised to do for him). A promise of a gift, for example, is not consideration because no form of mutual exchange takes place. So, if either you or your employer fails to keep the promise (the terms) in the contract, then that person will have 'breached' (broken) the contract. When one party breaches the contract it is said that he has 'defaulted'. This means that the other party can assume he is no longer bound by his obligations to the defaulting party. Thus, an employee who breaches a contract can be dismissed from his job. (See section on Dismissal, later.) The innocent party may also sue the defaulting party in the civil courts, either at the local county court or in the High Court, either for damages, an estimated sum of his financial losses, or for 'a decree of specific performance' when the court orders someone to fulfil his promised obligations under the contract. The former remedy is the more common one. So, if an employer does not pay you the wages he promised you, you may sue him for the amount he owes you, and possibly for the court costs as well.

The law of contract based on the common-law principles can be open to abuse, so over the past twenty years, Parliament has introduced statutory measures to protect the employee from losing his job at the slightest provocation, and to improve working conditions in general. There have been a succession of Acts of Parliament, the most important being the **Employment Protection (Consolidation) Act 1978** amended by the **Employment Acts of 1980** and **1982**. The Employment Protection (Consolidation) Act 1978 came into force after a considerable amount of consultation between the government, the trade unions and the employers' representatives. The Act lays down the minimum rights of those employees who normally work 16 hours a week or more. It does not apply to those who are self-employed, to apprentices, or to those who contract out or sub-contract their trade or services. Other Acts of Parliament which may affect an employee are:

Equal Pay Act 1970
Sex Discrimination Act 1975
Race Relations Act 1976
Health and Safety at Work Act 1974
Trade Union Act 1984
Employment Act 1988

There is also statutory provision for national insurance and taxation. Statute law always has supremacy over the common law which means that **the terms of the contract you have with your employer can never take away those rights that have been laid down by Parliament**, but your contract may give you additional rights, such as holiday entitlement and pay, which, contrary to popular belief, are not covered by any Act of Parliament.

Going to Work

How does the law operate?

Many of the rights and obligations provided by the common law and legislation will affect you as soon as you go to work. How the law operates is illustrated in the cases below and in the questions and answers which follow each case.

CASE 1:

Written statement of main terms and conditions of employment – holiday entitlement – proper notice – fair and unfair dismissal – race discrimination – written wage slips – expenses out of wages

Kashmir is 17 and has been working as a waitress in the Gorygrub Restaurant for eleven months since leaving college. The manager, Mr Bull, pays her £50 a week out of which she is required to pay for her waitress's uniform and shoes. One morning, without warning, the manager tells her she is dismissed. When Kashmir asks why, he replies that his customers don't like being served by 'coloureds'. He gives her a week's pay *in lieu* of notice. On counting the money Kashmir realises that he has not given her some holiday money, about £30, which she had been promised, but this is difficult to prove because she has no written contract and Mr Bull has not always given her a written pay slip with her wages.

Should Kashmir have asked for a written contract when she was taken on by Mr Bull?

It is always a good idea to get SOMETHING IN WRITING in order to find out the employer's policy concerning notice, holidays, sick pay and overtime. Within thirteen weeks of starting her job at Gorygrub Restaurant, Kashmir could have asked Mr Bull for a **written statement of main terms and conditions of employment**, even if he was not prepared to produce a signed contract, and he would have been legally obliged to give it. Although the statement itself is not a contract and does not have to be signed by anyone, it could have provided useful evidence of what Mr Bull and Kashmir had agreed about her holiday pay at the time Kashmir was offered the job, especially as there is no Act of Parliament which tells Kashmir what her holiday pay should be. Had she been 21 or over, because she worked in the catering industry she would have found that her basic rates of pay were fixed by the **Wages Council** of the Department of Employment, and she could have checked her position with the Wages Council in her area.

Example of a written statement

The following gives an example of a possible form of a written statement of main terms and conditions of employment under the Employment Protection (Consolidation) Act 1978. Part I of this statement sets out particulars of the terms and conditions on which I *(name of employer)* am employing you *(name of employee)* on *(date on which statement is issued)*.

Part II of this statement sets out information on disciplinary rules, whom you should contact if you wish to appeal against a disciplinary decision or to take up a grievance, and the subsequent steps to be followed in the disciplinary and grievance procedures.

Your employment with me began on *(date)* and, by virtue of paragraph 17 or 18 of Schedule 13 to the above Act or the Transfer of Undertakings (Protection of Employment) Regulations 1981, your previous employment with *(name of previous employer or employers)* counts as part of your continuous period of employment which therefore began on *(date continuous period of employment commenced)*.

or

Your employment with me began on *(date)*. Your employment with your previous employer does not count as part of your continuous period of employment.

Part I

1. You are employed as a *(insert job title)*.

2. Pay will be *(insert scale or rate of remuneration, or the method of calculating remuneration and intervals at which remuneration is to be paid)*.

3. Hours of work are *(give normal hours and any other related terms and conditions)*.

4. Holidays and holiday pay *(give sufficient details to enable entitlement, including accrued holiday pay, to be precisely calculated)*.

5. Incapacity for work *(state terms and conditions relating to sickness or injury and sick pay — if none, say so)*.

6. Pensions and pension schemes *(state terms and conditions or refer to relevant handbook or other document which is reasonably accessible to the employee — if none, say so)*.

7. Amount of notice of termination to be given by:
   a) the employer is *(insert period)*
   b) the employee is *(insert period)*.

Fixed-term contracts should state date of expiry instead.

Part II

1. The disciplinary rules which apply to you in your employment are *(explain them)*.

or

The disciplinary rules which apply to you in your employment can be found in *(reference should be made to a handbook or other document which is given to the employee with the written statement and additional note, or, if that is not practicable, can be read by the employee in a place to which access can be gained without difficulty)*.

2. If you are dissatisfied with any disciplinary decision which affects you, you should appeal in the first instance to *(name of the employee to whom the appeal should be made or the position held, for example supervisor)*.

3. You should make your appeal by *(explain how appeals should be made)*.

or

The way in which appeals should be made is explained in *(refer to an accompanying handbook or a document which is reasonably accessible to the employee)*.

4. If you have a grievance about your employment you should apply in the first instance to *(give the name of the employee with whom the grievance should be raised or the position held, for example personnel officer)*.

5. You should explain your grievance by *(explain how grievances are to be raised)*.

or

The way in which grievances should be raised is explained in *(refer again to an accompanying handbook or, if necessary, a document which is reasonably accessible to the employee)*.

6. Subsequent steps in the firm's disciplinary and grievance procedures are *(explain them)*.

or

Details of the firm's disciplinary and grievance procedures are set out in *(refer to an accompanying handbook or, if necessary, another document which is reasonably accessible to the employee)*.

Note: These separate stages can of course be telescoped where, for example, the same person is the first to be approached for appeals against disciplinary decisions and for grievances, or where the method of application for both is the same.

7. A contracting-out certificate under the Social Security Pensions Act 1975 is/is not* in force for the employment in respect of which this written statement is being issued.

*Delete as appropriate.

Figure 4.2 An extract from the Department of Employment leaflet *Written statement of main terms and conditions of employment*

Going to Work

The law and written statements As we have already seen a contract of employment does not have to be a written and signed document, but whatever is agreed between you and your employer – even if it is stated verbally – is your contract. However, the **Employment Protection (Consolidation) Act 1978** entitles an employee to a **written statement of main terms and conditions of employment** (See Figure 4.2) after thirteen weeks of continuous employment with the same employer. This statement sets out the particulars of pay, hours of work, holidays and holiday pay, sick pay, pension schemes, period of notice, and various disciplinary rules (other than those relating to health and safety at work). The employer is only obliged to give a written statement when the employee requests it, and then he must not refuse to supply one.

Holidays Although the European Council has recommended a minimum four-week holiday (July 1975), there is no law which guarantees a minimum holiday to every worker in Great Britain. Your legal rights are those terms which have been agreed between you and your employer or between the employer and the trade union (when there is one). Often trade unions agree basic terms for particular industries.

Public Holidays. There are two kinds of public holiday in England and Wales, **common law holidays** such as Christmas Day and Good Friday, and **bank holidays** such as 1 January, Easter Monday, May Day and the last Monday in August and Boxing Day. Bank holidays are either fixed by the Banking and Financial Dealings Act 1971 or are holidays which are declared by Royal Proclamation. Generally, an employee cannot insist on not working on a public holiday. Only certain groups of workers in banks and some factories are given the right to the time off. These include **young people between 16 and 18 years** who work in factories and who are entitled to bank holidays, with the exception of those who work in factories where milk, cheese and fish are prepared for sale or preservation, or where fruit and vegetables are canned, or young people engaged on a factory maintenance scheme. Generally, there is no statutory right to pay on bank holidays not worked. There is no statutory requirement for the holiday to be given on an alternative working day; however, in practice, this is usually done.

Wages Councils Wages Councils were originally set up to assist workers who are unlikely to have trade-union protection, those in catering, retail shops, hairdressing and tailoring industries. The Councils ensured the right to basic pay, minimum holidays and holiday pay. Since 1986 the Wages Councils' powers have been reduced and today they mainly secure a minimum pay for workers of 21 and over in these industries. This means that young people between 16 and 20 years have lost this protection. It is possible to apply to a Wages Council either to check you are getting the basic terms or to lodge a complaint against your employer if you are not getting them. The address of your area *Wages Council* can be obtained either from the Department of Employment or from a Citizens Advice Bureau. However, note that at the time of writing there is a government proposal to abolish Wages Councils. If this is carried out, it will become very difficult for low-wage earners in certain industries to retain fair terms and conditions of employment

Was Kashmir given proper notice of the termination of her employment?

Kashmir had been in Mr Bull's employment for more than four weeks so she was entitled to either a week's notice or a week's pay *in lieu* (in place of) notice. As it happened, Mr Bull has complied with the law in this respect. However, he should have put his reason for dismissing her in writing and normally prior warning of notice is considered to be a reasonable requirement under common-law principles. If Kashmir had been guilty of 'gross misconduct' she could have been dismissed instantly without notice or pay *in lieu* of notice, but there seems to have been no evidence of misconduct on Kashmir's part.

Giving proper notice Under the 1978 Act minimum periods of notice related to the employee's duration of continuous employment are laid down. An employer is normally required to give one week's notice to anyone who has worked for him for four weeks or more; two week's notice after two years; three weeks after three years and so on until a maximum period of notice of twelve weeks is reached for twelve years or more. Pay *in lieu* of the appropriate notice may be given as an alternative.

Employers are required to put their reason for dismissing a person in writing, usually in a letter addressed to the person. Although the law does not stipulate that a warning be given prior to the written notice it is generally accepted that this is a reasonable thing for the employer to do – but this would depend on the circumstances giving rise to the dismissal. A person can be dismissed on the spot without the statutory notice or pay *in lieu* when he or she has been found guilty of 'gross misconduct'. **Gross misconduct** must be behaviour of a very serious kind such as malicious damage or abuse, violence towards others, theft or fraud, which has taken place in the course of the work. Dismissal for misbehaviour of a less serious nature, such as persistent lateness for work, taking long tea-breaks, or not doing work properly, would require the normal statutory period of notice and the written reason.

An employee may give only **one week's** notice whatever the duration of the work period. However, it is usually expected of an employee to give longer notice where this is stated in his or her contract of employment.

Going to Work

Could Kashmir have made a complaint of unfair dismissal against her employer?

An employee who has not been given proper notice and a lawful reason for the dismissal may pursue a claim for unfair dismissal by an application to an industrial tribunal. But this would only apply to employees who have completed two years of continuous employment with the same firm or company. Therefore, on the ground of improper notice, Kashmir could not have taken her case to the industrial tribunal for a fair hearing because she had only worked eleven months with Mr Bull. Unfortunately, there are a few unscrupulous employers, like Mr Bull, who follow this practice of employing young people and then evade their legal responsibilities to them by dismissing them before they have met the normal qualifying rule of two years' employment. Kashmir, however, may be able to rely on the **Race Relations Act 1976,** which forbids anyone to discriminate against a person on grounds of race, colour or creed. Mr Bull gave as a reason for dismissing Kashmir that 'his customers did not like being served by coloureds'. He would appear to be infringing the Race Relations Act, and since the qualifying rule of two years' continuous employment does not apply to this Act, the chances of Kashmir succeeding with her complaint would seem to be very strong.

The termination of an employment contract A contract may be terminated in a number of ways, the most common being an ending of the contract by agreement. This occurs quite naturally when a person gives in his or her notice and the employer accepts the notice. Another form of termination by agreement is when a fixed-term contract, for example one or two years, comes to its prescribed end. An employment contract may also come to an end through a frustration, i.e. performance of the contract by the parties becomes impossible, such as in a redundancy situation, or where the workplace becomes flooded or is burnt down. On the other hand an employee may be dismissed from his or her place of employment.

Fair and unfair dismissal **Dismissal is usually considered to be 'fair'** if the employer can show the reason was:

- related to the employee's conduct;
- related to the employee's capability or qualifications;
- redundancy (i.e. your job or firm no longer exist);
- a statutory duty or restriction which prevents employment being continued, e.g. unsafe premises;
- some other substantial reason which could justify the dismissal. This could apply to someone who has taken a prolonged sick leave, or who develops an illness or disability and would be permanently unable to carry on with the work he was employed to do:

- going on strike.

A case which is an example of an unfair dismissal is *Lister v. M. Thom & Sons Ltd (1975)*. In this case Mr Lister was employed as a foreman fitter/driver. He mostly performed the duties of a fitter. Following a dispute at work, he was told that unless he obtained a HGV driver's licence he would be dismissed. It was held that, since Mr Lister's contract of employment made no reference to such a term, a dismissal based on his lack of qualification would be unfair. The more colourful case of *Pepper v. Webb (1969)* provides an example of a fair dismissal. Here, a head gardener, who, when questioned by his employer on arrangements for a greenhouse during his absence, replied, 'I couldn't care less about your bloody greenhouse or your sodding garden.' The gardener's standard of work had been deteriorating over the past three months. It was held that his summary dismissal was fair, not because of his vulgar language, but because by refusing to obey 'lawful and reasonable instructions' from his employer, he had broken his contract.

Dismissal is generally considered to be 'unfair' if the employee can show that the reason was:

- being a member of the trade union and taking part in its activities; or
- on grounds of a person's race, sex or religious belief.
- the employer had not been 'fair' under the provisions of the Act.

An unfair dismissal may also be considered where an employee has felt compelled to resign against his personal wishes because of certain conduct of the employer. An instance of this could be where an employer frequently gets himself drunk and becomes impossible to work with. This is referred to as **constructive dismissal.**

The two-year qualifying period **Employees who have not completed 2 years' continuous employment with the same employer cannot complain of unfair dismissal.** However there is no qualifying period of employment (or age limit) for those complaining of unfair dismissal on account of:

- trade union membership and related legitimate activities;
- failure to join a trade union, whether it be covered by a closed-shop agreement or is a non-independent trade union (i.e. company controlled);
- racial or sex discrimination.

The procedure for making a complaint Most firms operate their own internal disciplinary appeal procedure before which an aggrieved employee can appear pending dismissal. If the

Going to Work

dismissal still goes ahead after the appeal is heard, then you can take your case to an **industrial tribunal**. The procedure is explained in Chapter 10. But before taking this step, *seek advice* from your trade union or the Citizens Advice Bureau.

Wrongful dismissal This should not be confused with 'unfair dismissal'. **Wrongful dismissal** is where an employer dismisses an employee in breach of his or her contract of employment. Generally this will happen either when the employer dismisses the employee without giving the proper notice to which he or she is entitled, or when the employer does not follow the disciplinary procedure that is in the employee's contract of employment.

The main differences between unfair dismissal and wrongful dismissal are shown in Table 4.1:

Table 4.1 Differences between unfair and wrongful dismissal

Unfair dismissal	*Wrongful dismissal*
The employee's employment has been unlawfully teminated (along the lines outlined) and the employee can complain about the reasons for dismissal.	This is a claim for damages – usually unpaid money – against the employer. The reason for dismissal is not considered by the court.
The claim is brought in an **industrial tribunal.**	The claim is brought in the **county court** for claims between £10 and £5000. The **High Court** will hear other claims.
A tribunal can make an order which will give the employee his or her job back. *Or* the employee can get compensation for the loss of job.	The court will not give back the employee his or her job. The compensation claimed can only be for loss of payment *in lieu* of notice.*

---

* Since 1989, it has been possible to make a claim for pay in lieu of notice to an industrial tribunal. In *Pename Ltd v. Paterson (1989)* the Employment Appeal Tribunal (EAT) ruled that where an employer withholds pay in lieu of notice this can be regarded as a 100 per cent deduction from wages. The employee can therefore make a claim to an industrial tribunal that unpaid pay in lieu of notice is an illegal deduction under *S. 1* of the Wages Act 1986. *NB.* The Wages Act says that when an employee can complain to an industrial tribunal about an illegal deduction s/he is excluded from having the right to sue in the courts for unpaid wages.

Race and sex discrimination at work To discriminate unlawfully means to treat a person less favourably than he or she would otherwise be, simply because of his or her race, sex or married status. An employer may not recruit, promote or treat someone in a firm on the basis of one of these held prejudices, only on the person's suitability for the work.

- The **Race Relations Act 1976** makes it unlawful to discriminate, directly or indirectly, on the grounds of colour, race or ethnic or national origins or nationality or citizenship. For example, if an employer **directly** discriminated by advertising a job 'for whites only', or **indirectly** discriminated by forbidding the wearing of headgear where the nature of the job did not justify such a restriction thereby preventing certain racial groups such as Sikhs working in his company, it would be a breach of the Act. On the other hand, it could be lawful not to employ a Sikh who refuses to wear statutory safety headgear while being employed down a coal mine or on a construction site. Positive race discrimination may be allowed in certain circumstances, for example where a Community Centre wanted to employ someone of Caribbean origin to assist in an area where there was a large population of youths of Caribbean ethnic origin.
- **Sex Discrimination.** There are three interrelated Acts, to counter sex discrimination, the *Equal Pay Act 1970* and the *Sex Discrimination Acts 1975 and 1986*.

The Equal Pay Act A woman must have equal pay for work of equal value, whether she is working alongside male workers or replaces a man in a certain job. 'Equal value' does not mean that the jobs have to be identical but that they are not significantly different, requiring similar skills, experience and qualifications. The question of equal pay for women was referred to the European Court of Justice by Wendy Smith. She was a stockroom manager who was paid £50 per week. She discovered that her predecessor, a man, had received £60 per week. The tribunal and Court of Appeal dismissed her case on the ground that the two had not been employed at the same time doing the same work; however, the European Court held that men and women should receive equal pay for work of equal value even if one preceded the other, provided they were doing work which was 'the same or broadly similar' (*MaCarthys Ltd v. Smith (1981)*. More recently, there has been the important case of *Hayward v. Cammell Laird Shipbuilders Ltd (1988)* in which the House of Lords held that a woman cook could claim equal pay with male painters and joiners because, on comparison, her duties were of equal value to theirs, and therefore the terms of her contract must not be less favourable than theirs. Ms Hayward became the first person to win a case under the Equal Pay Act where jobs done by

Going to Work

men and women, although different in character, were considered to be of equal value.

The Sex Discrimination Act 1975 was originally designed to prevent unlawful discrimination against women in respect of advertisements, recruitment, employment, education and training, and job promotion, but, today, the Act may also apply to men. In employment it is also unlawful to discriminate because a person is married. As with the *Race Relations Act*, the law recognises both direct and indirect discrimination:

- **Direct discrimination** arises when **a person of one sex is treated less favourably than a person of the other sex because of their sex or marital status**. For example when advertising a job employers may not state 'for men' or 'for women' unless there is a genuine occupational requirement for a person of a particular sex, such as in acting, or for a post in a single sex establishment such as a prison.
- **Indirect discrimination** arises when **a condition or requirement is applied which is detrimental to one sex and not to the other**. For example to refuse to employ or promote a person with small children is likely to put a man in a more favourable position than a woman for the post or promotion. It is also unlawful for interviewers to question a woman about her family circumstances, about her relations with her husband and about what she is going to do about her children while she is at work, unless the same questions are validly asked of male candidates.

Sex discrimination laws also include incidents of sexual harassment, such as in the case of *Strathclyde Regional Council v. Porcelli (1986)*. Mrs Porcelli, a science technician at a school, was sexually harassed by two male employees at the school as part of a campaign to make her leave, by brushing against her, by vulgar verbal abuse and by interfering with her work. It was held that unlawful discrimination had occurred because she had been the subject of 'less favourable treatment' of a sexual nature; a man would have been less likely to have received the same kind of harassment. The **Sex Discrimination Act 1986** amended the 1975 Act to comply with a ruling of the European Court in the case of *Marshall v. Southampton and South West Hampshire Health Authority* (1986), which established a woman's right to work to a retirement age of 65 as can a male employee. However, the 1986 Act is still unequal, it does not give the pension and redundancy rights to a woman to which a man is entitled, neither does it give a man the automatic right to retire at 60. The Act also exempts small firms and private households from the provisions held in the 1975 Act.

Under both the **Race Relations Act** and the **Sex Discrimination Acts**, it is unlawful to **victimise** anyone who has brought an action, or made allegations of a contravention, under the Acts, or provided evidence in connection with an action or allegation. It is also unlawful to **segregate** the races or sexes without a lawful reason.

The Commission for Racial Equality and the **Equal Opportunities Commission** have been set up to monitor the Acts against discrimination. They can investigate cases of complaint and they have powers to issue notice to employers warning them against discrimination.

Wage slips

Should Mr Bull have given Kashmir a written pay-slip each time he paid her wages?

Yes, he should give Kashmir and all his employees an itemised pay statement whenever he pays them.

The law and pay At any age a person's income belongs to him or her. **Employment law requires employers to give their employees an individual pay statement at or before the time of payment**. The statement must set out the following details:

- **Gross pay** – the full amount earned for the weekly or monthly pay period;
- **Net pay** – or take-home pay – the amount received after deductions of National Insurance contributions, income tax, and where applicable, contributions to an occupational superannuation scheme;
- **The cumulative totals of both your earnings and tax** paid to date for the current tax year (from April to April);
- **a record of your National Insurance contributions** and number;
- **your income tax code.**

Any variation of the amounts or of the deductions should be explained on the slip.

Deductions from pay

- **National Insurance Contributions** must be paid by everyone in employment from the age of 16 who earns more than a certain amount called the 'lower earnings limit'. The amount you pay depends on how much you earn when above this limit. Your employer also pays a contribution for every person on his payroll who earns above the limit. The money is used by the government to finance the National Health Service and the welfare benefits system. Once you pay

Going to Work

National Insurance, you may qualify for various State benefits, such as sickness and unemployment benefits (see Chapter 5).
- **Income Tax** Everyone who earns an amount that comes above the statutory tax allowances is requred to pay income tax. If you have more than one income they are totalled together for the purposes of paying tax. The allowances are sometimes changed on Budget Day, when the Chancellor of the Exchequer takes certain economic measures for the country as a whole. The single person's allowance at the time of writing is £3005. This means that the amount you earn above this figure becomes taxable at 25 per cent.

Example:	You earn £6365 a year	£6365
	Single Person's Allowance	**£3005**
	Taxable pay	**£3360**

The tax you pay will be **25 per cent of £3360 = £840 for the year**. This is deducted directly from your earnings in weekly or monthly instalments on a PAYE (Pay as You Earn) system. Other allowances include sums for dependents and some expenses. Your local Tax Office will help you to sort them out even if the district tax office nominated to you is in another part of the country.

Form P45 When you leave an employer you must make sure that you are given a leaving certificate, a form P45 which shows your tax code number, your total earnings and the tax paid for the current tax year. If the employer doesn't give you a P45, notify the benefit office who will write to the employer and ask for one.

Form P60 This is a form on which your employer gives details of all your earnings and the tax you have paid in one tax year. You will receive a P60 at the end of every tax year. Always keep your P60 in a safe place. If you lose it you will NOT be given another one.
- **Occupational Superannuation Schemes** These are special pension schemes run by large companies and firms for their employees. It is also possible to enter into a privately run scheme which ensures a pension for retirement. Those schemes, which are 'contracted out' of the State Pension Scheme, usually offer considerably better terms than the State-run scheme. Joining one of these schemes does not exempt you from paying the basic National Insurance contribution.

Is it reasonable to expect Kashmir to pay for the clothes she is expected by her employer to wear for her job?

There are a number of jobs in which the employee is expected to wear special clothes, such as in the business of hotel and catering. The general rule is that the employer, and this includes Kashmir's boss, Mr Bull, should either supply the special clothes or uniform or give the employee an allowance for them.

If Mr Bull is wilfully refusing to pay Kashmir's holiday money and to pay for her uniform, what remedy has she under the law?

The items of holiday money and uniform allowance are relevant to the terms of the employment contract, which means that Kashmir would have to seek a remedy not at an industrial tribunal but at the **county court**. Industrial tribunals do not normally have the powers to consider a breach of contract but the county court does have this power. Going to court may cost money and be very time-consuming, but it is the ultimate solution if all else fails. (See Chapter 10 for details of the county court and its small claims procedure.)

Young trainees and health and safety at work

CASE 2:

Apprenticeships – minors' employment contracts – self-employment – accident at work – sick pay and statutory entitlements – contributory negligence – the Health and Safety laws

Jim, aged 17, has been apprenticed with Power Machines Ltd – an engineering firm – for just over a year. Although he quite likes the work, he has decided that he doesn't like being bossed around by the Chief Technician and he is also disgruntled because he has discovered that his friend, Bob, who has a similar apprenticeship with Aerospeed Ltd in the next town, gets £15 a week more pay. He has come to the conclusion that he has learnt enough about his trade to set up a small business of his own. When he explains this to George, his boss, and offers to give in his notice, George says he cannot leave and that he is obliged to stay for the whole term of his three-year apprenticeship. Jim is downhearted and angry, and argues that he is sure he saw on a television programme that people under 18 need not be bound by their contracts. George replies that this does not apply to apprenticeships so he may as well forget what he saw, and that if Jim

Going to Work 81

was unhappy with his job, he had the chance to go during his three-month probationary period at the beginning of the apprenticeship. Jim storms back to the workshop and fails to see that some rain has leaked through the roof and on to some electrical equipment he had been testing. Disregarding the safety precautions stated on the equipment, he switches it on and receives a severe electric shock and suffers burns on his hand and arm. It is some time before he can return to work.

Is George really within his rights to make Jim stay the full term of the apprenticeship against his wishes?

Yes. Jim is the subject of what is termed in law as a **'fixed-term contract'**, which means that one of the fundamental conditions of his apprenticeship is that he has promised to fulfil a stipulated term of training in return for George giving that training. Such contracts are governed by common-law principles and Jim would be unable to rely on the Employment Protection (Consolidation) Act 1978 and the procedures it lays down for terminating employment. So Jim is obliged to stay unless George agrees to release him from his contract. The point that Jim raises about those under 18 not being tied to their contracts is generally correct, but if Jim had listened more carefully to the television programme he would no doubt have been told that this general rule does not apply to educational and training courses which are considered to be beneficial to the young person, and George's apprenticeship would certainly fall into this category of minor's contractual liability.

Apprenticeships Apprentice contracts – often called **indentures** – have to be in writing and signed by both parties and usually by the apprentice's parent or guardian as well. A fundamental term of this agreement would be that the apprenticeship runs for a specified period of training and both parties are bound to this promise. The fixed term usually runs for one, two or three years and is more often than not linked to a day-release or block-release examination course at a college of further or higher education or a college of technology. The fees for such courses may be paid by the employer and this is why a trainee is obliged to stay the term and cannot resort to the termination of employment conditions of the 1978 Act. **An apprentice can only be released from the contract under the following conditions:**

- During the probationary period, either party may withdraw from the obligations imposed on him/her.
- By the mutual agreement of the parties.
- If the employer can show the trainee is unsuited to the work and would not benefit from the training; or if the apprentice fails any required examinations. Re-sits are usually permitted.

- If the trainee wilfully misbehaves or is disobedient to the terms and obligations of his/her contract, then s/he is in breach of the contract and can be dismissed by the other party, the employer, and can even be sued by him for breach of contract, but very few employers are prepared to go to these lengths.

Minor's liability In general people under 18 cannot be sued for breach of contract. They can, however, enter into contracts (and be liable if they breach them) for 'necessaries' such as food, clothing lodgings etc. They can also be sued on **beneficial contracts of service**, where the minor gains some education, training, experience or instruction which is beneficial to his or her future career. This includes apprenticeships if these are beneficial, and the contract is binding on both the employer and the trainee. In *Roberts v. Gray (1913)*, an infant, Gray, a trainee billiards player, made a contract with Roberts, an adult, in which Gray was to go on a world tour, playing exhibition matches against a famous player. A dispute between the pair arose and Gray refused to go. Roberts sued for the expenses he had incurred. *Held:* that this was a breach of a valid contract as the training and experience Gray would have received on the tour would have been beneficial to his career as a billiards player, and Roberts was successful in his claim for damages against Gray.

Generally contracts of employment are binding on both the employer and on the minor.

General rights and obligations Apprentices have some employment rights in the same way as other workers. They can, for example, belong to a trade union, have time off work for certain activities, be suspended on medical grounds, be entitled to maternity rights, and rely on the laws regarding discrimination at work. An apprentice's rights on insolvency of the employer (i.e. if the employer becomes bankrupt) are the same as those of other employees – he or she can claim what is owing to him or her.

Can Jim stay and improve his wages?

Jim will have agreed a scale of pay which would have been a condition of the contract, so there may be very little he can do about increasing his pay. The fact that his friend Bob gets more with Aerospeed Ltd is largely irrelevant. Bob may have a more generous boss or his firm may be larger and make bigger profits, or there may be a stronger union at Aerospeed. However, the majority of industrial apprenticeships are expected to comply with a minimum scale of rates which are laid down by various industries' **National Joint Councils**, which are governed by agreements with the TUC. Jim could check with the National Joint Council or his particular industry that he is not getting

Going to Work

less than the minimum rate for his age. However, there may be one snag to this; if his boss, George, is not a member of the National Joint Council, then there is nothing Jim can do except to get George to agree to an increase if he will.

Apprenticeships' pay   In practice most apprentices' rates of pay are covered by collective agreements, by National Joint Council or Wages Council orders. These rates are often less attractive than for other employees doing similar work. The reason for this is that the apprentice is learning the job. In most cases the rate of pay will be laid down in the indenture along with any travelling or other expenses and details of day-release. No educational grant is available for apprentices. Apprenticeships mostly exist in the industries of engineering and hairdressing.

Youth Training Scheme (YTS)   Today the Youth Training Scheme is a more likely means of acquiring the education and training for a job than an apprenticeship. Set up in 1983, and today run by the Training Commission, the YTS is designed to provide training opportunities for all 16 and 17 year olds who have left school and have no job or other training opportunity. For 16 year olds it consists of 2 years' work experience which includes 20 weeks off-the-job education or training provided either by the local authority or privately by an approved training organisation or employer, and for 17 year olds one year of work experience and a minimum of 7 weeks off-the-job education or training. Other eligible groups are 18 to 21-year-old school-leavers who are disabled or under 18-year-old girls who have been pregnant and unable to train. When the young person has completed the training s/he receives a certificate which records what s/he has achieved on the scheme, which in most cases is a recognised qualification such as the Business and Technical Education Certificate (BTEC), the Scottish Vocational Educational Certificate (SCOTVEC) or a City and Guilds Certificate or credits towards one.

YTS trainees and the law   Like apprentices, YTS trainees are not protected by the Employment Protection (Consolidation) Act 1978. Instead, all trainees get a training agreement spelling out their rights and responsibilities and giving such details as pay, hours of attendance, holidays and sick pay, and to whom to complain when things go wrong. YTS trainees:
- are only paid a minimum pay allowance which is not subject to income tax or National Insurance contributions;
- must not be made to work more than 40 hours per week and they must attend the hours of off-the-job education or training allotted to them. They cannot usually work overtime; if they do they must be paid at the overtime rate that an employee would receive; if a young

person is asked to work weekends, evenings or unusual hours, the managing agent must seek the permission of his or her parents;
- are entitled to between 18 an 20 days' holiday per year;
- can be given up to three weeks' paid sick leave before losing their allowance. A sick note must be sent in after seven days of absence;
- are entitled to have time off for interviews without losing their training allowance;
- must observe the Health and Safety laws and regulations at work in much the same way as apprentices and employees are required to do (see below).

See also update, p. 272.

The small business

If Jim did succeed in securing his release from his apprenticeship what are his chances of setting up in a business of his own?

Until Jim is 18 his chances are practically nil. Conducting a small business requires entering into numerous contracts for buying and selling materials and commodities, insurance cover, property and so on, and being a minor, he is a strong liability risk. For the same reason it is unlikely he would be able to borrow money with which to start up the business. Even at the age of 18, to set up on one's own as a self-employed person is not easy to accomplish. Many people believe, as Jim does, that to set up as one's own boss is a desirable thing to do. In fact, it not only requires a certain amount of business acumen but also a considerable knowledge of one's own trade or profession, so in Jim's case, he would be advised to complete his apprenticeship, become suitably qualified and get some work experience (and be paid for it) for a few years. Then, if he still feels he would like to become self-employed, he would have a better chance of success, as the public are more likely to take a qualified and experienced man more seriously than an unqualified teenager with a mere two years' experience behind him. Then, he should seek professional advice on setting up a business from an enterprise agency.

Self-employment Anyone who sets up as a sole trader or partner risks bankruptcy if his business fails and he will be liable for all his debts not only out of his business account but also out of his personal savings and property. He would also find it difficult to borrow money in the future – for a house mortgage, for example. In a limited company the shareholders' and directors' personal liability is limited to their shares, and their private capital and income is protected from the company debts.

It is for these reasons and others listed below that to set up in a business on your own you must either have plenty of capital of your own

Going to Work 85

or be able to borrow a large sum from your bank or some other creditor. You cannot borrow money unless you can convince the bank manager or creditor that your proposed business has a good chance of succeeding and eventually becoming profitable. This also applies to government grants and loans for setting up a business. The financial outgoings of a small business or a self-employed person can be a considerable drain on your earnings and profits. The usual outgoings are:

- **National Insurance** – You will be expected to pay Class 2 contributions unless your earnings are below a certain limit for this class of contribution, and these count for claiming basic sickness benefit, basic invalidity benefit, a basic retirement pension, basic maternity allowance, and a basic widow's benefit. They do not count for unemployment benefit. This means that if you have little or no income coming in over a certain period you would not be able to claim unemployment benefit. Neither would you be able to claim income support unless you declare yourself no longer self-employed and therefore available for work for an employer. You may voluntarily pay additional contributions to raise the level of these entitlements above that of the basic rate but the cost of the contributions is very high. If you earn generous profits or gains from self-employment you will be penalised again by having to pay a larger Class 4 contribution.
- **Income Tax** You will not be able to escape paying income tax either. Your profits for the year will be assessed and the normal tax deductions and allowances will apply. Self-employed people are entitled to claim their personal allowances for the heating and use of a room or building, tools, special clothing, books and other such items that are required of the work they do. An Inspector of the Inland Revenue will want to see a record of your accounts, so if you have no head for bookkeeping and keeping similar records, it is a good idea to employ an accountant to do it for you. He can also advise you on how to save paying unnecessary income tax and the fee you would have to pay him could well be offset by the savings he might advise you to make.
- **Value Added Tax** Any business which has a turnover of £25 400 or more over the year is liable to pay VAT. A form VAT1 has to be filled in and sent to Customs and Excise.
- **Insurance Cover** Anyone who is self-employed should protect himself and his business for when things go wrong. So you should insure against fire, theft and other damage to your premises; against liability for claims for faulty work, accident or claims under the Health and Safety Act made against you, and also against the possibility of your own long-term sickness and injury and unemployment. The premiums are fairly high but insurance is a very essential safeguard against bankruptcy and poverty.

- **Credit repayments** on loans, property and hire-purchase transactions.
- **Professional fees or subscriptions** Sometimes these are compulsory in your profession, e.g. lawyers in order to practice must pay an annual fee to the Law Society; or they may be voluntary payments, e.g. a builder may subscribe to the Federation of Master Builders, and can put the Federation's name on his headed notepaper. Belonging to such an organisation may reassure the public of the standard of the service you give them, and complaints by the public about you can be referred to the associated organisation and you can then be struck off their list if the complaints are substantiated. The powers and the action that these trade and professional organisations practise vary considerably, some being far more effective than others.
- **Solicitors and accountants fees** You will require the services of a solicitor from time to time and especially if you have to purchase leasehold premises for your work. Also, as suggested above, it is desirable to employ an accountant. There could also be surveyor's fees.

The work premises See under *Health and Safety at Work Act 1974* and the *Offices, Shops and Railway Premises Act 1963*.

Enterprise agencies Anyone thinking of becoming self-employed should always seek advice prior to embarking on their course. This can be obtained either from the Department of Employment, who run a special counselling service, including advice about government incentive loans, or from a local private enterprise agency; also some local authorities may run an advisory service. Your Jobcentre will help you to find such advice.

Sickness entitlement

Will Jim receive any money while he is ill and away from work?

First, Jim must look at his contract of employment. If George runs a firm's scheme for paying employees who are away from work because of illness or injury, details of this should be contained in his terms and conditions of employment. George is then under an obligation to pay him some or all of his pay for a stipulated period of time as laid down in the contract. Unfortunately, although many employees do benefit from such a scheme many apprenticeship contracts do not include provisions for sick pay. Neither are there any welfare benefits especially for apprentices. Nevertheless, the law does require George to pay Jim **statutory sick pay (SSP)** for twenty-eight weeks under certain conditions, one being that the employee is paying Class 1

National Insurance contributions and has a full year of contributions paid in the previous tax year (April to April). Once Jim has checked his entitlement to SSP, he should inform George straightaway that he is incapable of work, and submit medical evidence of his incapacity. On the fourth day he should make sure George receives a 'self-certificate' and by the seventh day a doctor's sick-note. Then after the first **three waiting days** – for which no SSP is paid – he should be paid SSP for up to twenty-eight weeks while he is ill. He will only be paid for **'qualifying days'**, that is, the days he would normally work. If Jim's injury becomes a lasting disablement or disfigurement, he may after fifteen weeks be entitled to an **industrial disablement benefit**. But this is unlikely to happen in Jim's case unless he loses a hand or an arm and is unable to carry out his job as before. He should endeavour to return to work as soon as possible as he could be fairly dismissed for a prolonged absence through illness if George could show that this was reasonable. SSP can be paid only where the employee has paid the right amount of National Insurance contributions. If Jim has not paid any contributions because his earnings are too low or his year's contributions are incomplete, then his only alternative is to claim a special sickness benefit for an industrial accident from the DSS. The fact that Jim disregarded the precautionary statement on the equipment need not necessarily exclude him from claiming the benefit, which in normal circumstances is a contributory benefit.

State benefits for sickness and industrial injuries
Payments for sickness and industrial injuries are many and varied; they can be classified under two headings – **contributory benefits** and **non-contributory** benefits. Contributory benefits are only paid to the employee who has paid the right kind of National Insurance (NI) contribution over the right period of time (usually over the tax year previous to the date of your claim – but this should always be checked). Non-contributory benefits have to fit other requirements and are not based on NI contributions.

Contributory benefits for men and women

Statutory sick pay Since April 1983 all **employers** have been required to pay statutory sick pay (SSP) for the first twenty-eight weeks to employees who are off work because of illness or injury, including industrial injury. Many employers operate the statutory scheme in conjunction with their own sick pay scheme, so the rules and procedure can vary from organisation to organisation. The calculation of sick pay is complicated and in many instances confusing, so if you are in doubt, it is always wise to check your entitlement with your employer, personnel

```
┌─────────────────────────────────────────────────────────────────────┐
│                  CONFIDENTIAL   Payroll No. W/M ..................  │
│                                 Dept. ............................  │
│                                                                      │
│                                                                      │
│                    SELF CERTIFICATION CLAIM FORM                     │
│                                                                      │
│         This form must be completed in the presence of your departmental super-
│   visor/head, on your return to work, to claim sickness payment for up to (and including)
│   seven calendar days at the beginning of a period of sickness.       │
│                                                                      │
│   1.  I certify that I was unable to attend work                     │
│                                                                      │
│       from.......................day........................date (1st day of sickness)
│                                                                      │
│       to   .....................day........................date (day of return to work)
│                                                                      │
│       i.e. .....................working days, because I was incapacitated through
│   illness.                                                           │
│                                                                      │
│   2.  The nature of my illness was:                                  │
│                                                                      │
│       ...............................................................│
│       ...............................................................│
│                                                                      │
│   3.  If you are claiming that this illness is due to an injury  ┌──┐│
│       while at work, please tick this box.                       └──┘│
│                                                                      │
│   4.  I *did/did not attend a *Doctor/Hospital with regard to my illness.
│                                                                      │
│       Name of Doctor .................................................│
│                                                                      │
│       Address of Surgery/Hospital ....................................│
│       ...............................................................│
│                                                                      │
│   5.  I wish to claim payment for the above period of my sickness and confirm that the
│       above information is true and correct. I confirm that I understand the rules of the
│       sick pay scheme.                                               │
│                                                                      │
│       Signed ........................   Date ........................│
│                                                                      │
│       Name ..........................   Department ..................│
│              (BLOCK CAPITALS)                                        │
│                                                                      │
│   *DELETE WHICH NOT APPLICABLE                                       │
│   ───────────────────────────────────────────────────────────────────│
│   This form must be countersigned by the departmental supervisor/head and the top copy
│   sent to Wages Administration/Personnel Department.                 │
│                                                                      │
│       Signed ........................   Date ........................│
│                                                                      │
│       Name ..........................                                │
│              (BLOCK CAPITALS)                                        │
└─────────────────────────────────────────────────────────────────────┘
```

Figure 4.3 An example of a self-certification form for claiming statutory sick pay from your employer.

Going to Work

department, staff association or trade union official. Failing any of these, try your local DSS (National Insurance) office or Citizens Advice Bureau, who will answer any individual's problems.

The general rules for **employees** are:

- If you work for an employer and pay Class 1 National Insurance contributions you will usually be able to get SSP for up to twenty-eight weeks of sickness in a tax year. You will be excluded from the scheme once you have reached statutory retirement age, or if you have been taken on by your employer for a set time of less than three months.
- You have to let your employer know you are sick or injured and incapable of work. Let him know at once either by telephone or in writing. If you are sick for less than four days in a row you will not get SSP – the first three qualifying days in a period of incapacity for work are 'waiting days' and, whatever the length of your sickness, no SSP is payable for them (although your employer may pay you through his own scheme).
- Your employer is entitled to ask for any reasonable evidence that you are incapable of working for him. So, if you are sick for seven days or less, he can ask you to fill in a self-certificate. This can either be a form supplied by your employer or the form SC1 which is a state self-certificate available from doctors' surgeries, hospitals and local DSS offices. If you are sick for more than seven days, your employer will expect a sick-note from your family doctor. You will only be paid for **qualifying days**, that is, the days you would have worked had you not been ill. These are normally the days of the working week if you work full-time, but qualifying days need not necessarily be from Monday to Friday, they can vary where a worker does shift work or works part-time on certain days of the week.

SSP is paid at one of two weekly rates, and then calculated to the number of **qualifying days** of each week. The rate which is related to your average earnings is set annually by the DSS.

If your incapacity for work is likely to continue after the twenty-eight-week period, then a week before it expires you may make a claim for sickness benefit or for invalidity benefit.

Sickness benefit If you are not eligible for SSP, you get state sickness benefit for up to twenty-eight weeks whether you are employed, self-employed or unemployed. To get the benefit, employees must have paid enough full-rate Class 1 NI contributions, and self-employed must have paid sufficient Class 2 contributions. If you are off work because you contracted an industrial disease or were injured at work, then it is usually possible to get Sickness Benefit, even if you have not paid enough contributions. You cannot claim sickness benefit if you are getting SSP or unemployment benefit.

Invalidity benefit Invalidity benefit is made up of **invalidity pension** and **invalidity allowance**. Invalidity pension is paid when sickness benefit finishes if you are still incapable of work because of serious disability. Invalidity allowance is an additional payment given to people whose illness began when they were still under 60 (for men) or under 55 (for women). If you qualify for Invalidity Benefit at the end of the twenty-eight weeks of SPP and/or Sickness Benefit your Social Security Office will pay it automatically.

Maternity rights Statutory Maternity Pay (SMP) is available to women who work while they are pregnant. The woman must have been earning enough to be paying Class 1 NI contributions; she has to have been employed by the same employer for at least six months, and she must be employed in the 15th week before her baby is due, i.e. 26 weeks of pregnancy. Women who cannot get SMP may qualify for a weekly **Maternity Allowance** from their Social Security Office if they have been recently employed and have paid standard-rate Class 1 or Class 2 NI contributions for at least 26 weeks during a set period. Both SMP and Maternity Allowance can be paid for up to 18 weeks. Women who have not paid NI contributions get no help. Women on Income Support or Family Credit may apply for **Social Fund Maternity Payment** to help with maternity expenses, but this is only available at the discretion of their local DSS Social Fund Officers.

Maternity pay and leave Women employees who are about to have a baby may qualify for maternity leave and pay from their employer. If eligible, a woman can receive nine-tenths of her normal pay for six weeks while she is away and have her job back, providing she notifies her employer in advance that she intends to return. There are other complex rules of eligibility which can be explained by the Department of Employment leaflet No. 4, *Employment Rights for the Expectant Mother*.

Non-contributory benefits

These include **Severe Disablement Allowance** for people who have not been able to work for at least 28 weeks and have not paid sufficient NI contributions, and **Industrial Disablement Benefit**, a cash benefit for any employee who has become disabled or is unable to work because of an accident at work or because of a certain illness caused by the nature of his work, e.g. industrial diseases such as pneumoconiosis and byssinosis and occupational deafness. The benefit you get is related to the severity of the disablement.

These are just a few of the available benefits. Other welfare benefits are described in Chapter 5. The Department of Social Security issues a wide range of leaflets which give details of the various benefits you can claim. There is a special **Young People's Guide to Social Security (FB 23)**.

Would Jim be able to claim any lump-sum compensation for the personal injuries he has suffered?

An accident at work is taken very seriously by the law and employers have to comply with certain health and safety regulations. There are also provisions to make sure that the injured person receives some money, some of which are the benefits outlined above. Jim, however, may feel he deserves compensation or damages for the injury he has suffered in the form of a lump sum of money. Jim would have to sue George privately in a civil court action, and would have to show that the accident happened at work when he was doing something he was employed to do, and that George was to blame. In such a case Jim would be well advised to seek the advice of a solicitor or his trade union.

Jim would have to consider his case very carefully because he would have to rely on the common law **tort of negligence** (tort = civil wrong) and this means that **he would have to prove to the court that his injuries were caused by his employer's negligence.** It is true he could show that George had failed to repair the roof of the workshop and should have foreseen that rain coming through the roof would come into contact with electrical equipment making it dangerous for members of his workforce to use. George had not complied with his duties under the **Health and Safety at Work Act** in this respect. However, Jim may have to exercise some caution, because George could make a counter-claim against Jim for negligently switching on the appliance without reading the precautionary notice, and could allege that he contributed to his own injury. The outcome of such a case would depend on what the judge decided. If he found that both parties were negligent then the damages would be allocated in proportion to each party's share of the blame, so if the judge decided they were equally to blame, the amount of damages each party was claiming might be cancelled out by the other. If, on the other hand, the judge decided that one party was slightly more to blame than the other, then the damages would be reduced and awarded to the other party accordingly. In this case, George's liability would appear to be slightly stronger than Jim's because he failed to keep his workshop safe, but Jim would only receive a small proportion of the damages for which he has hoping because of his own **contributory negligence**.

A civil claim for personal injury

A claim may only be made when you have a right to compensation, that is, as a result of the injury you have lost money in some way such as time off work, hospital fares, torn clothes, etc. These may be quantified with additional damages that the court determines having regard to all the circumstances. For example where a young person has been injured in an accident and is disabled for life, the defaulting party would have to compensate for the life-style the injured person would have had, had not the accident happened. You cannot claim damages if you have lost nothing.

Tort of negligence When making a claim for a personal injury in the civil courts, you take a private action for negligence against the person who was responsible for your injury.

Negligence is one of the most important and common torts of law. The plaintiff suing in negligence must prove three points for a successful claim:

- **That the defendant was under a duty of care to the plaintiff,** e.g. an employer is under a duty of care to his or her employee; a manufacturer is under a duty of care to supply commodities that are safe for the public to use; one road user is under a duty of care not to injure other road-users; teachers owe a duty of care to their students; the list is endless.
- **That there has been a breach of that duty**, i.e. the defendant has been careless or merely disregarded to do something which he should reasonably have done in the circumstances of the case, based on the idea that he should have foreseen the likely injury to the other person by his act or by his omission to do something.
- **That as a result the plaintiff has suffered damage.** The 'damage' can be physical, mental or financial, or any combination of these. Financial only when there has been either physical damage causing the financial loss or where there has been a specially close legal relationship, such as something close to a contractual relationship.

Contributory negligence The **Law Reform (Contributory Negligence) Act 1945, Section 1 (1)** provides that:

Where a person suffers damage as a result partly of his own fault and partly of the fault of any other person or persons, a claim in respect of that damage shall not be defeated by reason of the fault of the person suffering the damage, but the damages recoverable in respect thereof shall be reduced to such an extent as the court thinks just and equitable having regard to the claimant's share in the responsibility for the damage.

This means that anyone who contributes partly to his own injury because of his own carelessness will lose a proportion of any damages that he is likely to have claimed from the negligent party. Common examples of this are non-compliance with health and safety rules by both the

Going to Work 93

employer and employee, or where a pedestrian carelessly steps in front of an oncoming car which is being driven in excess of the statutory speed limit for that road. In such a case the court may find that the employer or pedestrian was 20 per cent to blame for the injuries he suffered and accordingly award him damages 20 per cent less than he might have had against the employee or negligent driver. Sometimes the 'fault' of the other person or the company that you are suing is difficult to prove. There are many people of the opinion that we in Britain should introduce a 'no fault' system of compensation for all accident injuries as is practised in countries such as Germany.

Insurance Cover Many companies, firms, and other organisations insure themselves so that they can meet any negligence claims made against them. Likewise all drivers of vehicles on the highway *must* insure themselves in the event of accident and damage to their cars, third persons, and themselves on the road. In cases where the insurance cover is not sufficient to cover all your losses or you cannot be successfully indemnified for some reason or other, then you can resort to a civil court and make a claim in the tort of negligence, as outlined above.

Health and Safety at Work

The Health and Safety at Work Act 1974 is based on the principle of mutual responsibility of management and workers alike to be aware of the importance of achieving high standards of health and safety at the workplace. The scope of health and safety legislation includes all persons at work, whether they be employers, employees, or the self-employed. The first concern is to do everything possible to prevent the occurrence of accidents and occupational ill-health. The second concern is to ensure that everyone using the premises and dangerous substances on it should co-operate to exercise every care to keep their workplace safe and healthy not only for themselves but also for other members of the public who may be affected by the work activities. The legislation covers such things as:

- **protective clothing** – eye-shields, respirators, overalls
- **safe clothing** – no loose ties, belts or hair near machinery; sensible footwear; head covering when working near food
- **protection of dangerous machinery** with guards or fencing; adequate warnings and signs
- **strict supervision and handling of all flammable materials and toxic substances**
- **the instigation of proper fire precautions**
- available **first aid** and medical attention.

Do not fool about

Accidents can be caused by fooling about, so don't indulge in horse-play at your place of work. Remember one slip could be enough to cause regret for the rest of your life.

Do not throw things or meddle with switches or levers; you may cause serious harm to yourself and to others. Remember that compressed air is a powerful working tool—not a toy; don't play around with it, it could be very dangerous.

Do not meddle with machinery

Do not touch machinery unless you have been told to do so and have been instructed in its use. If there is a fault, report the matter to your supervisor and get proper advice and help. Do NOT attempt to fix it yourself.

Do not interfere with, or interrupt, other people who are using machinery; distraction can be dangerous. Take particular care when near moving machinery and DO NOT remove any protective guard or fencing, except under supervision.

Figure 4.4 Health and Safety at Work – an extract from a leaflet for young workers, produced by the Health and Safety Executive

Going to Work

When an accident occurs, it must be reported at once to someone in authority and a record of the accident and when and where it occurred should be made by the employer – most workplaces are under a statutory duty to keep an **accident book** for this purpose. Even apparently slight accidents should not be overlooked because more serious complications may emerge at a later date and a person will want to claim his or her industrial injuries benefits and many other entitlements from the recorded date of the accident. Many accidents at work can be caused by people behaving foolishly such as not paying attention to cleanliness after coming into contact with poisonous substances, not being tidy, leaving objects on the floor for other people to fall over, lifting heavy objects without help or proper instructions on how to lift them, and indulging in horseplay. Also, **warning notices should always be heeded**.

In 1989 the *Control of Substances Hazardous to Health Regulations* were introduced to place a duty on employers to protect people at work from substances they might use, such as chemicals, solvents, dusts, fumes, oils, cleaning agents and micro-organisms.

The Offices, Shops and Railway Premises Act 1963 It is the responsibility of the occupier or owner of working premises to ensure the requirements of the Act are met. In shops, offices and railway premises the temperature must not fall below 16°C (60°F) after the first hour in the rooms where people work. There must not be overcrowding, and first-aid facilities must be available in the event of an accident at work. Other provisions include an adequate supply of drinking water; effective supplies of either fresh air or air conditioning; suitable and sufficient sanitary conveniences and washing facilities including a supply of hot and cold water; lighting which must be comfortable to the eyes, and clean premises. There must also be adequate fire precautions.

The Factories Act 1961 makes similar provisions for people who work in factories. Factories must be kept at a 'reasonable' temperature, dirt and refuse must be cleaned away every day, and fresh air must move freely through the building. There should be clean and sufficient toilets, a place to wash, drinking water and first-aid facilities. The premises must be safe with adequate fire precautions.

The role of trade unions

CASE 3:

Vicarious liability in tort – trade unions

Sally is a full-time employee of Power Machines Ltd. As a qualified mechanic she is employed to carry out repairs and maintenance on machines already sold to customers of the firm. This means that she does a great deal of travelling as part of her job and for this purpose she is supplied with a transit van by her boss, George. Sally has a notice by the driver's seat warning her not to carry unauthorised passengers – that is, anyone not connected with the business – in the van. Sally, however, decided to take her boy-friend Malcolm to a football match one afternoon in the van when she should have been working. On the way home the van was involved in an accident in which Malcolm was severely injured and permanently disabled. He claimed that the transit van had faulty steering and he decided to sue Power Machines Ltd for damages. George angrily reprimanded Sally and told her that since she was doing what she was not employed to do when the accident took place, she should be the party whom Malcolm should sue. He also said that he would consider taking some disciplinary action against Sally for disobeying the firm's ruling on 'no passengers'. Sally replied, why shouldn't she have a bit of fun on the side, when normally she's good at her job. She said she would take the matter to her union. When she was on the way to see the shop steward, she met one of the more militant members of the union, Joe, and told him of George's threat. 'Don't worry, sister', said Joe, 'We'll get the lads to give you some backing even if it means downing tools.'

Whom should Malcolm sue – George as the boss of Power Machines Ltd or Sally as the driver of the van?

The first question Malcolm must ask himself is to what extent George is **vicariously liable** for the tort, or civil wrong, of his employee, Sally. Vicarious liability means that in some circumstances one person can be liable for the torts committed by another even though he did not commit the wrongful act himself. The general rule is that a boss, or master, is vicariously liable for the torts of his employee, or servant **committed during the course of his employment**. Other questions Malcolm must ask are, was the wrongful act expressly or by implication authorised by George the master? Or was Sally doing something which she was not authorised to do or which was not a proper part of her job? Clearly in this case, Sally disobeyed George's

Going to Work

rule not to take an unauthorised passenger in the van. In doing this, she was acting 'outside the proper course of her employment' and by taking Malcolm out in the firm's time she was – to use a judicial phrase – 'on a frolic of her own'. This means that Malcolm would be better advised to sue not George in an action for vicarious liability but Sally in a private action for damages for his personal injuries. However, there is the question of the alleged faulty steering and it is possible that George may have to take some of the blame for not keeping his firm's vehicle in a roadworthy and safe condition even though this was Sally's job as the regular driver of the vehicle. If Malcolm was able to show this by getting an independent report on the state of the van at the time of the accident, then he might find that he could take separate actions against both Sally and George, for their negligence.

Vicarious liability

In certain circumstances one person can be held liable for the torts of another even though he himself did not commit the tort in question. The most common circumstances of this is where there is a **master-and-servant relationship**. The modern interpretation of the 'master-and-servant' relationship is that of employer and employee (not independent contractor). This is usually where the employer controls the work and the working conditions of the employee, supplies his place of work and his tools, pays National Insurance for him and where the employee's income tax is paid under the PAYE (Pay-as-you-earn) scheme.

If an employee commits wrong **in the course of his employment** and injures someone, the victim can sue both the employer vicariously and the careless employee. The policy behind this rule is to ensure that the victim is properly compensated. It also makes the assumption that employers should select responsible employees and supervise them properly.

In *Century Insurance Co. v. Northern Ireland Road Transport (1942)*, the driver of a petrol lorry was transferring petrol into an underground storage tank. He struck a match to light a cigarette and this caused an explosion resulting in great damage to the garage. **Held:** that the driver was negligent in carrying out his authorised work, and his employers were vicariously liable.

In *Beard v. London General Omnibus co. (1900)* a bus conductor drove a bus negligently and collided with the plaintiff. It transpired that the conductor was not authorised to drive the bus. **Held:** The employers were not liable as the servant was employed as a conductor and not as a driver and was therefore forbidden to drive buses. He had acted outside the course of his employment.

Vicarious liability will only apply where the employee is doing his job properly but is not acting in an authorised manner. If he injures someone doing something he is not paid to do, fooling around or going on a 'frolic of his own', he is solely responsible for his own actions.

If an employer does have to pay damages because of vicarious liability, he can in turn ask the employee to indemnify him or take disciplinary action against him.

Liability for independent contractors The general rule is that an employer is not liable for the torts of an independent contractor or a servant employed by the contractor. Independent contractors are usually liable for their own torts.

How far can Sally's trade union be of assistance to her?

This would depend on the kind of agreements already laid down and practised between the management of Power Machines Ltd and the trade union. If she is a member of the union, Sally is entitled to go to the firm's elected shop steward who is there to talk over any member's grievance, give her advice, and where necessary negotiate between her and the employer. A union official can also arrange for tribunal representation for any member who requires this service, but, normally the union will only intervene on a worker's behalf if it is convinced a member is being treated unfairly or unlawfully by the management of the place of work. In Sally's case a lot may depend on the kind of industrial relationship which George and the union enjoy. If the relationship is a good one, then the union is unlikely to assist Sally with her grievance because, on the face of it, she was acting unreasonably as an employee. However, the union would ensure that any disciplinary proceedings taken against Sally were in accordance with the firm's grievance procedures. Also, the union may request an investigation into the safety of the firm's vehicles. If Sally herself is away from work as a result of the accident, the union can also advise her on sick pay and other welfare benefits. If the union does not have a very good relationship with the management, then there is the danger that any strong disciplinary moves George takes against Sally may bring about some form of industrial action but under the **Trade Union Act 1984,** this would be unlawful unless the strike was endorsed by a majority vote in a ballot of the membership.

Trade unions

Trade unions are many and varied, representing something over 10 million people in the UK (1984 figures). A trade union is defined in the

Going to Work

Trade Union and Labour Relations Act 1974 as 'an organisation consisting wholly or mainly of workers whose principal purpose is the regulation of industrial relations with employers or employers' associations'. All individual trade unions are affiliated to the **Trade Union Congress** (TUC) which holds an annual conference to discuss issues affecting them and to re-examine their common aims.

The common aims of the trade unions include:

- negotiating maximum wages, better working conditions and job security for their members
- ensuring that their members get the benefits, such as redundancy pay and industrial injuries benefits, to which they are entitled
- providing legal advice and services such as tribunal representation, to their members
- participating in appropriate public bodies, e.g. the National Economic Development Council (Neddy).

Union officials and their duties Union officials such as shop stewards and staff representatives, can take 'a reasonable' amount of paid time off work for their duties and activities. (What is a 'reasonable' amount of time will depend on such factors as the size of the firm, the number of members, and the work and economic pressures on the firm.) These would include: matters concerning members, appearing before tribunals, lecturing new employees, and attending approved industrial training courses. ACAS have published a Code of Practice, which gives guidance on how the rules are to be applied.

Union members Union members can take a 'reasonable' amount of unpaid time for their union activities, but sometimes employers may agree to pay members in certain important circumstances. If an employer refuses members time off, the employee can complain to an industrial tribunal within three months. The tribunal can order the employer to award compensation to the aggrieved member.

Members of the police force, the armed services, and those engaged in official secrets and security are not allowed to be members of a union, or take industrial action.

Once you become a member you are expected to attend union meetings, obey the constitutional rules and pay an annual subscription. Unions have the right to discipline or expel a member from the union if he does not comply with the rules of membership.

Trade unions build up educational and training funds for their members and also strike funds to help members in the event of a prolonged strike. Some unions also run insurance schemes, and generally aim to protect their members from unemployment and poverty.

The law and trade unions **Taking industrial action** This area of trade union law is controversial and often changes because it is fraught with political overtones. Your trade union may require you to go on strike and to picket. **Picketing** is only lawful for the purpose of peacefully obtaining or communicating information (by word of mouth or by leaflets or banners, etc.) or peacefully persuading any person to abstain from working, or to give support to the dispute. Anyone who goes beyond peaceful picketing is acting unlawfully. The **Trade Union and Labour Relations Act 1974** does not allow pickets to stop vehicles so that they can communicate with the driver to persuade him from entering the employer's premises. In practice, however, the police use their discretion to allow the stopping of vehicles provided this is done in an orderly manner. You can only picket your own place of work. This means that 'secondary picketing' at someone else's place of work is illegal and the employer of that firm can obtain an injunction to stop the pickets. Often the law breaks down and disorder ensues when people picket in excessive numbers either to stop people going to work or to stop the collection or delivery of goods. The prolonged miners' strike of 1984 was an example of excessive picketing, unlawful obstruction and intimidation of people who wished to go to work.

Trade unions intensely dislike any legislation which they allege interferes with their right to take industrial action. Other people including many politicians feel they have a duty to curb what they see as 'mob rule' by 'strong-armed' unions, and want to see more legislation to protect other groups in the community. It is true that unions vary considerably in their bargaining strength, and there are certain groups, such as the nursing profession, who feel a strong duty not to go on strike in the interests of the patients who depend upon them. It is also possible for other members of the public or of other industries to suffer considerable hardship because of the actions of a powerful union.

Under the **Trade Union and Labour Relations Act 1974**, S.13 trade unionists were given statutory immunity from being sued for damages but only when they were acting 'in contemplation or furtherance of a trade dispute'. This section led to many interpretations of what is meant by a 'trade dispute'. The general view that it concerned the term of work, allocation of work, dismissals, discipline at work and the provision of union facilities, was often misinterpreted to suit the political or personal interests of certain individuals and groups. The **Employment Act 1980**, an amendment of the 1974 Act, was an attempt towards protecting firms who were not involved in the dispute but suffered heavy losses through secondary action, such as blacking and sympathy strikes, but not secondary picketing. The 1980 Act enables firms affected in this way to take action in the civil courts against a culprit union. The **Trade Union Act 1984** takes away the tortious immunity which would otherwise have been available under S.13 of the Trade Union and Labour Relations Act 1974, as amended, in respect of acts of inducing a person to break his employment contract or to interfere with its performance. S.10 of the 1984 Act says that where the industrial action is authorised or endorsed by a trade union without the support of the majority vote in a ballot, the act can be actionable in tort against the trade union on the ground that it induced a person to break a commercial contract or interfered with its performance. The employer can claim for his economic loss in the civil courts. The miners' strike of 1984, which was held for a year without a ballot of its union members, was unlawful. More recently the government has introduced the **Employment Act 1988** which many people believe interferes with the way trade unions may conduct their own internal affairs. Others argue that the aim of the Act is to protect individual trade-union members from unfair union practices. The Act enables all trade-union members the right to a secret ballot and to take his or her union to court if it attempts unballotted industrial action. It also sets down controls on the disciplinary procedures of unions towards their members, enabling a union member to take legal action against the union if it does not comply with the rules laid down in the Act and in previous trade-union laws. It also gives the individual member the right to inspect the union accounts. The Act has virtually wiped out the former 'closed-shop' agreement which required all employees of a particular industry to be a union member whatever their personal views about joining a union. The government are proposing further legal provisions for trade unions in a new Employment Bill.

Trade union immunity does not extend to **criminal law**. Members of a picket line who do not act peacefully can be prosecuted for breach of the peace, obstructing the highway or for insulting behaviour. The role of the police is to maintain law and order so; although the police have powers to limit the number of people on picket lines, they may exercise an element of discretion where technical infringements of the law takes place. On the other hand, the police have been accused of applying the law too forcefully where the pickets turn up in large numbers.

Exercises

1. Is there a legal remedy in the following situations? State the problem, what kind of advice you would seek and from where and, if relevant, in which court or tribunal you would ultimately seek a remedy.

    (a) You work in a shop and your employer refuses to pay you some holiday money to which you are entitled.
    (b) Your boss has accused you of meddling with some dangerous machinery and instantly dismisses you. You know that it was he who forgot to replace the guard.
    (c) You have been persistently late for work, and after two warnings by your boss, you were given a written notice of dismissal.

(d) You have been working for your firm for five months. You have never been given an itemised pay slip, nor have you been given a contract in writing.

(e) At the firm's Christmas party, which took place in the firm's time, you fooled around with the fuse box and switched out all the lights. An employee at the party tripped over some office furniture and severely injured her leg.

2. Can you solve the following problem?

   Marian, aged 24, has had a good job in publicity for four years. She is highly qualified and has often been commended for her efficiency and pleasant manner. The manager of her department, however, is of the opinion that a woman's place is in the home, and when he learns that Marian is about to get married, he begins to make life unbearable for her; he jeers at her at meetings saying such things as 'women can't think logically' and 'get your hands back into the kitchen sink where they belong'. When Marian attends an interview for promotion, the manager is on the interviewing panel and he openly questions her about her sex life and how many children she might have when she is married. The job goes to a male candidate who has less experience than Marian. On returning from lunch one day, Marian finds the manager half drunk and he threatens her and makes more abusive comments about her private life. Marian becomes very distraught and impulsively gives in her notice and walks out. Afterwards she regrets what she has done.

   Advise Marian on her legal position.

3. **Accident at work**

   (a) Read the following account of an accident at work.

   As supervisor of the workshop, you are required to **fill in the company's accident claim form.** Make a copy of the form illustrated in Figure 4.5 and fill in the relevant details.

   - **Details of the accident**
     Charlie Carpenter is employed in the Cutting Division of the Wood Company Ltd, who are a firm of furniture makers. His normal working day is from 8a.m. to 5p.m. with an hour for lunch starting at 12.30p.m.

     Charlie, who is a pigeon fancier, likes to go up on the roof of the factory in his lunch-breaks to catch pigeons. He knows he is not allowed up on the roof as there is a large notice to this effect on the factory notice board and also at the foot of the stairs leading to the roof.

     On 3 March of this year, while he was chasing a pigeon, Charlie slipped and fell through a ventilation shaft in the roof and on to some

Going to Work 103

machinery below. Fortunately, the time of the accident was about 12.45p.m. when the machines were not in motion, but Charlie happened to fall on to an unguarded saw and sustained severe cuts to his body and a broken arm. The guard had inadvertently been left off that morning, after a few repairs had been done to the machine. The Machine was of the Liver Blade Saw type and manufactured by Cuttam and Co. Ltd.

Two workers nearby, Ivor Heart and Tony Goodman, who were playing a game of cards over their lunch, saw Charlie fall, and while Ivor stayed with Charlie, Tony ran off to fetch the foreman, Tim Tough, who was in the works canteen in the next building. Tim Tough immediately arranged for a car to take Charlie to the casualty department of the nearby hospital. Later, he made sure that the guard was replaced on the machine.

- **You, as supervisor** had to hear the stories of Ivor and Tony in order to fill in your report. You also know that Charlie has not been back to work since the accident, he is still at home recovering from his injuries.
  (b) Discuss how the accident report might be used to decide (i) statutory sick pay and state benefits, and (ii) a personal injuries claim.

4. Write a letter offering a job to a successful applicant stating the terms and conditions of employment either in the letter itself or on a separate sheet with a covering letter. Remember, you are offering the job, to someone who might accept or reject your offer. If your offer is accepted, a contract is formed.

5. (a) Prepare and give a **brief talk** to new employees on the health and safety standards of your place of work. Invent the details.
   (b) **Draft a Safety Notice** for your school or college.

6. Study this extract and then answer questions (a) to (e) which follow:

Psychiatric nurse Derek Owen, aged 46, who was sacked at Walsgrave hospital, Coventry, after refusing to be involved in administering electrical shock treatment, lost his appeal against unfair dismissal in the Appeal Court yesterday, Lord Justice Bingham said that the final decision in such matters was that of the doctors and it was the duty of the nurses in all but the most exceptional cases not to intervene.

(*The Guardian*, 20 December 1986)

```
┌─────────────────────────────────────────────────────────────┐
│                    ACCIDENT REPORT FORM                      │
│                                                              │
│  NAME OF INJURED PERSON (Block Capitals) ..................  │
│  DIVISION (Block Capitals) ................................  │
│  PARTICULARS OF ACCIDENT                                     │
│  1.  Where did the accident occur? ........................  │
│      Date ........................ Time ..................  │
│  2.  Date reported ................. To whom reported .....  │
│  3.  State (a) the cause of the injuries (full information)  │
│      ....................................................    │
│      (b) the nature of the injuries ......................  │
│      ....................................................    │
│  4.  State fully what the injured person was doing when the accident
│      occurred and was it authorised ......................  │
│      ....................................................    │
│  5.  If machinery is involved state type, maker, part causing injury and
│      whether in motion at the time of the accident .......  │
│      ....................................................    │
│  6.  State action to prevent recurrence ..................  │
│      ....................................................    │
│  7.  Has person resumed work? Yes/No. If 'Yes' give date .. │
│      If 'No' state date on which injured person was first absent ....
│      ....................................................    │
│  8.  Any other relevant details, e.g. did the injured person resume
│      work on the day of the accident after any necessary rest or
│      treatment?                                              │
│      ....................................................    │
│      ....................................................    │
│                                                              │
│  WITNESSES to accident 1.                                    │
│                        2.                                    │
│  Supervisor's signature .................... Date ........  │
└─────────────────────────────────────────────────────────────┘
```

Figure 4.5   An example of an accident report form

(a) Why was Derek Owen sacked? (2)
(b) To what extent must an employee obey orders? (3)
(c) Explain what is meant by constructive dismissal. (4)
(d) Explain what is meant by unfair dismissal. (6)
(e) To what extent should the law imply rights and duties into a contract of employment? (10)

LEAG GCSE Examination June 1988 (Paper 2)

7. *GCSE assignment suggestions*

(a) Re-read the problem of Marian in question 2 above, and consider not only how Marian may be advised on her legal rights but also how, in her case, she might resort to an Industrial Tribunal and the kind of procedures she would undergo. Also consider:

(i) What are the advantages of an Industrial Tribunal over an

Going to Work   105

        ordinary court of law for settling disputes of this type?
        (ii) Is there any stage, on appeal, when Marian might have to resort to the main court system?
- (b) How successful have the Equal Pay Act and Sex Discrimination Acts been in achieving equality for women?
- (c) How effective is the Race Relations Act in achieving its specific aims of equal opportunity?
- (d) To what extent have the laws relating to employee protection advanced or taken away the rights of the young person?
- (e) Trace the laws relating to the freedom and restraint of trade-union activity.

Role play asignments

1. *Either* complete the details on form IT 1 (Figure 4.6.) and use it, *or* enact the case imagining what might have taken place from the time the dispute arose to its final conclusion at an industrial tribunal. Use facsimile copies of the IT 1 forms for the applicant and the respondent (see Fig. 4.6) and the illustrated plan of an industrial tribunal (see Fig. 10.10) to simulate a tribunal room in your classroom. The hearing could be recorded on a video or cassette-tape recorder and played back to the class or group for criticism and comment.
2. Simulate a General Election **television programme** or a **public meeting** in which two MPs of opposing parties (played by students) debate the question of whether or not more legislation should be introduced to curb the activities of the trade unions. Students who form the audience can be asked to write a **press report** on the arguments put forward.

Suggested visits

Industrial tribunal – generally open to the public, but a telephone call in advance to announce your arrival is advisable.

Citizens Advice Bureau or Department of Employment – by arrangement only. Here the wide range of leaflets available could be shown to the students, and questions answered. Alternatively, a guest speaker from these organisations could be arranged.

County court – it is always essential to discuss the visit in advance with an official of the Clerk's Office. The judges do not sit every day in most courts and many cases are settled out of court before the proposed hearing is due to take place. The official can advise on the best time and the most suitable case for your needs.

FOR OFFICIAL USE ONLY		
Received at COIT	Case No.	Code
	Initials	ROIT

Application to an Industrial Tribunal

Please read the notes opposite before filling in this form.

1 Say what type of complaint(s) you want the tribunal to decide *(see note opposite)*.

Unfair dismissal

2 Give your name and address etc. in CAPITALS *(see note opposite)*.

Mr/~~Mrs~~
~~Miss/Ms~~   Jeremy Smith

Address
2 Queen's Square
Shiretown
Wessex

Telephone   —

Date of birth 1st April 1967

3 Please give the name and address of your representative, if you have one.

Name   Mrs B. Jones

Address
Community Law Centre
Howards Street
Shiretown,
Wessex.

Telephone   03366 1234

4 Give the name and address of the employer, person or body (the respondent) you are complaining about *(see note opposite)*.

Name   Mr Len Tankard

Address
Prince Albert
Restaurant,
High Road,
Shiretown, Wessex.

Telephone   03366 5678

Give the place where you worked or applied for work, if different from above.

Name

Address
as above

Telephone

5 Please say what job you did for the employer (or what job you applied for). If this does not apply, please say what your connection was with the employer.

Waiter

IT 1 (Revised August 1986)   Please continue overleaf

Figure 4.6 Applying to an industrial tribunal

Going to Work

6 Please give the number of normal basic hours you worked per week.

Hours [ ] per week

7 Basic wage / salary £ [ ] per [ ]

Average take home pay £ [ ] per [ ]

Other bonuses / benefits £ [ ] per [ ]

8 Please give the dates of your employment *(if applicable)*

Began on [ ]

Ended on [ ]

9 If your complaint is **not** about dismissal, please give the date when the action you are complaining about took place (or the date when you first knew about it).

Date [ ]

10 Give the full details of your complaint *(see note opposite)*.

11 Unfair dismissal claimants only (Please tick a box to show what you would want if you win your case).

[x] Reinstatement: to carry on working in your old job as before

[x] Re-engagement: to start another job, or a new contract, with your old employer

[x] Compensation: to get an award of money

You can change your mind later. The Tribunal will take your preference into account, but will not be bound by it.

Signature: Date:

5 No Job

Figure 5.1 Looking for work

For many young people leaving school or college, unemployment is a big problem. The chances of finding work or acquiring further vocational training cannot always be guaranteed and will depend a lot on where you live. Youngsters of the 1980s and 1990s are entering the work-market at a time when there is widening world competition. The situation in Britain is affected because other countries are making cheaper goods than ours and are competing with us on the world markets. Also many computerised machines are doing the jobs people used to do, so fewer people are needed to produce the goods we sell.

No Job

Many young people do find work, while others may register for a place on a training scheme. It may have taken them several months to find a job or a training place; it may not be quite what they want, but at least these young people have the advantage over the unemployed of gaining work experience and possibly learning a useful skill and earning a wage. Other young people wisely return to further and higher education or to some other type of training scheme in order to become skilled and thereby improve their chances of getting work in the future. However this is not the obvious solution for everyone.

This chapter aims to explain the ways and possibilities of getting money, training and work, and the legal implications of these. It explains the social security entitlements for those looking for work or work experience. We shall also consider the position of those in part-time and full-time education. We shall do this by looking at the cases of two typical school-leavers, Les who wants a job on leaving school, and Meeta, who is taking three 'A' levels and aims to go on to higher education.

Les and Meeta have each decided to seek advice from their local Citizens Advice Bureau. Below are the transcripts of their interviews.

Figure 5.2   Seeking Advice from the Citizens Advice Bureau

A scenario: at the Citizens Advice Bureau

The following interviews could be adapted for a role-play exercise. In addition to this, interviews can be recorded either on close-circuit television or cassette tape, and played back to the class or group for commentary and discussion. Leaflets mentioned in the interviews are obtainable either from the DSS, Careers Office, or a CAB, and can be used in the role play.

1. Les's interview

How to 'sign on' – income support – ways of getting work or work experience

Les: *I'm nearly sixteen and leaving school at the end of the summer term. I shall be taking some GCSE exams but, frankly, I don't expect to get very good results. To tell the truth I can't wait to leave school and earn my own living. I'm prepared to take any kind of work, or, failing that, something through the Youth Training Scheme. Can you tell me about signing on, I'm not sure how to go about it?*

Interviewer: If you were over 18 you would have to go to your local unemployment office, but since you are under 18 you 'sign on' or register for work at your local careers office. Just after your 16th birthday you should have had your **National Insurance Number card** posted to you. You did? Good! Printed on it was your **personal National Insurance or NI number**. This number you

Figure 5.3 The National Insurance Numbercard

No Job

will keep all of your working life and possibly beyond that – you will need it to sign on, you can't claim benefits without it, and when you get a job your employer will need to know your NI number. So don't forget to keep your card in a safe place. Now, coming back to your question, at the careers office, you will be interviewed by the officer there and he will ask you to fill in a form stating that you are 'actively seeking work' and will take on any job that is offered. No one can claim either income support or unemployment benefit without this formality; it is a condition of receiving state benefits that you are prepared to accept work if it is offered, and if you refuse work you risk losing your benefit.

Les: *I see. What's the difference between unemployment benefit and income support?*

Interviewer: You only receive unemployment benefit when you have been employed and have been paying national insurance contributions over a certain period before claiming, usually a full year's contribution in the previous tax year. Income support is a benefit available from the Department of Social Security (DSS) to help people who either have no work or who work less than 24 hours a week, and who do not have enough money to live on. You don't have to pay national insurance to get it, but it is means-tested; that means that the money the claimant already has is taken into account when deciding how much s/he should get. For example, if you have any savings over £3000 and under £8000 the amount of benefit you receive will be reduced according to how much savings you have. If you have savings over £8000, then you would not qualify for the benefit – I see, Les, that you are shaking your head rather vigorously!

Les: *Too true. I'm skint! Once I've 'signed on' will I be able to claim income support just to tie me over while I'm looking for work?*

Interviewer: Unfortunately, most 16 and 17 year olds are not eligible for income support, unless they come into one of the categories for people who don't have to be 'available for work', such as single parents, pregnant women and the long-term sick – which, Les, you clearly aren't. Income support may be paid on a discretionary basis to certain under-16-year-old claimants for whom refusal would cause exceptional hardship, such as those who are in care, orphaned, or genuinely estranged from their families, and those whose parents cannot look after them for some good reason – for example, the parents may be in prison, in hospital for some time, or unavoidably away from home. I take it you don't come into any of those groups? However, if you leave school during or at the end of the summer term, your parents will receive child benefit for you until the end of December.

Les: *Does that mean that, if I stay on at school until I am 16, I would be able to claim income support as soon as I leave?*

Interviewer: Unfortunately not. The date from which you can claim will depend on when you leave school. Let me see, you say you leave school at the end of the summer term in July. That means you will have to wait until the first Monday in September before you can claim. The government expect your parents to look after you as if you were still on a school holiday until then. Similar rules apply at whatever time you leave school; if you leave at the end of the autumn term you can make your first claim from the first Monday in January and if you leave at the end of the spring term you can claim from the first Monday after Easter Monday.

Les: *If I am unemployed at 18 I may then claim income support. How would I claim?*

Interviewer: You would claim by going to your Unemployment Benefit Office and when you sign on ask for an income support claim form. A 16 year old who comes into the categories that I've just mentioned would go to his or her careers' office. You will be given an addressed, postage-paid envelope to send the completed form in to your local social security office. Once the application is processed through the system, and I warn you, this may take ten days or much longer, you will be paid your benefit by girocheque – this is paid by the unemployment office. Your girocheque will either be posted to your home address or you may have to collect it from the post office. And I'm afraid that is not the end of it, you may have to attend the unemployment office regularly to sign that you are still unemployed, actively looking for a job and available for work, but this will only apply if you live within six miles of your benefit office. They will tell you what day and time to attend. Of course, once you find work, you must tell the unemployment office and your benefit will be stopped.

Les: *Earlier on you mentioned something about being able to claim benefit and work 24 hours a week. Is that something I could claim?*

Interviewer: Only if you have children. The twenty-four hour rule applies only to working families with children. If one partner – the husband, wife, one parent or partner in a common-law relationship – works for 24 hours or more a week, then that family are entitled to Family Credit. Family Credit is a special tax-free benefit to assist families on low incomes, and both employed and self-employed people may claim. The amount the family gets depends on the joint income coming into the family, and allowances are given according to the number and age of the children in the family.

Les: *I see. Now getting back to my particular query. If I can't get a job, will I have to join the YTS programme?*

No Job

Interviewer: While you are under eighteen and have no income, the answer is, yes. The idea behind the Youth Training Scheme is that it guarantees a place for everyone between 16 and 18 who has not got a job, or loses a job, and hasn't enough money to live on. The scheme is meant to enable you to acquire skills and a recognised qualification or a credit towards one. Admittedly, the training allowance you receive is very modest; it is slightly improved in the second year of your training.

Les: *I know I have to register for YTS at the local Jobcentre, but there aren't many places around this area. If I get a place away from home, do I receive any extra money?*

Interviewer: You get assistance with travelling expenses, and, if you have to stay in board and lodgings or in hostel accommodation, you should get income support on top of your training allowance. If you find a place to rent, as a tenant, you can apply for housing benefit to assist you with rent and your community charge. This is available from the local authority in which you are a tenant.

Les: *Is it possible to change a YTS place if you don't like the first place you're given?*

Interviewer: It is possible to change a YTS place, but usually the reason you are required to give is that you think a change would help you. You would have to talk it over with the person responsible for your training or the careers officer. If you leave of your own accord, you would lose entitlement to a Bridging Allowance.

Les: *What's a Bridging Allowance?*

Interviewer: It's a small sum of money, at the moment £15, which is paid to any youngster for up to eight weeks if he or she either changes a YTS place, is waiting for one or loses a place and has to re-apply for another. Incidentally, Bridging Allowances are not paid to a young person whose parents are still receiving Child Benefit on his or her behalf.

Les: *Frankly, YTS is the last resort for me. The pay is so poor. How can I find work? I'm not fussy – anything will do so long as I can get started. Well, to be honest with you I'm better working with my hands than my brain.*

Interviewer: And I have to be honest with you, most employers are looking for youngsters who do have some skills, training or work experience. However, the only thing you can do is to keep looking. Don't give up too easily. First make regular visits to the Careers Office, Jobcentre and other employment agencies – something may have come in just the day you happen to be there. Also scan the job advertisements in the local and national newspapers and shop windows, and it's a good idea to keep your ears open – a lot of people find jobs by hearing about them from a relative, friend or someone else. For example, perhaps a local builder or supermarket is looking for someone eager to learn the trade. Sometimes it's a good idea to write to firms and companies and other organisations and send them details about yourself; if they can't find you a job straight away they may like the sound of you and keep your name on a file until something turns up. Whatever you do you should aim to get work experience. It may mean taking anything for the time being. For example, you may be offered a short-term job, say at Christmas time or in the summer, or some casual labouring. These can add up to 'work experience'. Of course, the obvious way is to register for the Youth Training Scheme.

Les: *You may prove to be right in the end. Anyhow, thanks for your advice. Once I've decided, I may come back to talk about my rights either as an employee or a YTS trainee.*

Interviewer: We'll be pleased to see you, Les. We are here whenever you need our help. Good luck!

Note: For an outline on social security benefits and additional information not mentioned in this interview, see pp. 119–22.

2. Meeta's interview

Students in advanced, and non-advanced education – grants – other financial help

Meeta: *I am 18 and I am taking 'A' levels this coming summer. I've already talked over my future course of study with my school careers advisor and my teachers, who have advised me to apply for a place at university through UCCA (the Universities Central Council on Admissions) and to some polytechnics. But there are one or two things I should like clarified about getting a grant and generally paying my way as a student. For example what are my chances of getting a student grant?*

Interviewer: If the course you have chosen is full-time or a sandwich course – these, as you probably know, are courses which combine full-time study with periods of full-time training and work experience in industry or commerce – then you may qualify for what is called a **mandatory grant or award**.

The two words 'award' and 'grant' are often used interchangeably, but the regulations make a distinction between them; an **award** covers both your maintenance, paid directly to you, and your tuition and course fees, which are paid direct to the university or college, whereas a **grant** only covers the maintenance element.

Mandatory awards and grants are only available for certain designated courses, usually in the higher education sector for such courses as yours leading to a university or CNAA (The Council for National Academic Awards) degree, or courses for the Diploma of Higher Education, for Higher National Diploma courses, and other such courses which are comparable with a degree or a similar course of study of any length. The Department of Education and Science offers free, a good guide, **Grants to Students**, which lists the types of course which qualify for a mandatory grant and also those for which you may only get a discretionary grant from the local authority after you are 19. It's worth getting a copy from your Careers Office, or we may have some copies here at the CAB. In your instance, Meeta, your proposed course of study would qualify you for a mandatory award, but there is another factor you will have to take into account, and that is your parents' income. You won't necessarily get the grant in full or you may not even qualify for it at all. The amount you will receive will be determined on your parents' income and on how many other children in your family are in higher education. This will be assessed by your local authority. There is now no minimum grant so you could be totally dependent on your parents – except for tuition fees which are paid for everyone by the local education authority. The best advice I can give you is to get your application for a mandatory award to the local education authority in the area in which you live as soon as you can. The best time to apply is between October and February in the academic year before you leave your sixth form.

Meeta: *Will the amount of award I get be more if I have to live away from home?*

Interviewer: Yes. The grants are calculated according to an assessment of your needs called **maintenance requirements**. These consist of a basic maintenance grant plus any additions to fit your particular circumstances, so students living in a hall of residence or in lodgings while studying at a higher education establishment will get an extra living allowance built into their grant. The amounts can vary, for example, if you study in London you will get a larger living allowance than someone who studies outside the London area. Also excess travelling expenses above a given figure can be reimbursed by the local authority. But a special application must be made to them. A copy of the DES booklet on student grants will give all the up-to-date facts you want to know on grants and on excess travelling expenses.

Meeta: *Yes, I will get a copy. Now can you tell me, is there any kind of state benefit I can get while I am at university or polytechnic?*

Interviewer: Generally speaking students on full-time courses of advanced education are excluded from benefit in term-time. This is because the grant is assumed to cover this, and also because full-time students cannot be available for work – a government requirement of signing-on for income support. While you are receiving a standard grant you will not get benefit in the short vacations at Christmas and Easter either, whether you live at home or not. Again the reason given is that there is an element in your grant to cover these short vacations. The long summer vacation, however, is not normally covered by the grant, so if you satisfy the normal DSS rules of being over 18 and being available for work, then you may make a claim for this period. The rules, however, don't apply to students who are unable to work, such as those who are lone parents or have some disability which keeps them from working, they may claim income support at any time if they are on low means. If, Meeta, during the long vacation you continue to live away from your parents' home and you are in lodgings and paying rent, you may also qualify for some housing benefit. It's worth an enquiry at the DSS in the area where your lodgings are.

Meeta: *I see. Of course, I may have to face up to the possibility that I won't achieve the 'A' level grades I need for going into higher education. If I did some part-time study to improve my grades, would I get any financial help then?*

Interviewer: You won't get a grant for non-advanced study if you are over 18. However, income support is available if you study for no more than 12 hours a week. This is referred to as the 12-hour rule – you may have heard of it? The scheme only applies to people in educational courses not above 'A' level or the equivalent level. Unfortunately, there is a snag, you will have signed on that you are available for work so if a job turns up during the course of study you must be willing to take it. The alternative choice is to pay the fees yourself.

Meeta: *Do you mean to say that if I'm on a part-time course and willing to take an exam at the end of it to improve my chances, I'd have to give it up if a job came along? Seems ridiculous to me!*

Interviewer: I agree, but unfortunately I'm not responsible for the rules. In fact there has been a lot of controversy over what was meant by 'part-time' – whether it should include homework or not? So, in August 1984, the DSS came up with another regulation to clarify the point. **Part-time education is now defined as the hours spent in supervised study–work, examination, projects which do not exceed 12 hours a week.** This takes into account study-time spent both on and off the education premises. However it does not include meal-breaks and unsupervised study.

Meeta: *But isn't there something else which is called 'the 21-hour rule'?*

Interviewer: Yes, this is another highly criticised regulation. If you are 18 and over, you can increase your part-time supervised study hours to twenty-one a week, but only after you have been receiving income support, sickness benefit or been on a Youth Training

Programme immediately before you start the course. If you have been on benefit since the first Monday in September after leaving school in July, you will not be eligible for part-time study under the 21-hour rule until January. As the majority of college courses commence in September, this means that you join the course either a term late in January or wait the year round to the following September. Neither can this anomaly be overcome by attending for 12 hours for the first term, as the 21-hour course must be a different course from the 12-hour course. Frankly, the best course of action for anyone seeking to train for a career outside the education system is to go for a job with built-in training. Many companies, banks, lawyers' firms, the police-force, and even the armed forces, provide excellent career opportunities for young people, and it is worth enquiring about these at your careers' office or watching the career pages of the quality newspapers.

Meeta: *You've given me much food for thought. I am now more determined than ever to get good 'A' level grades so that I can go either to university or to a Poly. Thank you for the information.*

Interviewer: You're welcome, and good luck with your studies, Meeta!

Note: At the time of writing there are government plans to introduce loans to replace student grants for advanced full-time courses.

Some things you ought to know

Signing on

National Insurance Numbercard About the time you leave school you will be sent your NI Numbercard. This will have your personal National Insurance Number on it. Both your employer and the DSS would need to know your number, so always keep your card in a safe place and take it with you when you sign on or whenever you begin a new job, or if you have to claim any benefits. You will keep this number for the whole of your working life and also in retirement when you claim your pension. If you do not know your number, it can be obtained from the local DSS office.

Where to 'sign on'?

You register for work ('sign on') at your local Careers' Office on leaving school or college. If you're 18 and over, you go to the Unemployment Office. To claim **income support** you are required to fill in the coupon on leaflet *SB 1*. The leaflet is available from post offices, the DSS or CABx. If you can't sign on

Figure 5.4 Useful leaflets for those leaving school, published yearly by the DHSS

for work because of illness, get form *SC 1* from your doctor's surgery, a hospital or a Social Security Office.
For **Family Credit** get and fill in form *FC 1*, available from post offices, the DSS and CABx, and claim by post from DSS, Government Buildings, Warbreck Hill Road, Blackpool, FY2 0YF.

Which benefit? This is the title of a useful booklet, *FB2* which is published by the DSS and updated by them every April. It lists all the benefits available to the public at large, saying how much they are and giving a few details about the right to claim on each one. It also gives the number of leaflets of specific benefits. These booklets are available from your local DSS or from the CAB. **Remember, the onus is on you to apply.**

Other useful leaflets for school-leavers:
NI196 – lists all the social security benefit rates.
FB23 Young People's Guide to Social Security

In Britain the social security scheme is paid for by national insurance contributions and taxes. There are many kinds of benefits – some you get in return for paying national insurance contributions, and others are paid to people who do not have enough money to live on, are sick or disabled. The social security benefits largely fall into two groups; those based on your own national insurance contributions and those that are 'non-contributory'.

Benefits based on NI contributions
- Unemployment Benefit
- Redundancy payments
- Statutory Sick Pay (SSP) and Sickness Benefit
- Industrial Disablement Benefit
- Invalidity Benefit
- Statutory Maternity Pay (SMP) and Maternity Allowance

Unemployment Benefit

To get unemployment benefit **you must have paid enough NI contributions, or been credited with them, in one or both of the two tax years before the year of the claim.** You must also be actively seeking work and available and able to take up any job offered you. If you are a student in full-time or higher education you may be able to get unemployment benefit for the summer vacation if you meet these rules. Once you become unemployed, or on the first day of the summer vacation if you are a student, contact your nearest Unemployment Benefit Office and take your **P45** form with you if you have one. Then you may register to find work at any Jobcentre or employment office.

Some groups of people may be disqualified from claiming unemployment benefit even though they have paid all the necessary NI contributions:

- Anyone who has left their previous employment voluntarily, without good reason; those who have no other job to go to, *or* who have been dismissed for misconduct will not be paid unemployment benefit for up to 26 weeks. (If they apply for income support, this will be reduced by 40 per cent for the first 26 weeks for the same reasons.)
- Anyone on strike may only claim for his or her dependents but not for him or herself during the period that s/he is on strike.

Keeping up your national insurance contributions It is important to keep up your NI contributions, otherwise your right to benefits in the future can be affected. Usually, when you are unemployed you will get contribution credits instead of having to pay contributions, and these keep up your contribution record. Credits can count for several benefits but you must have paid some

Table 5.1 A GUIDE TO SOCIAL SECURITY non contributory benefits

Income support	*Premiums* Additional payments for special groups	*Other*
A basic element of income support is **personal allowances,** which cover certain housing costs for: single people couples lone parents dependent children and young people **Disabled groups** are entitled to various extra benefits and allowances	Family Lone parent Pensioner Higher pensioner (aged 80 and over) Disabled Severely disabled Disabled child	**Family Credit** (See Ch. 5, Case 1) **Housing Benefit** To assist with rent, mortgage interest **Residential Home Care costs** are set at certain levels to assist the elderly in residential homes **Widow's Pension**

Note: Rates are not shown as these are changed annually. Always enquire before you claim.

No Job

contributions while in work. All young people, whether on YTS or not, are automatically awarded Class 1 credits for NI Retirement Pensions purposes up to and including the tax year in which their 18th birthday falls.

Special Class 1 credits can be awarded for the period on YTS if you make a claim for sickness benefit. If you don't get unemployment benefit you can usually still get credits if you continue to claim regularly at the unemployment benefit office.

Income support

Income support is a means-tested, or income-related, benefit paid by the Department of Social Security to assist people who have no or very little money to live on. With a few exceptional cases (see Case 1 above), it is only available to people who are 18 years of age and over. Income support can be paid on top of other benefits, like unemployment benefit, and part-time earnings, if after certain calculations, the total income of the claimant reaches a certain level of benefit laid down by the DSS. It can also be reduced by 40 per cent of the total for 26 weeks if claimants have voluntarily left their jobs without another job to go to, or if they have been fairly dismissed from their jobs.

Income support acts as a 'passport' to other benefits. A claimant or his or her dependents will automatically qualify for such things as free school meals, free prescriptions, free dental care, vouchers for spectacles, free milk and vitamins, and maximum housing benefit.

Appeals Sometimes you may have to insist on your welfare rights. If you think you are not getting what you are entitled to, you can appeal by filling in a form within 21 days at the benefit office.

The Social Fund

People, who are faced with an exceptional expense they are unable to meet out of their regular income support, may be able to get a payment from the Social Fund. There are several types of payment and loans available for which they may apply.

- **Funeral Payments**, to help with funeral expenses, and **Maternity payments** to help to buy items for a new baby, are available to anyone receiving income support or Family Credit. Some people claiming housing benefit may also claim for a funeral payment.
- **Community Care Grants** are given to help those people in a priority group who need support to lead independent lives in the community and who are receiving income support, such as the

elderly, the disabled, families in distress (e.g. those who are looking after a chronically ill relative) and those leaving institutional care. The grants are lump-sum payments given at the discretion of the Social Fund Officer.

Unlike the Social Fund loans (below) these payments do not have to be repaid by the claimant, with the exception of the **Funeral Payment** which must be repaid out of any money and property left by the dead person.

- **Loans issued by the DSS have to be repaid, without any interest charges**, in gradual instalments into the Social Fund. A **Social Fund Officer**, acting on discretionary guidelines provided by the Secretary of State, decides whether the claimant should receive a loan, how much the loan should be and the rates of repayment of the loan. His or her decision rests on the yearly budget each Social Security Office is given for its particular area. Because of this first-come-first-served system, the Social Security Officer has to set aside money for priority cases. If the money runs out before the end of the Social Security year of allocation, then the claimant will be unlucky. However, in practice, most Social Fund Officers keep some of their budget in reserve for very deserving cases.

  There are two kinds of loan – **Crisis Loans** and **Budgeting Loans.**

- **A Crisis Loan** is intended to cover the short-term needs of anyone who needs financial help to meet the expenses of an emergency or disaster, such as the loss or destruction of their possessions and property in a fire, flood or burglary. It may also be used to cover emergency travel expenses for someone who is stranded away from home, or some other unexpected emergency. It is one of the few lump-sum payments which is extended to anyone on low means; the claimant does not have to be on income support to receive a crisis loan.

- **A Budgeting Loan** is only available to any person or couple who have been getting income support for at least 26 weeks. If the claimant(s) have savings of £500 or over, this is taken into account when deciding their application. People who are disqualified from getting unemployment benefit because they are involved in an industrial dispute, will not qualify. A maximum and minimum payment is set down by the DSS. A budgeting Loan can be obtained for such things as: replacing worn out clothes, bed-clothes, furniture, cooker, washing machine and other essential household items, and getting necessary household repairs done. It cannot be given to pay off other debts, or fines and is not available for items like training expenses.

Work Experience Schemes

Work Experience Schemes are changing all the time, so, if you are interested, always enquire at your local Jobcentre to see what is on offer. The most important schemes are:

- **Youth Training Scheme (YTS)** – for unemployed 16 and 17 year olds, run by the Training Commission, who provide local staff to supervise the proper running of the training. Local YTS schemes are run by Approved Training Organisations, known as 'managing agents', who can be employers, colleges, private training organisations, local authorities, voluntary organisations or a consortium of these (see pp. 83–4 on the law relating to YTS trainees).
- **Employment Training Scheme.** This scheme, also organised by the Training Commission, is designed for the unemployed who are 18 and over to improve their chances of getting a job. It provides both work experience and off-the-job training, sometimes through a Jobclub (which take on long-term unemployed, including 17 year olds), or a Restart course held at a local college or by a private agency. The training usually lasts for six months. Training allowances and bonuses are available to assist the costs of lodgings, child care, and for any special clothes and tools required for the job.
- **Enterprise Allowance Scheme:** This scheme is available for anyone from 18 to retirement who is receiving either unemployment benefit or income support and wants to set up in a business on his or her own. The applicant must have been unemployed for at least eight weeks and must have £1000 or more to invest in the new business or be able to raise it by loan or grant.

Table 5.2 Places where help can be obtained

Place	Help Given
• Careers Office	Advice on jobs, training, TS etc.
• Citizens Advice Bureau	Anything
• Employment Office–Jobcentre	Advice on jobs, training schemes
• Unemployment Benefit Office	Unemployment Benefit, credits
• Social Security Office (DSS)	NI leaflets, claim forms for social security benefits
• Housing Department (Local Authority)	Advice on rents, community charge, and housing benefit
• Local Education Authority	Grants and major awards for students

Written and role play exercises

Letter-writing

1. *Either* (a) Find a job advertisement in a newspaper or at the Careers Office. Write a letter of application and enclose your *curriculum vitae* (often referred to as a CV), *or*
   (b) Look in the *Yellow Pages* for the address of a firm for whom you would like to work. Write to the firm a speculative letter (one in which you enquire after a job) and enclose your CV.

   ### Notes for guidance
   (i) How to write a **letter of application** – make some reference to the advertised post you are applying for, where and when you saw it, express your interest, and refer to the enclosed CV.
   (ii) How to write a **speculative letter** – make reference to the firm and the kind of job or chance they may offer you, enquire if they have any vacancies they can offer you now or in the future, express an interest and say why. Enclose your CV.
   (iii) How to write a **curriculum vitae (CV)** – a CV is a formal list of all the details about yourself which are of interest to the prospective employer. On it you would give the following information:

   > Name, address, telephone number
   > Date and place of birth
   > Status – whether married or single
   > Education – qualifications obtained and about to be obtained, present course or job, length of time you have been there, previous experience, if any
   > Special interests

   At the foot of your CV give the names and addresses of TWO or THREE referees: one (or two) able to give an account of your educational or work experience and progress, and one able to give a character reference.

   Think of ways of setting out these details in a neat, clear and coherent manner. Type it out on a **word-processor** if you have access to one.

   It is always a good idea to make several copies of your CV so that it is ready to send to several prospective employers.

No Job

Form filling and interviews

(a) Complete application forms:
  (i) for a college of further education, a polytechnic or a college of higher education.
  (ii) for claiming income support

  To the teacher You may be able to get permission to reproduce the application form of an appropriate college or polytechnic for part (i) of this question, and make copies of the form attached to the DSS leaflet SB1 Income Support for part (ii).

(b) **Interview – role play** Once you have filled in your form, simulate an interview either at the Careers Office, Unemployment Benefit Office or at the appropriate college or polytechnic.

A Do-It-Yourself or Class Quiz (30 obtainable marks)

		Marks
1.	You are given a national insurance number when you leave school. How?	1
2.	Where do you register for work on leaving school?	1
3.	At what age would you normally receive income support?	1
4.	If you leave school at Easter from which day can you claim benefit?	1
5.	What is the savings limit which bars people from receiving income support (a) altogether?; (b) in part?	2
6.	Suggest three ways in which you can look for work.	3
7.	What is a mandatory award?	1
8.	Give any instance where a student in full-time education can claim income support.	1
9.	How does the DSS define 'part-time' education?	2
10.	Who sponsors and organises the Youth Training Scheme?	1
11.	What duration of training does the YTS guarantee: (a) a 16 year old, and (b) a 17 year old?	2
12.	What is a Bridging Loan?	2
13.	What NI contributions must you have paid to receive unemployment benefit?	2
14.	Who may be disqualified from receiving unemployment benefit for 26 weeks from the date of their claim?	2
15.	Does the YTS trainee have a contract of employment?	1
16.	Does a YTS trainee pay tax and national insurance?	1

17. Name **two** benefits based on NI contributions.	2
18. Name **two** benefits that are non-contributory.	2
19. What is the title and number of the booklet which lists and describes all the available benefits?	2
Total	30

GCSE assignment

Consider the way in which available welfare benefits assist any one group of people, e.g. the under 16s, families, the unemployed, the elderly or the disabled. Try to assess the kind of help they do receive and also what they don't receive and, in your opinion, should get. (To assist you, certain DSS booklets are available for each of these groups.)

To answer this question you also may have to consult the section on Housing Benefit in Chapter 6.

Suggested visits

Careers Office or the Jobcentre – to be introduced to the signing-on procedures and to look at job vacancies and their respective qualification requirements.

Suggested speakers

Careers Officer
Unemployment Benefits Officer
An official from the Training Commission.

6 Somewhere to Live

Figure 6.1 Leaving home

Sooner or later it becomes the cherished desire of most young people to leave home and to set up somewhere either on their own or with a friend or group of friends. Other youngsters don't give the matter very much thought and are quite content to stay in their parents' home perhaps until they decide to get married. There are those, of course, who are compelled to move away either to get work or to spend a few years at a university or at some other higher education establishment.

Unfortunately, finding somewhere to live is not easy and moving into a place of your own can be fraught with difficulties, such as being able to pay your way, getting on with other people, and being able to fathom the complex housing laws. The consequences of not knowing what to do could leave you homeless. It is easy to get conned, especially if you intend to rent a bed-sit, flat or house from a private landlord, and in a strange district you might feel even more exposed and gullible to exploitation. So it is a sensible measure to think about the matter seriously, find out all you can, plan well and be forewarned. Homelessness should be avoided at all costs.

The two ways of acquiring a place to live are by buying a flat or house or by renting a place. The majority of young people do not have enough money to buy a place of their own and generally have to resort to finding some kind of rented accommodation. Whichever way you acquire a place, the law of contract will apply. If you buy you will enter into a contract of deed in the form of a **Deed of Conveyance** which has to be 'signed, sealed and delivered' at the point of purchase. This usually requires the services of a solicitor or a licensed conveyancer. All rented accommodation is subject to the common law of contract. Certain types of rented accommodation are also governed by various Rent and Housing Acts. Nonetheless the four essential elements for the formation of a contract must exist. By accepting the offer to rent you enter into a **legally binding agreement** with the landlord or landlady. In return for the **consideration** of being able to dwell in the accommodation, you undertake to pay rent. The transaction, being a business agreement, assumes **an intention to create legal relations**. If, however, you went to live with a relative or friend as a companion and paid no rent, this would be regarded not as a business agreement but as a **social or domestic agreement** – there is no consideration and the law would not recognise an intention to create legal relations in these kind of circumstances – there would be no legally recognised contract. Where a landlord-and-tenant contract does exist, certain terms and conditions will be agreed; some are self-evident: you will be required to pay the agreed rent at the agreed time, weekly or monthly, and you will be expected to behave with reasonable care while on the premises. The **Rent Acts of 1957 to 1974,** the **Housing Act 1980** and **Housing Act 1988** make special protective provisions for the majority of tenants but not for all. The law relating to rented accommodation is extremely complex and would be impossible to explain in full in a book of this kind. The case studies and information presented here are meant to be no more than a helpful guide. **It is always advisable to seek proper advice immediately prior to taking the first step towards finding somewhere to live.**

Rented accommodation

CASE 1:

Rented accommodation – accommodation agencies – shared accommodation – tenants and landlords – notice to quit – rent assessment committees – housing benefits

Barry and Bess are surprised to discover that they will both be going to new jobs in Shiretown, some 40 miles away from their present homes. Barry has been offered a job with good prospects to train as a sales clerk in a big expanding company which means that he will have to settle in Shiretown for a period of several years. Bess, on the other hand, is going to Shiretown for only one year to train as a computer programmer before being sent to some other part of the country. Barry is anxious to find some accommodation which he can rent on a long-term basis, and he wonders whether Shiretown council would find him a single person's flat. His prospective employers have written to say they have another trainee who is prepared to share some private rented accommodation with Barry if he would like to take this opportunity. Barry has discussed the matter with his mother but she suggests he should make other enquiries before taking this step. 'Whatever you do, you don't want to end up paying high rent for some hovel with rising damp,' she has warned him. Bess, in the meanwhile, has decided that she must get some short-term accommodation either in a hostel or by renting a small flat or bed-sit.

Would Shiretown Council house Barry?

It is very unlikely that Shiretown Council will house Barry. Most local authorities operate a residential qualification requirement for housing people; this means that a person who wishes to be housed by the council must have lived in the district for a specified number of years. The specification varies from district to district – it may be one, two or even more years. Also – because Barry is over 18 – the local authority is under no statutory obligation to house him. However, he can enquire at the Housing Department of Shiretown Town Hall to see if he can put his name on the housing waiting list. Some local authorities have a policy of providing single-person accommodation but the demand far exceeds the supply, and Barry would probably have to wait two, three or even more years before being housed – if he is lucky. Under normal circumstances, Barry cannot expect to be housed by the council.

Should Barry accept the invitation to share privately rented accommodation?

To share privately rented accommodation has the obvious advantage of two or more people paying a share of the rent. However, Barry should also be aware of the disadvantages of the idea. First of all, he must be able to get on well with and to trust the other person. Even the best of friends can fall out over minor irritations when they are in close daily contact. Barry should feel absolutely confident that he and the other trainee could get on well together, and that the other trainee is a person who is prepared to stand by his obligations to pay the rent and to share the other bills for electricity, gas, water, internal repairs and so on. If the other trainee walks out one day or decides to leave the tenancy because he can't afford the rent, then Barry will have to face up to finding the trainee's half of the rent as well as his own, and be left to settle all the debts. He could sue the defaulting party but this may not get him very far.

How can Barry go about finding rented accommodation for himself? And what should he guard against?

Barry could write to a number of addresses in Shiretown, or better still, visit the town at least twice before commencing his new job and make a few personal enquiries. The company for whom he is to work may keep an accommodation list for employees moving into the district, so he could begin with this possibility – generally the Personnel Department will advise him.

Alternatively, he could enquire at any of the advice centres in the town such as a Housing Advice Centre, a Housing Aid Centre or a Citizens Advice Bureau – the addresses of which he can get from the Town Hall. These organisations may find him temporary accommodation, such as bed and breakfast and hostel accommodation, which would enable him to live in Shiretown while he looks around for more suitable accommodation.

A fairly common way of finding accommodation in a different district is to use one of several **accommodation agencies**, the names and addresses of which can be obtained from a CAB, the library and sometimes the Town Hall. If Barry uses an accommodation agency, he must be on his guard. The agency should not ask him for a 'registration fee' or for any payment for a list of addresses. If it does then he should not deal with that agency. However, it is quite legitimate for an agency to charge for any work it does for Barry in order to accommodate him, such as telephone calls, letters and other administrative work. The general practice of reputable firms is to charge the client a sum that is equal to twice the weekly rent of the flat, room or house that has been found for him or her. This covers the first down-payment of rent and the cost of administration fees. **So if Barry is asked to pay any large sums he should seek advice straight away before paying anything.**

Another method of seeking accommodation is by looking at advertisements in shop windows and in local newspapers, or as a last resort, Barry could advertise for accommodation, stating his particular requirements. Whatever accommodation Barry finds he should take a responsible adult, such as his mother, with him to look at it before accepting it.

How much of the law should Barry know if he is to rent from a private landlord?

This is where the law gets complicated because this will depend upon the type of tenancy (rented accommodation) Barry takes on. Most tenancies come within the Rent and Housing Acts, a few – such as bed-and-breakfast, hostels, and lodgings where the landlord lives on the premises and provides certain services such as cooking breakfast or doing the cleaning or laundry – do not. Barry will have to ascertain whether he is in accommodation which is protected by the Rent and Housing Acts or not. Also, he will have to ascertain whether he is a **tenant** – that is, someone who has a right of exclusive possession – or a **licensee** – someone who has been given permission to occupy the property. If he is not clear on these points he should seek advice straight away. Working out a person's status is not easy to establish. **The majority of tenants** whose premises are let as separate dwellings by a private landlord or a Housing Association are in what are called **assured tenancies**. Other groups, who live in council-owned property, have **secure tenancies**. Assured and secure tenants enjoy certain protection under the law. If Barry becomes an assured tenant, then, normally, he cannot be evicted – that is, asked to leave the premises – without a county court order if he has no wish to go, provided he pays the rent that has been agreed between him and his landlord and does not breach any of the duties of a tenant laid down by the Rent Acts and the Housing Act 1988. So, first, Barry must make sure he has enough money to pay the rent and that there is a record of the payments, this will take the form of a **rent book** if he pays his rent **weekly**, or a **receipt** from his landlord if he pays his rent **monthly**, and he should keep the receipts in a safe place. Other ways of breaching a tenancy contract may be by misbehaviour, damaging the property or being a nuisance to other tenants. So, if

Barry finds himself in accommodation protected by the law, the landlord will not be able to get him out if he pays his rent on time and is generally a considerate tenant.

If Barry is an assured tenant, what are the legal rights and responsibilities of his landlord?

A landlord of an assured tenancy must keep to the rent and terms, such as proposed future rent increases agreed with Barry and not harass Barry in any way to get him to move out against his will. Barry must guard against getting behind with paying his rent as he can be lawfully evicted if he gets three months in arrears. Barry's landlord has a mandatory right to possess his property if he needs the property as a main home for himself or for a member of his family, or if he wishes to redevelop the property and cannot do so with the tenant there. There are also a number of discretionary grounds on which the landlord may also act to remove Barry: he may move him to suitable alternative accommodation, and, more drastically, evict him if he has damaged the furniture or property in some way, made alterations to the property without his permission or has been a nuisance or an annoyance to adjoining occupiers. Under the **Housing Act 1988**, Barry's landlord may give anything from two weeks' to two months' notice depending on the ground he uses to repossess his property. The landlord of an assured tenant can only get possession by serving a notice which states that he wishes to have his property back. He has to use a special form, available from law stationers for the purpose.

If, at this stage, Barry agrees of his own free will to go, there will be no court order. If, however, Barry wishes to stay, then the landlord will be obliged to seek **a possession order from the county court**. Whether or not Barry's landlord will succeed in getting his order will depend upon the grounds he puts forward for getting Barry out. If he is successful and Barry persists on staying on in the property, Barry effectively becomes a trespasser and he can be evicted by the court bailiffs. The other legal responsibility of all landlords is to keep the premises safe (**Occupiers Liability Act 1984**) and in good structural repair.

Bess requires accommodation for a short term of one year. What should she do?

Like Barry, Bess could first make enquiries of her prospective employers, who, if they operate a regular training programme at their Shiretown branch, may be able to supply a list of short-term accommodation or even have a hostel of their own. Failing that avenue, then she could try the advice and accommodation agencies in the town, as Barry was advised to do. Also she could look at the advertisements in the local paper and in the shop windows.

What kind of accommodation should she look for?

Bess is obviously not interested in being tied down to long-term accommodation. She may be content with either a **bed and breakfast stay** or some form of **board and lodging** where the landlord or landlady lives on the premises and supplies her with a meal or two and keeps her room clean. Or she may prefer the communal atmosphere of a **hostel**, such as YWCA, if there is one in or near Shiretown. If she wishes to be a little more independent, she may consider looking for **an assured shorthold tenancy**. This is a tenancy where the property is only let out for a fixed period for at least six months. The landlord must formally notify the tenant of the shorthold term before the tenancy agreement is entered into. Bess and the landlord can freely agree the rent and other terms of the tenancy between them.

This does not mean that Bess has to remain for the term of the fixed tenancy; if she wishes to leave it earlier she can do so provided she gives the landlord proper notice. **An assured shorthold tenancy is only protected by the Housing Acts up to the termination date of the fixed term**. Bess's landlord will have to serve two months' notice to bring the tenancy to an end, and will have the right to evict Bess as a trespasser if she stays longer than the agreed period. Alternatively, under the Housing Act 1980, the landlord may grant another periodic or fixed term. As with all assured tenants, Bess can be asked to go during the period of tenancy if she fails to pay her rent or misbehaves in some way.

What are the legal rights and responsibilities of Bess's landlord if Bess is a bed-and-breakfast lodger or in a hostel?

The full protection of the Rent Act is not designed for anyone who is a boarder, the occupier of a hotel room or a hostel-dweller. The landlord, landlady or proprietor is bound only by common law contract where he or she provides **substantial attendances** or certain services for the tenant, such as cleaning, cooking a meal, or doing the laundry. So as long as Bess complies reasonably with the rules and regulations of the establishment, such as locking-up if she comes in late, putting lights out, not making an excessive amount of noise, not having drugs or other abusive substances on the premises, then she will be a welcome tenant and it is unlikely she would be asked to go. She must, of course, pay her rent. If, however, the landlord wishes her to leave, then he may serve a notice to quit in writing giving Bess 28 days or less in which to find alternative lodgings. No court order is necessary. If Bess outstays the term of notice, then she becomes a trespasser on the property and the landlord could take steps to serve a court order against her in the tort of trespass. The other legal responsibility of the landlord is to keep the premises safe.

If either Barry or Bess get into difficulties with paying their rent, is there anything they can do?

If Barry is an assured tenant, the rent he agrees with his landlord must be a '**market rent**'. However, if the landlord decides to increase the rent he must notify Barry giving at least a month's notice. If Barry does not agree with the proposed increase then he has three months in which to refer the rent on a prescribed form to the local **rent assessment committee**, a body of independent people with experience in legal and property matters who have been appointed by the Lord Chancellor and the Secretary of State. The committee will consider whether the increased rent is a market rent or not and Barry will have to accept their findings. If Bess is in an assured shorthold tenancy the rent will have already been agreed for the period of the tenancy; however, it could be increased if the agreement is renewed. If she ends up in bed-and-breakfast accommodation or in lodgings with services provided and her landlord decides to increase the rent, unfortunately she would have no recourse to the rent assessment committee or to any other appeal body.

Can Barry and Bess claim housing benefit to help them pay their rent?

This will depend upon a number of factors: the cost of their rent, what their weekly income is, and what the government decides is their needs allowance. The calculations are very complicated, but as both Barry and Bess are in new jobs their income is likely to be fairly low so it would be worth an application to the Shiretown Town Hall. They may well find that they do qualify for **housing benefit**. This is a weekly-paid cash help for tenants on low incomes. They may also find their income is low enough to qualify them for a Community Charge rebate.

Tenants and licensees People who rent property fall into **two categories of occupier**, a tenant and a licensee:

A tenant owns an interest in the land and has a right to occupy it. The landlord grants the right of exclusive possession over a certain property for a certain period of time. The tenant has the right to exclude anyone else including the landlord (council or private) from using the property as his own. The landlord, however, has some limited rights to enter the property, e.g. to collect the rent, empty the gas meter, and he reserves the right to enter to inspect or to do necessary repairs – usually after notifying the tenant of his intention to enter.

A licensee is someone who has been given permission to enter the property. A licence is permission to do something which would

Somewhere to Live

otherwise be forbidden. A licensee can stay on the premises for as long as the licence lasts. **When it ends, he or she becomes a trespasser.** A licensee may or may not pay rent, he or she may be a lodger, a visiting friend or relative who may enter and stay on the premises whenever he or she wishes.

NB Children under 18, and husbands and wives as parties to the matrimonial home, have a statutory right to residence and cannot be licensees unless a court order says otherwise.

The tenant and the law

The laws governing the various types of tenancy are very complex indeed, and where there is any doubt, advice should always be sought. The majority of tenants in rented accommodation are protected by the **Rent Acts of 1957, 1966, 1974** and the **Housing Acts 1980 and 1988** if no landlord lives on the premises.

Table 6.1 Tenancies since the Housing Act 1988 came into force

Types of tenancy	*Secure*	*Assured*	*Assured shorthold*	*Protected*	*Unprotected licencees*
	Council tenants Rent Act protected	(Private and Housing Association)	(fixed term)	(Tied houses, non-resident landlords – Rent Act protected before 1989)	B & b, hostel, hotel lease-holders, resident landlord
Notice to quit	28 days	2 months, or 2 weeks if right to possession	2 months or 2 weeks if right to possession	28 days, longer for tied tenants	28 days or as agreed, or at once
Protected by Court Order	Yes	Yes	No	Yes	No

The council tenant Many people rent a house from the local authority. It is difficult to evict a council tenant unless there is a long history of rent arrears. (The introduction of the certified housing benefit scheme in 1983 has eliminated the possibility of getting into rent arrears for those tenants receiving income support as their rent is paid direct for them and does not have to pass through their hands.) Councils, like private landlords, must obtain a court order. They must serve a preliminary notice on the tenants, and court proceedings cannot begin before four weeks after the notice is served. An illegal eviction by a council can be a criminal offence.

Service tenancy Where the tenant is the landlord's employee and lives with his job, such as a caretaker or an agricultural worker, the landlord does not have to have a court order to evict, although agricultural workers are given special protection.

Notice to quit A 'notice to quit' requires the tenant to leave the premises and 'to deliver up possession of' the house, flat or room. The notice to quit must be in writing or on a prescribed form. If the notice-to-quit requirements are not complied with, then the notice will not be effective and the landlord will be unable to evict. Pre-printed notices to quit can be purchased from law stationers.

Eviction of tenants The court will only evict an **assured** or a **protected** tenant under the terms laid down by the rent and housing laws:

- failure to pay rent; or being in arrears of rent
- harassment of other tenants or neighbours
- tenant's misbehaviour, causing damage to the property or making alterations to it without the landlord's permission
- using the premises for an illegal or immoral purpose
- taking in sub-tenants without the landlord's permission
- where the landlord requires the premises for his own use or that of a member of his family, or wishes to redevelop the premises
- where the landlord has found the tenant suitable alternative comparable accommodation for a similar rent
- where proper notice is served.

It is unlawful for a landlord to harass his tenants or the tenant's family in an attempt to get them to leave, or to get someone else to do it (see 'landlord's harassment of tenants' in Case 2). Tenants who defy court orders or who defy proper notice become liable in trespass. Court orders and the court bailiffs can remove them.

The Rent Officer and the Rent Assessment Committee

At one time the local Rent Officer played a crucial role registering fair rents for private tenants and their landlords, and the Rent Assessment Committee was a form of tribunal set up to listen to appeals on fair rent decisions and other related matters. Since the Housing Act 1988 came into force the respective roles of the Rent Officer and the Rent Assessment Committee have changed:

Somewhere to Live

- **The Rent Officer** still registers rents for those private tenants who were protected by the Rent Act 1977 up to January 1989 and for Housing Association landlords under the 1988 Act. Also since January 1989, the Rent Officer's duties have been extended to receiving housing benefit claims from assured, assured shorthold and other tenants and from licensees, whose tenancies commenced after January 1989. This includes agricultural occupiers, and people who live in caravans, mobile homes and on houseboats.
- **The Rent Assessment Committee**. An independent panel of lay-people with relevant expertise will listen to applications made by assured and protected tenants who think their rent increase is too high, and will fix a 'market rent' and it can say what the terms of the tenancy agreement should be. Once the Committee has come to these conclusions, the landlord cannot increase the fixed rent, including services charges, unless he has the agreement of the tenant.

Housing Benefit

The Housing Benefit scheme is run by the local authority and is aimed at helping people on low incomes or income support, with their housing, hostel or bed and breakfast costs. The scheme covers items such as rent, mortgage interest payments, leaseholder's ground rent and service charges. For income support claimants the two benefits are dealt with together: once the social security benefits are calculated by the DSS, the housing benefit calculation is passed to the local authority for them to complete the claimant's entitlement. Other claimants apply direct to the local authority. Anyone with savings of £8000 or more cannot claim housing benefit, those with savings of £3000 or less get full relief; however, 'full relief' does not include repairs, household insurance, water rates, cesspit or septic tank charges.

CASE 2:

The rent book – repairs and improvements – multi-occupation – landlord's harassment of tenants

Barry is now working in Shiretown and has moved into a small two-bedroomed flat, which is one of four in a converted house. He shares the bathroom and toilet amenities with the other tenants. The landlord, Mr Flint, lives on the other side of the town and he sends an agent to collect the weekly rent. None of the tenants has been supplied with a rent book. When Barry pointed this out to the agent, the agent laughed cynically. 'You'll just have to trust us, won't you?' he said, 'Mr Flint doesn't bother with things like that'. Barry discussed the matter with a fellow-tenant, Stella. They also discussed the poor state of the roof which leaked water into their rooms and the state of disrepair to the water-closet which they shared. Stella told Barry she had been trying to get Mr Flint to attend to these things: 'But he just won't do anything about it,' she said. 'His answer is always the same, that the tenants will have to get together and pay for the repairs themselves. I don't think outside repairs are our responsibility, do you? But I'm not sure about the water-closet?' Barry decided to write to Mr Flint about the absence of the rent books and about the repairs. He told him he was legally responsible for these things. A week later after returning home from work he found that his electricity supply had been cut off and he was without lighting or hot water. On the table was a note telling him to get out of the flat. Barry immediately telephoned Mr Flint to protest. The next day he found that the locks on his door had been changed and all his possessions dumped outside.

Can Mr Flint refuse to supply a rent-book to his tenants?

If Mr Flint's agent arrives **weekly** to collect the rent and does not supply a rent book, then Mr Flint and his agent are committing a criminal offence which is liable to prosecution. Not only does the rent book provide a record of the payments, but it must also be in a prescribed form stating, the legal rights of the tenant, the name and address of the landlord, and the amount of the weekly rent the tenant must pay. A rent book is **not necessary where the tenant pays the rent monthly** but even then it is always advisable to get a receipt for every payment. In Barry's case, Mr Flint should be supplying a rent book to each of his tenants.

Can Barry, Stella and the other tenants, do anything about the state of disrepair to the roof and water-closet?

Ideally landlord-and-tenant contracts should set out in detail who is responsible for the repairs to the tenancy. It is generally assumed that the landlord is responsible for the external repairs and the sanitary repairs, and the tenant for the internal repairs. Also, there is a statutory duty on landlords under the public health laws to put right such things as dampness, defective roofs, sanitary fittings and drains, and ill-fitting doors and windows. Mr Flint is in breach of a statutory duty if he does not get the leaking roof repaired or replace the insanitary water-closet. Neither should he try to pass on the cost of these repairs to his tenants. Barry, Stella and the other tenants should report these matters to the Public Health Department of Shiretown Town Hall and they will serve on Mr Flint a notice to do the repairs. Because the premises is a multi-occupation – that is, there is more than one tenancy there – the landlord has additional statutory responsibilities for making sure that necessary works are carried out to the lighting, the water supply, ventilation, drainage and water-closets, cooking facilities, and fire regulations. Mr Flint will have 21 days in which to comply with the order. If he fails to do anything to the multi-occupation, the local authority may take over the control of the repairs and improvements, and recover the cost from him.

What should Barry do about his unlawful eviction by Mr Flint?

Barry is in an assured tenancy. It is, therefore, illegal if his landlord tries to by-pass the law by making life uncomfortable for him by cutting off his electricity. Also Mr Flint has no right to change the locks, or to go into Barry's flat or collect his belongings and dump them outside, without serving proper notice and seeking a court eviction. Barry, as a lawful tenant, has exclusive possession of the property. Any landlord who attempts to harass a tenant is acting illegally and the council have powers to prosecute. Barry should either report Mr Flint to the Town Hall straight away or he can take action himself in the civil court. He should seek help from the CAB or a Housing Advice Centre to advise him on the most appropriate course of action. Also, if he intends to keep the tenancy, Barry should keep in reserve the rent he would have paid Mr Flint had the unlawful eviction not happened, and he should be ready to hand it over once the matter has been settled.

Rent book and receipts for rent **The Rent Acts require landlords of protected and assured tenancies to supply a rent book where the rent is collected weekly**. Rent books must be to a prescribed format and can be bought at the larger stationers. Printed on the inside cover of a rent book are the legal regulations relating to the tenancy. The landlord is also required to fill in on the rent book particular items:

- a record of the weekly payments, signed by the landlord or his agent
- the name and address of the landlord
- the amount of the weekly rent.

Tenants who pay their rent **monthly** do not have to have a rent-book, but you should always get a receipt for every payment made, or keep your cheque-book stubs as proof of payment.

Repairs and improvements Landlords are more often required to be legally responsible for **repairs** than for **improvements** to their properties.

A repair includes putting right existing items such as a defective roof, a damp-proof course, the brickwork, the plastering on walls, the plumbing and worn-out fixtures.

An improvement includes putting in additional amenities such as a bath, central heating, extra electrical sockets, a gas fire, etc.

A landlord generally has some repair obligations under the terms of a tenancy agreement. Where there is a written agreement there may be a specific clause which details who is responsible for carrying out the repairs. The agreement, however, cannot override any statutory obligations imposed by an Act of Parliament. Some remedies under the Acts can be enforced by the tenant in a civil action, others may be enforced by the local authority in the magistrates court. Some of these statutes are:

- The **Housing Act 1961** which provides that in most lettings of less than 7 years, the landlord is responsible for **maintaining and repairing** the structure and exterior of the building; drains and gutters and external pipes, water, gas and electricity supplies, sanitary installations (sinks, baths, WCs) and heating appliances. The landlord can only be liable if he knows of the repair or it is brought to his notice by the tenant.
- **Housing Act 1985** This Act gives powers to local authorities to take action against landlords requiring them to carry out repairs where a house is either classed as 'unfit for human habitation' or where a house requires substantial repairs to bring it up to a certain standard. The aim of the Act is to ensure that all properties have certain basic amenities, such as an inside WC, a bath and hot water.
- **Public Health Act 1936** Under this Act a local authority may prosecute where the defects of a premises are 'prejudicial to health'. This covers items such as blocked or foul drains, dampness, defective roofs, leaking gutters, defective sanitary fittings, ill-fitting doors and windows, polluted water supply, defective foundations.
- **The Housing and Building Control Act 1985** secure tenants have the right to do and receive payment for repairs.

Multi-occupations   A multi-occupation is where a property (such as a converted house) houses several households. These may be:
- houses occupied by two households
- houses shared by several people who are not one collective unit
- where lodgers are taken in
- houses divided into self-contained flats.

Where there is a multi-occupation the local authority has powers to ensure that the landlord carries out suitable maintenance and repairs of the lighting, water supplies, personal washing facilities, drainage and WCs, facilities for storage, facilities for the preparation and cooking of food, ventilation and heating appliances. The landlord must also comply with fire regulations of escape and fire-proofing.

Occupiers' Liability Acts   The **Occupiers Liability Acts of 1957 and 1984** require all occupiers of premises to keep them safe and

Figure 6.2 Home improvements – an Office of Fair Trading leaflet

to take such care as is reasonable in the circumstances to prevent personal injury to whomsoever comes on to the premises. This includes lawful visitors and to some extent trespassers as well.

Landlord's harassment of tenants The **Protection from Eviction Act 1977** makes the harassment of any residential occupier an offence. 'Harassment' is any act which is done with the intention of causing the tenant to give up possession of all or part of the property.

This includes harassment either by the landlord, or by anyone acting on his behalf, which is intended to disturb the tenant and his family. Examples of harassment are cutting off the gas and electricity, locking the tenants out of the building, changing the locks, assault and abuse, deliberately taking up floorboards or removing tiles from the roof, removing light-bulbs and similar acts.

Illegal evictions The **Protection from Eviction Act 1977** makes it illegal to deprive a lawful occupier of all or part of the premises in which he resides.

There are two remedies for an illegal eviction of tenants. One is the remedy of **criminal** prosecution by way of the local authority, the result of which can be a fine or imprisonment. The other is a **civil law remedy**, where the tenant seeks an injunction and/or damages from the civil courts. The more usual and more effective practice is the civil action which aims to compensate the tenant and to restore him or her to the residence.

Nowhere to live

CASE 3:

Squatting – trespass – homelessness

A year has passed by and Bess has finished her training at Shiretown. She has moved on to Billchester, a large industrial town, where she has been placed in one of the firm's offices. However, she has not found anywhere to live. She is temporarily living in bed-and-breakfast accommodation but this is draining her small savings. A group of young friends have invited her to join their squat in some old properties on the edge of town. Bess is tempted to join them but she is afraid that the squat might be illegal and she does not want to find herself homeless.

Should Bess move into the squat?

Bess should first establish whether the squat is a licensed squat or not. Licensed squatters are on the property with the owner's permission. Generally the premises is a short-life property and the licensed squatter may remain there for the time being, and have services such as gas, electricity and water connected during the time he or she is using the premises and pay for it in the usual way. Licensed squatters are not protected by the Rent or Housing Acts and must leave when asked to go. An unlicensed squatter, on the other hand, is a trespasser and has no legal right to be on the premises. If the squat is licensed then Bess should find out how long the squat is likely to last; she does not want to find herself homeless if

Somewhere to Live 143

she is required to leave the squat before she has found a place of her own. If the squat is not licensed then she would be ill-advised to join her friends there.

Would not the local authority be under statutory obligation to house Bess if she became homeless?

The answer is no, unless Bess could show she had a 'priority need' to be housed. The **Housing (Homeless Persons) Act 1977** does not put adults of 18 and over into the priority-need category unless they are in very poor health, physically or mentally, or if a woman is pregnant. Since none of these applies to Bess, the local authority is under no statutory obligation at all to house her under its emergency regulations. However, she can make enquiries at the Housing Department at Billchester Town Hall to see whether the council would put her on the waiting list for a council flat. Some local authorities do provide single-person units in their housing programme but the queues are invariably long and the wait may take several years. Also, Bess may not meet the residential requirement for putting her name on the list.

The law and squatting There are two distinct groups of squatters:

(i) **Licensed squatters** are those who are on another's land with his permission. The homeless may become licensees of short-life property for the time being. They are not protected by the Rent and Housing Acts as other tenants are.
(ii) **Trespassing squatters** are those who occupy premises without the owner's permission. They are trespassers and can be asked to leave. If they refuse the owner can take reasonable steps to get them out, or resort to the law to get them evicted. The **Public Order Act 1986** permits the police to take steps to remove and, if necessary, summarily convict, groups of two or more trespassers from land which they have unlawfully entered with the common purpose of residing there for any period. Reasonable steps must have first been taken by the lawful occupier to ask them to leave.

The Housing (Homeless Persons) Act 1977 A person is homeless if he or she has no accommodation with his or her family or others who may house him or her, and where he or she has no means of renting available accommodation. The Act also requires the homeless person to have a **priority need**. People in this category include:

- a woman who is pregnant, or someone with one or more children under the age of 16, or under the age of 19 if they are receiving full-time education, who might reasonably be expected to live with him or her

Figure 6.3 A squat in south London

- people who become homeless through no fault of their own; for example, their home is threatened or has been destroyed by fire, flood or other disaster
- people above retirement age or who are particularly frail or in poor health or vulnerable for any reason such as senility
- people who are mentally handicapped or physically disabled, or who are deaf or dumb
- other groups of people who are vulnerable, such as battered women and homeless young people who are at risk of sexual and financial exploitation.

The Act does not normally apply to adults of 18 and over unless they come into any of the above categories.

'Intentionally homeless' A key clause of the Act which is being applied more rigorously than ever before in the face of increased homelessness is the one of 'intentional homelessness'. If a local authority believes a person has made himself homeless with the intention of getting council accommodation, then the authority can refuse to house a

Somewhere to Live 145

homeless person even if he is in one of the priority-need categories. Only those who have become homeless through no fault or action of their own will be considered for 'emergency housing' under the Act. A person who chooses to sell his house or who has lost it because of wilful and persistent refusal to pay rent would in most cases be regarded as having become homeless intentionally. However, where a person was obliged to sell because he could not keep up the mortgage repayments or got into rent arrears because of genuine personal and financial difficulties, then the 'intentional' clause would not apply.

Buying a home of your own

CASE 4:

Buying a house or flat – the conveyance – surveyor's report – leasehold and freehold property – community charge – public and private nuisance

Jasmine, who is 19, has been left a small sum of money in her late grandfather's will. She has managed to get a job as a typist but after getting some further training and experience hopes to become a managerial secretary and improve her salary. She expects to buy a place of her own. In an estate-agent's window she has seen – advertised for £85,000 – a small flat which she likes and would like to purchase. She knows, however, that house-buying can be a hazardous business. Her cousin Ashby bought a house and then found dry-rot under the floorboards and had to pay hundreds of pounds putting the matter right. She also recalls the case of a neighbour who became unemployed and could not meet the high cost of running the house and paying the mortgage. She wonders if there are any measures she can take to prevent these kind of things happening to her. Also, she wonders about her legal responsibilities once she became a property-owner.

Will Jasmine be able to afford to buy a place of her own?

Jasmine will have to do her sums very carefully. There are three basic things she should check. They are: (i) has she enough money for a deposit? (ii) can she afford the mortgage repayments and other bills out of her earnings, and (iii) would she be able to afford all the extra charges that go with buying a house or flat? Since Jasmine's grandfather has left her some money, she may be able to pay a deposit on a small flat. A **deposit** secures a conditional interest in the property; the **mortgage** is the sum of money which is lent to the purchaser to meet the remainder of the cost of the property and which must be paid back over a stipulated number of years. The payment of the deposit does not secure the property straight away. At this stage of the negotiations, the sale will be 'subject to contract'; this allows either the buyer or the seller to withdraw from the agreement without legal liability. So, if Jasmine's solicitor or licensed conveyancer in his search finds something amiss concerning the flat, then Jasmine can withraw from the sale and have her deposit returned.

Once the contract is signed then the parties are bound to the transaction. The deposit is generally 10 per cent of the agreed price, so if the agreed price for the flat remains at £85000 Jasmine will have to find a deposit of £8500. There are many schemes for first-time house-buyers – some run by local authorities and others by various building societies. Jasmine would be advised to shop around to see what they have to offer. The schemes aim to reduce the down-payment but this means that there will be more mortgage repayments to pay but this might not worry Jasmine as she hopes to increase her future earnings. The second step Jasmine should take is to check that she can afford the mortgage repayments. The chances of obtaining a mortgage may depend on a number of factors – on the demand for mortgages at the time and the state of the money market, on the current interest rates, and on Jasmine's own ability to meet the repayments out of her monthly salary. She would have to convince her prospective lenders of her job security, and she would have to declare her salary to them so that they can calculate the maximum mortgage they would lend her. Finally Jasmine would have to allow for the extra charges of buying a property, such as the solicitor's or licensed conveyancer's fee, land registry fee, the building society's evaluation fee and a surveyor's fee.

What other costs should Jasmine take into account when she is in the flat?

Jasmine will need a few extra pounds to buy essential pieces of furniture, utensils, cutlery, crockery and other such items. She should also insure both the flat and the contents to protect herself against the event of theft, fire or storm damage and so on. Also, she should make sure that she can meet the community charge and the water, gas and electricity bills, repair bills and also the cost of food and cleaning items. Paying the bills is an important part of being a householder; failure to pay the community charge can mean a magistrates' court summons, and non-payment of other bills a county court summons. Jasmine may be able to reduce her community charge bill if she qualifies for community charge rebate. Also she will be liable for a ground-rent charge if her property is **leasehold**. This does not apply to **freehold** property.

Figure 6.4 Buying a flat

How can Jasmine avoid buying a house with hidden structural flaws?

Jasmine clearly does not want to be faced with the problem her cousin Ashby experienced, so she should engage a surveyor to look over the property and give her an **independent surveyor's report** – it is worth the surveyor's fees, especially if he finds some major fault. Jasmine may then either withdraw from the sale or instruct her solicitor or conveyancer to request a reduction in the asking-price of the flat. If Jasmine relies on the building society's surveyor she should remember that this is usually confidential to the building society and is not a full structural report, although for a nominal fee the building society's surveyor will submit a copy of his report to her. If Jasmine finds that the flat is structurally unsound and needs a number of improvements done to it, she should look elsewhere for something less costly to repair.

What could Jasmine do if she suddenly and unexpectedly found herself unemployed and unable to keep up the mortgage repayments and her other bills?

This is a grave risk that many people take when they enter into a mortgage agreement. Jasmine may find she will have to sell the property and find rented accommodation, but this should be as a last resort because the period of unemployment may not last very long, and it may also be very difficult to find rented accommodation where she wants it. First, she should inform the building society or whatever creditor is lending her the money. Once she has signed on as unemployed, or for income support, then she should apply to the DSS for help with the repayments. Mortgage repayments include both the capital return (of the money lent) and the interest payable to the lender for lending it. Under the scheme she may get half the interest payments of her mortgage paid for the first six months of being unemployed, after which the scheme covers all the mortgage interest repayments, but she will get no help with paying of the capital-return portion of her payments. She will have to try and meet the rest of her bills as best she can and, if in difficulty, apply for a loan under the DSS Social Fund Scheme (see Chapter 5).

What are the other laws Jasmine should observe once she is a property-owner?

She should keep her premises safe for anyone who enters it, although she is not liable if her visitors do anything foolish and bring about their own harm or injury (**Occupiers Liability Acts 1957 and 1984**). Also she should observe the local bye-laws and **public nuisance** laws which require occupiers not to be a nuisance to their neighbours by having noisy parties in the early hours of the morning; persistently revving-up cars; doing car repairs on the pavement outside the premises, or obstructing the pavement in some way or having an overhanging tree or hedge which is either a nuisance to pedestrians or obscures the view of passing drivers. Bye-laws also govern the smokeless zones of certain areas and the lighting of bonfires at certain times – these can be checked with the council. Also, laws concerning **private nuisance** may apply if Jasmine allows her trees to become a nuisance to her neighbours or if she harbours anything on or in her premises which disturb the neighbour's lawful use and enjoyment of their property.

The mortgage A mortgage is the sum of money you borrow enabling you to pay the vendor the full cost of the house or flat you are buying. The money has to be paid back to the lender, or **creditor**, such as a building society, local authority, bank or insurance company, over a specified period of time, usually 20 or 25 years and sometimes 30 years. There are various mortgage options so it pays to ask around the building societies, banks and other creditors. If you have money deposited with a building society you may get preferential treatment. Make sure you get

Somewhere to Live

the best mortgage to suit your particular set of circumstances. The main options are:

- **Repayment mortage,** either from a building society or the local authority. This is where each monthly repayment pays off some of the **capital loan** (the money you've borrowed), and some of the **interest** (the money that the creditor earns by lending you the money). In the early years you pay back more interest than capital, but as the years go by you pay less interest and more of the loan. A repayment mortgage is the cheapest form of mortgage and is a good option for people who pay tax on their income, because the interest on a repayment mortgage is tax deductible, which means that tax-payers get tax relief up to certain levels.
- **Endowment mortgage** from a building society or an insurance company. The monthly repayments are generally higher than those for a repayment mortgage because the borrower takes out a life-insurance policy for the period of the mortgage. Then either at the end of the period or on the death of the borrower, if earlier, the creditor pays out on the policy and thereby discharges the mortgage. Some of these endowment mortgage schemes are 'with profits' which means that you pay slightly more each month and receive a lump sum in addition to having the mortgage paid off.
- **Council mortgages** A few local authorities run schemes generally aimed at the first-time buyer or the council-house tenant who has an option to buy his or her house. It is worth an enquiry at your Town Hall or Civic Centre.

The conveyance Most house- or flat-buyers put the work of the conveyance into the hands of a solicitor although since 1985 building societies, banks and other licensed conveyancers are permitted to do this work. **The conveyance is the transfer of ownership of the property**. The duties that a solicitor or conveyancer will undertake include drawing up the contract of sale and carrying out the conveyancing; checking that the vendor of the property has a legal right to sell it; finding out whether there are any planning proposals for the area; finding out what you can do and cannot do with the property (you may not be able to trade from the property or keep livestock in your garden) and checking on the existence of rights of way. The solicitor or conveyancer will also see that you pay a land registry fee and stamp duty, if any. Some individuals try to save the cost of a conveyance fee by undertaking the conveyancing for themselves, but this is not advisable unless you have the time and are sufficiently experienced to do it.

The surveyor It is a wise policy to have the building surveyed by an independent surveyor. A surveyor may save you a great deal of money if he discovers major structural faults. He can also be liable in the tort of negligence if he does his job carelessly. Some people rely on the report of the building-society surveyor, but you should bear in mind that the building-society surveyor is more concerned with the financial value and re-sale prospects of the property than with hidden structural faults. However in recent years the building societies have given a more detailed structural survey as an optional extra for a standard fee. Moreover the Royal Institute of Chartered Surveyors (RICS) has been encouraged to produce a new form of survey – the **House Buyers Report and Valuation**. This is a half-way house between the minimum valuation report and a full structural survey. The *pro forma* document offers an adequate compromise for the majority of housebuyers. The report will give details of any damp, the state of decorations, the condition of the roof timbers, etc. It will not, however, constitute a full structural survey on the property. If the property is **brand new** the **Building Regulations (1976)** under the **Public Health Act 1936** require structural minimum standards and a builder can be liable if faults appear.

Ownership of land

Property is classified as personal property and 'real' property which is a term used for land and building. Land can be owned **freehold** or **leasehold**.

A **freeholder** owns the land and the building on it until he passes the ownership of it on to another. He has fairly wide powers to do what he likes on the land. Most owner-occupied houses are freehold.

A **leaseholder** owns the flat or house on the land and has a right to occupy it for a fixed period of time. During this time the leaseholder pays ground rent to the freeholder of the land. Most flats are leasehold. When the lease runs out, it can either be renewed, usually at a higher rent, or terminated. It is now possible for the majority of settled leaseholders to buy the freehold of their homes under statutory provision.

Community charge

On 1 April 1990 domestic rates were replaced with the community charge or 'poll tax'. Almost everyone over 18 is required to pay a sum of money to their council to cover the cost of the services it provides. Every council decides the level of its community charge each year, and each person is responsible for paying his or her own 'poll tax'. Certain groups of people do not have to pay, such as long-stay hospital patients, people in residential care, hostels or religious communities, the severely mentally impaired, prisoners and people living rough. Students over 18 pay 20 per cent of the standard community charge in the area where they study. Rebates are also available for the less well off through the community charge scheme. A wilful intention not to pay can result in a magistrates' court summons and, ultimately, imprisonment.

The community charge and students in further education Students at school or in further education who are studying 'A' levels or similar level courses are exempt from paying the personal community charge until their 20th birthday. The course must include an average of 12 hours or more of teaching per week. However, the exemption does not apply if the student is sponsored by an employer in preparation for or during employment, or in association with a YTS scheme. Students in full-time advanced education pay 20 per cent of the personal charge.

Water Rates are paid to the local water board.

Insuring your home and the contents

Once you have purchased a property and bought some furniture for it, you are strongly advised to insure both the flat or house and the contents (your furniture, personal belongings such as clothing, jewellery, video and TV, and other items of value). You insure the property against the event of a fire, flood or storm to enable you to replace or repair the damage. You insure the contents against damage, loss or theft.

There are many insurance companies and insurance brokers who will give you a quotation. Shop around, but take care to examine what you are getting for your money. Carefully examine the exemption clauses. The cheapest quote may not always be the best.

The law and the occupier

No one can do exactly as he or she pleases with his or her home or property. The law may regulate the use to which your flat or house may be put – it may be purely for residential purposes only, and it must not become too overcrowded. Planning permission has to be obtained from the local council for any substantial alteration or extension. Also the **Occupier's Liability Acts 1957 and 1984** require an occupier to be legally responsible for the safety of anyone who comes on to the premises – visitors, postmen, window-cleaners, etc., and you must not be a nuisance to those who live near you or to those members of the public who pass by your home.

Your local council may have issued a **tree preservation order** protecting one or more trees on your land. This makes it illegal to cut down those trees.

Being a good neighbour

The tort of nuisance Nuisance can be of two kinds, public nuisance and private nuisance:

- A **public nuisance** is some unlawful act or omission which endangers or interferes with the safety or comfort of the public generally or somehow obstructs the exercise of a common right. The 'public' may consist of everyone at large or three or more people. It is, for example, a public nuisance to obstruct the public highway; to park cars on the pavement; or to allow a factory to emit excessive fumes or dirt or to create excessive smells, smoke or noise on your own property which are likely to cause discomfort to persons in the locality. Local bye-laws cover some of these public nuisances.

A public nuisance is a criminal offence, punishable at common law. Most public nuisance cases are dealt with by the **Environmental Health Department** of the local authority. A nuisance can be reported to the Environmental Health Officer who will investigate the complaints and if necessary prosecute the offender. It is also possible to take proceedings yourself against the offender in the Magistrates' Court.

- **A private nuisance** is an unlawful interference with a person's use of his or her property, or with his or her health comfort or convenience, or with the enjoyment of his or her land generally. Common instances of private nuisance are overhanging trees or root encroachment on to a neighbouring property; noise; fumes; smells; dirt; damp; straying dogs; and anything which would materially interfere with the neighbour's lawful use and enjoyment of his property. The nuisance has to be excessive and persistent for it to be actionable, the general rule of the courts being that neighbours should learn to 'live and let live' or to 'give and take' so, for example, the normal noise of children's play would not be actionable.

A private nuisance is only actionable in the **civil courts**, and some damage to health, comfort or convenience must have occurred to enable one occupier to sue another.

NB There are proposals to introduce stronger laws and penalties against neighbours who play their radios and televisions above acceptable limits of noise and who allow their dogs to bark incessantly.

Exercises

1. What is meant by (a) an assured tenancy and (b) a secure tenancy?
2. Explain the law with respect to: (a) notice to quit for assured tenants, (b) harassment by the landlord, and (c) a registered rent.
3. Explain and distinguish between: (a) freehold and leasehold land, (b) public and private nuisance, and (c) a tenant and a licensee.
4. Advise the following on the best method of borrowing money to buy a house: (a) a single person who pays a considerable amount of income tax, and (b) a person who wishes to take out a life insurance policy with the mortgage.
5. How might the law apply in the following circumstances:
    (a) You are looking for a place to rent for an indefinite period.
    (b) You want accommodation for a few months in another town.
    (c) You need financial assistance with paying rent.
    (d) You have been invited to join some squatters in a house scheduled for demolition.

Somewhere to Live

(e) Your landlord has not given you a rent book.
(f) The flat you have just bought has its WC in an outhouse in the back yard.
(g) You are a wife whose husband regularly gets drunk and beats you. In desperation you leave home taking the baby with you. You hope the council will find you somewhere to live.
(h) You deliberately get into arrears with your rent in the hope that your landlord will evict you and you will be rehoused by the council.
(i) The only area you have for doing repairs to your motorbike is on the public pavement outside your flat.
(j) Your neighbour comes into your garden and leaves his wheelbarrow there without your permission.

Assignments

1. **An advertisement letter and telephone call.**
   (a) Imagine that you are either Barry or Bess and wish to advertise for accommodation in the *Shiretown Gazette*. Using no more than twenty words, devise a suitable advertisement.
   (b) You are a landlord or landlady who writes a letter of reply to the advertisement giving a description of the accommodation terms, and other relevant details.
   (c) As Barry or Bess telephone the landlord expressing your interest in the accommodation being offered and arrange a time to view it.

2. **Form filling**
   Obtain a mortgage form from either a building society, bank or the council. Carefully note the details of the information that is required. Imagine you are Jasmine and, inventing any relevant details, fill in the form.

3. **The household budget** (recommended for integrated study)
   Get some leaflets on different mortage schemes and make a note of the different interest terms being offered, the amount of the monthly repayments (you could calculate this by working out the interest). Check the monthly repayments against a person's estimated average weekly earnings. Then budget how much you would spend on gas, electricity, community charge, water rates, insurance, food, clothing, household items, and any other necessary expenses.

4. **Community survey**
   Get hold of, or draw, a black-and-white street plan of your district. Making use of different colours and symbols, mark on it the

following items: Council Housing Department, Rent Office, estate agents, property shops (if any), accommodation agencies, hostels (if any), solicitors' practices, Housing Advice Centre, CAB or similar advice agencies. Comment on their respective locations.

5. **GCSE Question**
   Study this extract and answer the questions which follow:

   > Young couples in the Borough of Shiretown have been given the right to rent an assured tenancy under a new Housing Association scheme. Couples who have been in the tenancy for five years may purchase the tenancy from the Housing Association under a repayment mortgage scheme.

   (a) What is an assured tenancy? (3 marks)
   (b) What legal rights exist under an assured tenancy for (i) the tenants, and (ii) the landlord? (5 marks)
   (c) What is a repayment mortgage? (2 marks)
   (d) Set out the differences in the legal position between a couple renting a house and a couple buying a house. (10 marks)
   (e) How may an occupier of either rented or owned property legally be a good neighbour? (5 marks)

7 Family Law Quiz

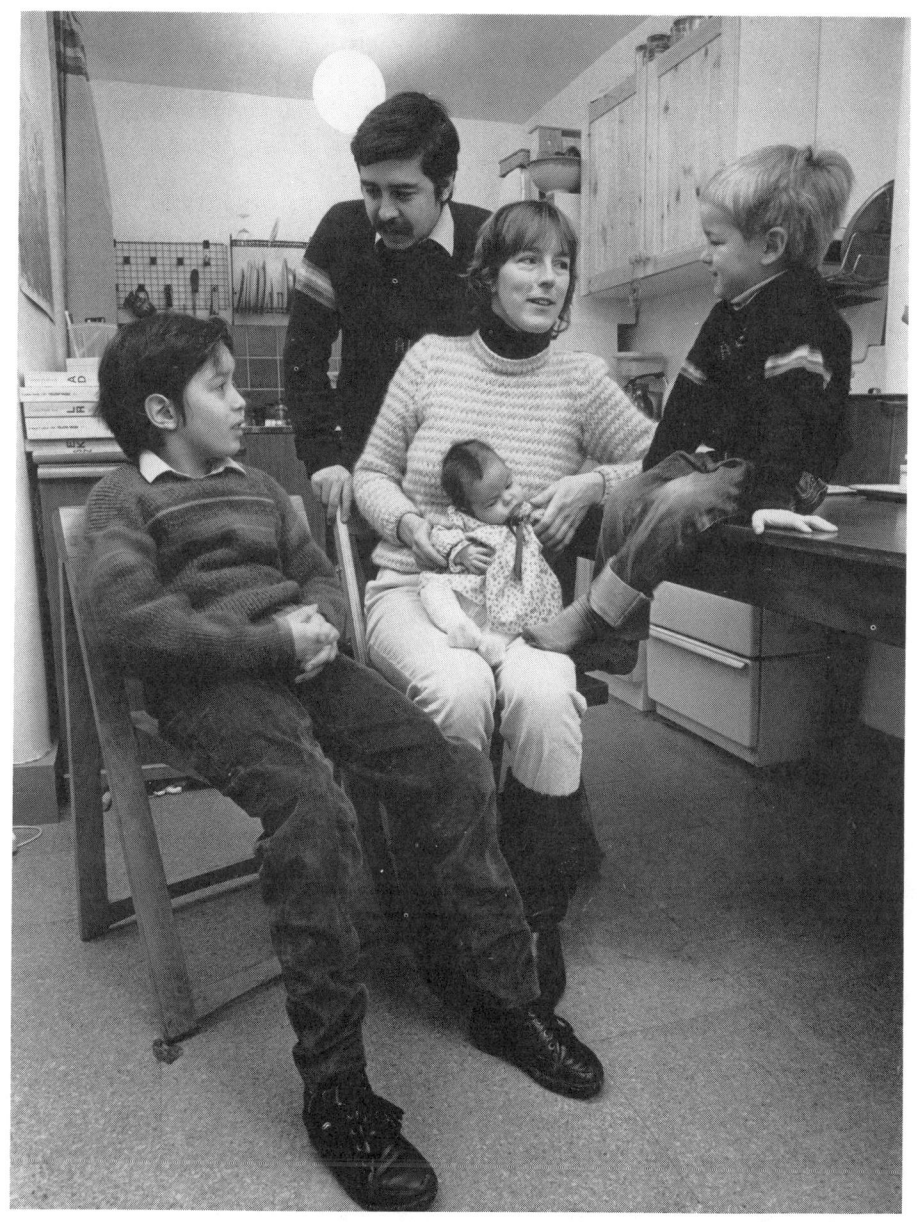

Figure 7.1 A British family today

The family has long been recognised as the most important social unit of a civilised society. Both the state and the Church regard marriage as a desirable institution for keeping the family together, for ensuring mutual responsibility among the old and young within the family and for protecting the interests of its individual members. Consequently, marriage and the family unit are governed by rules which are both legal and moral. In modern-day society some couples choose to establish a family unit without the formality of legalising their union by way of a state-registered marriage. Some couples and their children cannot always rely on the same laws as married couples may, although many laws will still affect them. The interests of children are generally paramount. Parents must see that their children are educated between the ages of five and sixteen; parents are under a duty to maintain the child within the scope of their means, and to look after the general welfare of the child. Parents are given a wide field of choice, they have the right to choose the child's name, the child's school and religion, and to discipline and correct the child by moderate corporal punishment. Most parental rights and legal responsibilities cease when the child reaches his or her eighteenth, sometimes sixteenth, birthday.

Quiz

Below is a quiz on family law. Test your knowledge by answering **True** or **False** to the following statements. The answers, with additional information, are given on pp. 158–71.

Marriage   True/False

1. No one may marry before the age of 18.
2. The marriage ceremony must take place in a registered building.
3. The Church of England, as the established Church, is the only religious body licensed to register a marriage.
4. If either party is suffering from mental disorder at the time of the marriage, the marriage is invalid.
5. People who are judicially separated can remarry.
6. It is impossible for a party to remarry unless the other spouse has either died or s/he has divorced him or her.

Divorce

7. The law recognises only one legal ground for divorce.

Family Law Quiz　　　　　　　　　　　　　　　　　　　　　　　　　　　*157*

True/False

8. The couple seeking a divorce have to have been married for two years.
9. You should always use a solicitor if you decide to file for a divorce.
10. Neither party is free to remarry until the 'decree nisi' has been granted.

Children

11. Unborn children can have no rights.
12. A parent who fails to look after a child will be prosecuted.
13. Parents have the right to decide when their children travel abroad.
14. It is a criminal offence, not a civil wrong, for one parent to snatch a child from another without lawful authority.
15. An adoption order cannot be made without the consent of both the natural parents of the child.
16. A father of an illegitimate child has no parental rights over the child.
17. Children can be fostered by a private arrangement as well as by the local authority.
18. Parents have no right to appoint a guardian to look after their child on their death.
19. Any child made a ward of court has to remain so until s/he is 18.
20. When parents separate the mother has custody of the children and the father must pay maintenance for them.
21. Contraceptive advice to a girl under 16 cannot be given without a parent's consent.

Death and succession

22. No one can draw up a will until s/he is 18.
23. No one may act as executor to a will until s/he is 21.
24. When a person dies without making a will, all the possessions s/he leaves goes to the next-of-kin.
25. An illegitimate child has the same rights to his/her natural parent's property as a legitimate son or daughter.

Total 25

Answers and additional information

Question no.	True/false	Additional information
1.	F	**Marriage** Normally no one may marry before the age of 18 but 16–17 year-olds may marry with the consent of their parents. If the consent is refused or there are no parents alive, a minor who wishes to marry can apply to the local magistrates' or county court for permission. The court, having heard all the facts, has powers to overrule the parent's decision. The court will consider such matters as the financial position of the couple and whether they can support themselves.
2.	T	Weddings in the main are required to take place either in a Church of England (the Anglican Church) or in a Superintendent Registrar's Office or in the building of some other religious denomination. They may also take place on a ship at sea. A wedding outside the Church of England requires a superintendent registrar's certificate and licence. Notice of the intended marriage must be given to the superintendent registrar by one of the parties who must have previously resided for at least 15 days in the district of the registry office. The notice is put in a book which is open to the public to permit anyone who knows the marriage to be unlawful to say so. Certain related persons, either by blood or marriage, cannot be lawfully married: parents cannot marry their children, uncles may not marry nieces, nor aunts their nephews; however, first cousins may wed and a woman may marry her husband's brother, uncle or nephew, if her marriage has ended by divorce. Separated persons are also not free to marry. On the second working day after the giving of notice, the certificate and licence are issued. A

Family Law Quiz

Question no.	True/ false	Additional information
		registry office wedding is celebrated before a registrar and at least two witnesses. Certain prescribed words must be used during the ceremony and the marriage register signed by the couple, their witnesses and the registrar. The presence of a registrar is not necessary in the Anglican Church: the register must be signed and witnessed in the presence of the priest. Other religious denominations, such as Non-conformists, Quakers (Society of Friends), Jews, Hindus and Sikhs, may also register their places of worship for the solemnisation of marriages; however the ceremony must be conducted in the presence of a registrar. Moslem couples are required to have their marriage ceremony in a registry office in advance of their own religious ceremony because Moslem law recognises polygamous marriages whereas English law does not. A religious ceremony may take any form, provided the official words of marriage, used in a registry office are used and the registration of the marriage is witnessed.
3.	T	A priest of the established Church of the land, the Church of England, may, as an authorised person, conduct the solemnisation of a marriage in church without the presence of a registrar. Anglican Church weddings are generally preceded by the reading of banns announcing the intended match on three successive Sundays in the parish church of both parties before the respective congregations. The subsequent ceremony may become void if anyone comes forward giving a reason why the couple cannot lawfully be married. A couple may marry without any banns being called where a common licence is obtained from a bishop authorising the wedding celebration: at least one member of the couple must have resided within the parish for at least 15 days before the issue of the

Question no.	True/ false	Additional information
		common licence. In urgent cases, marriage by special licence, granted only by the Archbishop of Canterbury, is also possible: the licence enables the couple to marry anywhere at any time.
4.	T	In a situation, such as mental illness, where one party is unaware of what the ceremony is about, then there can be no voluntary commitment towards the marriage, and the marriage therefore would be deemed to be void. The standard definition of marriage, established in the case of *Hyde v. Hyde (1866)*, is a voluntary union for life by one man and one woman to the exclusion of all others. The law in this country not only requires a marriage to be voluntary it also requires it to be monogamous, i.e. one man and one woman.
5.	F	A spouse who is separated, either informally (by mutual agreement) or judicially (by court order), is not free to remarry while they know their marriage partner is still alive. A judicial separation has the same legal requirements as divorce, except that the partners are not required to be married for one year before suing (as with divorce) and neither partner can remarry.
6.	F	If a party to a marriage disappears and becomes so untraceable that the other party may reasonably believe his or her spouse is dead, s/he may then under the **Matrimonial Causes Act 1973 (S19)** present a request to the court to have it presumed that the missing spouse is dead and to have the marriage dissolved. Normally, the evidence that the petitioning partner is required to provide is that his or her spouse has been continually absent for seven years or more and that there is no reason to believe that s/he is living. Sometimes other kinds of evidence are accepted if the petitioning spouse has taken

Question no.	True/ false	Additional information
		considerable steps to trace the missing spouse. If the court is convinced, then it makes a decree of presumption of death and of dissolution of the marriage, and the petitioning partner is free to remarry.
7.	T	**Divorce** Under the law in England and Wales **the only ground for divorce is that the marriage has broken down irretrievably**. However, the person suing (the petitioner) must prove one of a number of facts to get the marriage dissolved. They are: • that the respondent (the other party) has committed adultery and the petitioner finds it intolerable to live with him or her; • that the respondent has behaved in such a way that the petitioner cannot reasonably be expected to live with him or her; • two years' desertion by the respondent immediately before the petitioner sues for divorce; • two years' continuous separation immediately before the petitioner sues, and the respondent agrees to the divorce; • five years' separation up to the time of suing. This may be the case where one party contests the divorce. Such a case is likely to be referred to the High Court. Before granting a decree for divorce, the court has to be satisfied that the evidence the parties produce is material proof of 'irretrievable breakdown' of the marriage.
8.	F	The courts in England and Wales have power only to dissolve the marriages of people who are legally domiciled in England and Wales or who have been resident here for a period of at least one year. A couple seeking divorce are expected to have been married for at least *one* year before either party files a petition. If there are exceptional circumstances,

Question no.	True/ false	Additional information
		such as wife-battering, which make it urgent for one party to get the marriage dissolved within the year, then the court may agree to grant the divorce earlier.
9.	F	It is not always necessary to use a solicitor, and even where it is, it is always advisable, initially, to talk over the problem with a CAB adviser or a Relate (marriage guidance) counsellor. This can put the couple in the right direction in their particular case and may save them a considerable amount of money. Many divorce courts today also have welfare officers who will advise those who have petitioned for divorce on matters connected to the divorce. In many cases, where the couple have agreed that divorce is the only solution to their marriage and are in complete agreement over what happens to the property, money and children of the marriage, then they may file for an **undefended divorce** at the county court without using a solicitor. Proper forms and a booklet on how to petition can be obtained from the county court itself. The procedure is cheap, generally quick and uncomplicated, and is often referred to as a 'Do-it-Yourself-divorce', and some such divorces, where children are not involved, may even be granted by post. However, a solicitor should always be used for contested or defended cases. This is where one party will not agree to the divorce going ahead or where there is disagreement over who should have the property or the children. Such cases are usually transferred to the High Court and they can become very lengthy and costly settlements.
10.	F	Neither party is free to remarry until the **decree absolute** is granted. Both

Question no.	True/false	Additional information
		undefended and defended divorce are governed by the same divorce law. For a period of six weeks to three months prior to the decree absolute, the court makes a 'decree nisi', which entitles the couple to apply for a 'decree absolute'. Between these two hearings, the divorce judge will consider the provisions for the children of the marriage and matters concerning the appropriate division of property.
		Children
11.	F	To say that unborn children have no rights is not strictly true if one looks at the laws relating to abortion, congenital diseases and surrogate motherhood.
		• The **Offences Against the Persons Act 1861** makes it an offence for a pregnant women or another party to procure a miscarriage or abortion. More recently, there have been attempts to make abortion legal for certain cases. In an attempt to prevent amateur backstreet abortions, which could be highly dangerous to the health and life of a pregnant woman, the **Abortion Act 1967** was introduced. The 1967 Act, amended, requires an abortion to be carried out by a qualified medical practitioner and carried out in a NHS or approved clinic. It also requires two medical practitioners to certify that there is either a substantial risk to the physical or mental health of the woman or her family, or a substantial risk that the child may be born with a physical and mental handicap. An abortion may be carried out only on women who have not reached twenty-four weeks of pregnancy.
		• If a child is born disabled as a result of negligence by someone other than the mother, either during her pregnancy or before the conception of her child, the

Question no.	True/ false	Additional information
		Congenital Diseases (Civil Liability) Act 1976 provides that, once born, the child can bring an action in the courts for damages against the negligent person. Minors may sue through an adult who represents his or her interests.
		• Surrogate motherhood is a process where one woman will conceive, either by natural or artificial means, a child for another woman who is medically unable to give birth. In response to the Warnock Committee, which was set up by the government to look into the questions of both surrogacy and embryo experimentation, Parliament passed the **Surrogacy Arrangements Act 1985**. The Act only went so far as to make it a criminal offence to run a surrogacy agency or to advertise such arrangements commercially; it did not outlaw private arrangements. In 1986 embryo experimentation was the subject of a failed Parliamentary private member's bill. This came after the report of a committee chaired by Baroness Warnock which recommended that research on foetuses should only extend to 14 days. The Government is currently introducing a Bill on embryo research. The new Bill provides for the setting up of a licensed body which will make sure that the law is observed by the researchers.
12.	T	Parents and guardians enjoy a basic right to look after their children, either themselves or by making arrangements for them to be looked after by other people. However, parents and guardians can be prosecuted if they abandon a child under 16 years of age, neglect and fail to give a child the basic necessities for life, expose a child to harm which is likely to cause the child unnecessary

Family Law Quiz 165

Question no.	True/ false	Additional information
		suffering or injury to health, sexually abuse a child or act cruelly to a child. Neglect and cruelty can include undernourishing their children, preventing their proper development, inadequately clothing them, or refusing them proper medical treatment. There is no law which sets an age limit at which children can or cannot be left alone; the only circumstances in which an age limit exists is where a parent fails to protect a child under 12 from the risk of burning. Prosecutions of parents are fairly rare – the ill-treatment must be severe; if a parent fails to look after a child it is more likely that the child will be made the subject of care proceedings.
13.	T	Parents have the right to decide when their children travel abroad and can also arrange their child's emigration, but not where the court has made a custody order. Where the court has awarded one parent custody of the child, difficulties may arise, especially if one parent threatens to take a child out of the country against the wishes of the other parent. Where a parent has custody, the other parent's permission or the court's authority is required to take a child out of the country.
14.	T	Anyone who abducts or kidnaps a child under 16, unlawfully taking them from the care of the person entitled to the child's care, commits a criminal offence. This includes child-snatching cases where one parent, without lawful authority, removes a child from the other parent who has custody. Legal difficulties arise when the child is taken abroad as the English courts have no powers in some countries who are not signatories to two international conventions which require countries to recognise each other's custody decisions. A court order can ensure, through the Home Office, that a watch can be kept at airports and seaports to prevent the child from

Question no.	True/ false	Additional information
		being taken abroad. It is also an offence to take a girl under the age of 16 out of the care of her parents, without their permission.
15.	T	Adoption orders cannot be made without both the child's natural parents' consent to the adoption, unless the court has good reason to dispense with one or both parents' consent.
16.	F	Up to the time of the **Family Reform Act 1987** the father of an illegitimate child had virtually no claim on his child, although the mother could sue him for maintenance. Since the 1987 Act, unmarried fathers have been able to acquire the same parental rights as married fathers. The Act is designed to eradicate the long-time distinction between legitimate and illegitimate children. In 1989 one in every four babies was born to unmarried parents. The Children Bill, currently going through Parliament, will enable unmarried fathers in England and Wales to acquire the same parental rights as married fathers but only in cases where the father and mother of the child draw up an agreement to share parental rights and duties.
17	T	There are two types of foster parents, those who are paid by the local authority to look after children in local authority care, and those who look after a person's child under a private arrangement made between the natural parents and the foster parents. Not unexpectedly, the law imposes some controls over private fostering of children. The local-authority social-services department has to be notified of the arrangement between two and four weeks before the child is fostered and within forty-eight hours in an emergency situation. The local authority has powers to prohibit a private fostering arrangement, to impose conditions such as the number of children foster parents have in their care and to monitor the fire precautions in the foster

Question no.	True/false	Additional information
		home. Any child under 16 may be fostered. The foster parents do not acquire any of the parents' legal rights over the child and the parents may recall the child at any time they wish unless the child has been made a ward of court or is in local-authority care.
18.	F	Parents have the right to appoint a guardian to look after their children in the event of the parents' death, even when the parents do not have legal custody of their children or their children are in local-authority care. This can be done either by deed or by will.
19.	T	Once made a ward of court, the child remains one until the age of 18. Maintenance or education orders, however, may be continued until the ward is 21. Anyone can apply to the Family Division of the High Court to have someone under 18 made a ward of court. The person does not have to be a relative. Such applications are made where the child is uncontrollable, or where another person is influencing or treating the child in such a way that the child is in physical or moral danger or both. The court has extensive powers over the important decisions of the ward's life, such as marriage, education, and control of property. An official guardian is appointed to ensure no major steps are taken without the court's agreement.
20.	F	It is not always the case when parents separate the mother is given custody of the children and the father has to pay them maintenance. The position may be reversed if the father is thought to be the proper person to look after the children and the mother is likely to neglect or desert them. Also, if the mother earns more than her estranged husband and is capable of supporting herself and the children, then the husband would not be expected to maintain them. Courts may either grant *sole custody* to the parent who is likely to look after

Question no.	True/ false	Additional information
		the child, which in the majority of cases is the mother, or *joint custody* which attempts to ensure that both parents make the big decisions regarding their children. There is also *a care and control order* which gives to one parent the responsibility for providing the child's daily needs. The parent who is not given custody of the children is usually given a right of access to the children, which means that they may see or look after the child at various appropriate intervals. This gives a particular right for the child to continue his or her contact with both parents. **Maintenance** is a financial payment or lump-sum settlement paid to the parent who looks after the children by the other parent. In most cases it is the father, earning an income, who pays the maintenance. Under the **Matrimonial Family Proceedings Act 1984**, he may only be required to pay maintenance to his children and not to the wife – she may only receive maintenance while the children are pre-school age, when she cannot be expected to leave them to go out to work. There is also the *matrimonial home* to consider. This is left to the judge to decide, who will consider each case according to its circumstances: he will regard the welfare of the children above all else. The general rule is that the woman, who normally gets the custody of any children up to the age of 18, is likely to remain in the home until the youngest child reaches 18. At that point, if the house is rented, the tenancy will be put in her name; if it is owner-occupied, she will be required to sell the property and share the proceeds with her former husband – it is assumed that by this time the woman is able to achieve financial independence. On the other hand, the judge may order an immediate sale so that each partner may begin afresh.

Family Law Quiz

Question no.	True/false	Additional information
21	F	A girl under 16 can obtain contraceptive advice and treatment without her parents' knowledge and consent, but only if the doctor who prescribes the advice and treatment thinks the girl concerned is mature enough to understand fully the situation and circumstances, and that it is in her best interest to give her the advice. This was the House of Lords' decision in the case of *Gillick v. West Norfolk Health Authority (1986)*. Mrs Gillick, mother of several daughters, objected to girls being given contraceptive advice and treatment without reference to their parents. She sued the Authority in respect of guidelines given to doctors who were giving such advice and treatment, but she lost her case. Notably, men who have sexual intercourse with a girl under 16 will be committing an offence. Young women over the age of 16 can obtain contraceptive advice and treatment without parental consent; however, even though a girl between 16 and 18 can give her consent to intercourse, this does not stop the local authority bringing care proceedings on the grounds that she is in moral danger, or her parents from taking wardship proceedings in the High Court to protect her.
		Death and succession
22	T	Anyone may draw up a Will once the age of 18 is reached. To be valid it must be properly drawn up and witnessed by two people. No witness can be a beneficiary although the executor(s) can. When making a will it is always advisable to consult a solicitor even if it means paying his fee.
23.	F	At 18 you may act as executor or administrator of a deceased person's estate whether s/he leaves a Will or not. A person who has left a Will may have named you as executor, which means that s/he has

Question no.	True/ false	Additional information
		appointed you to be his or her personal representative for the purposes of disposing of the estate (the money, property, investments, etc. that have been left) according to his or her wishes. A person who dies *without* leaving a Will is said to have 'died intestate'. This means that the next-of-kin will have to take on the role of disposing of the estate, but will first have to apply for a Grant of Administration in order to do this. Both the executor and the administrator of the estate must apply to the Probate Registry of the area of the deceased person for the court's permission to be personal representatives before disposing of the estate. Both may benefit from the estate. When administering another person's estate it is possible to do it yourself without the necessity of going to a solicitor. The Registry officials are usually very helpful. The appropriate forms for the Grant of Administration and Probate are available from either the Probate Registry or a Citizens Advice Bureau. At a CAB you can get advice and help with filling them in if required.
24.	F	When a person dies intestate his or her next-of-kin does not necessarily receive all the deceased's property and possessions, which are often referred to as the estate of the dead person. The **Administration of Estates Act 1925** (amended) lays down the way in which the estate should be distributed. First, all the deceased debts and funeral expenses are paid from the monies of the estate. The estate that remains is called the residue. The surviving spouse only receives the whole of the estate if there are no surviving children, parents, brothers and sisters of whole or half blood or their issue – all of whom have some claim on the estate. The law of succession is illustrated in **Table 7.1**. A person who makes a will generally has a right to leave his or her estate

Question no.	True/ false	Additional information
		to whomever s/he wishes; however, the contents of the will or an intestate succession can be challenged. The **Inheritance (Provision for Family and Dependents) Act 1975** permits certain persons who may not be provided for under the will to apply to the court for an order to be given some reasonable provision out of the estate. Those with the right to apply are the surviving spouse, a former spouse who has not remarried, a child of the deceased including an adopted or illegitimate child or some dependant who was treated as one of the family or was being wholly or partly maintained by the deceased.
25	T	The legal concepts of illegitimacy no longer exist. Children have the same rights, whether or not their parents are married.

Table 7.1 The law of succession when a person dies intestate

Surviving spouse No other relatives	Whole of estate
Spouse with children	The spouse takes the first £75 000 plus life interest in one half of the residue. The children share the other half of the residue, and, on the surviving spouse's death, the spouse's half of the residue. The share for children under 18 is kept in trust until they reach the age of majority.
Surviving children No spouse	Take absolutely all the estate regardless of other surviving relatives
Spouse without children, but other relatives of the deceased alive	The surviving spouse takes the first £125 000 plus one half of the residue. Surviving parents would share the other half. If there are no surviving parents, the half they would have had is shared between surviving blood or half-blood brothers and sisters of the deceased, and then their issue
No spouse, children or other close relatives	Grandparents and aunts and uncles may inherit, and non-blood dependants of the deceased. If no relatives survive the intestate, the estate passes to the Crown as *Bona Vacantia*. This means that the property is disposed of and the proceeds paid to the Exchequer. It is possible to recover the proceeds at a later date if an unknown relative makes a claim

Exercises and assignments

1. How do you think the following problems might be resolved:
    (a) Jane's husband has left her. They have three children, whose ages are 9 months, 3 years and 7 years. There is a mortgage for the house which is in the joint names of Jane and her husband. Jane would like a divorce.
    Would your answer be any different if
    (i) Jane applied for a judicial separation? or,
    (ii) Jane was an alcoholic and was in the habit of neglecting the children?

(b) Larry, aged 9, has been taught by his parents to steal so that his parents have money with which to buy drugs to satisfy their own drug addiction.
(c) Patrick has died intestate. He leaves a wife, an aged parent and a married brother. He also leaves several debts. How will his estate be administered?

2. **Class debate or a GCSE assignment**
   Motion: Parents should have more legal controls over the lives of their 16-year old sons and daughters.

3. **GCSE course work**
   Examine *either* (a) the legal rights of the unborn child, *or* (b) the legal rights of children under the age of 16.

8 Citizenship and Civil Liberties

Figure 8.1 A passport for subjects of the European Community

Citizenship

Citizenship means that a person is a member of a particular state or country. Without it a person would be 'stateless' and have very little status in the world at large. Citizenship therefore is linked with our having 'nationality'. Nationality is the legal attachment (or belonging) of citizens to a nation as a result of birth, descent, naturalisation or marriage. As a condition of belonging to a nation duties of allegiance to the state are required of us and in return we expect protection by the state.

The subject, or member, of a state is required to pay allegiance to the state by being prepared to defend it and fight for it in times of war; and pay taxes and other dues for the general running and defence of the state, and generally be loyal to it. In return each subject is entitled to protection by the state. In Britain every adult citizen enjoys the right to choose who governs by being able to vote at Parliamentary and local elections. British nationals have the right to a passport and can move freely in and out of the country.

Domicile

A person's domicile is determined by two elements – the person's actual residence, and the intention to remain there. A person's domicile does not necessarily comply with his nationality – for example, a British subject may be domiciled in Germany because his work requires him to live there. Married women generally take the domicile of their husbands, although the **Domicile and Matrimonial Proceedings Act 1973** provides that a married woman may acquire a domicile independently of her husband. Minors normally take the domicile of their fathers unless they are illegitimate, then they may take the domicile of their mother. Minors with separated parents take the domicile of the parent with whom they have set up home.

Nationality and immigration

Before 1949, British subjects were all people who had been born in the UK or any part of the Commonwealth or colonies. They could move in and out of Britain freely. Since 1962 there have been many legislative moves to control immigration to Britain. The most recent Acts have been the **Immigration Act 1971**, the **British Nationality Act 1981** and **Immigration Act 1988**.

The **Immigration Act 1971** repealed all previous immigration laws and introduced a new concept of 'patriality' into citizenship. This meant that only patrial people – generally all citizens of the United Kingdom and colonies who were born, registered, adopted or naturalised citizens, or whose parents had been born in the United Kingdom, had the right of abode in the United Kingdom. A woman married to a patrial could also claim patriality. Registration to become a citizen became discretionary on application to the Home Office.

The **British Nationality Act 1981** redefined nationality. It came into force in January 1983 and divided British citizens of the UK and colonies into three classes of citizenship – British, British Overseas, and British Dependent Territories.

Of these, only a **British citizen** is a full British subject who has the right of abode in the UK. The citizen, or his or her parent or grandparent, must be a citizen of the UK or colonies by birth, adoption or naturalisation, or have been resident in the UK for five years. (This does not include student residence.) If neither parent of a child is British at the child's birth but later becomes British or settles in Britain, then the child can be registered as British. In any case registration is an entitlement if the child lives in Britain until s/he is 18 years old.

A **British Dependent Territories citizen** is a former non-patrial citizen of the UK and colonies, who was, or whose parent or grandparent was, born, naturalised or registered in an existing Dependency or associated state at the time of the Act. The British Dependent Territories citizens will only have a right of abode in the territory from which they originate (i.e. the Cayman Islands, Hong Kong, etc.). **British Overseas citizens** are all the remaining non-patrial Commonwealth citizens who are neither British citizens nor Dependent Territories citizens. The British Nationality Act does not affect or deal with any of the civic duties and privileges of those citizens, such as the right to vote, to serve on a jury and to take employment in the public service. It does mean, however, that their children cannot automatically become British. **Both British Dependent Territories citizens and British Overseas citizens** may acquire British citizenship after five years' residence in the UK. (This does not apply to residence as students or student nurses.)

The **Immigration Act 1988** requires British and Commonwealth citizens who have settled in the UK since 1973, and who wish to bring in their wives and children to settle here, to show that they can be maintained and accommodated once they arrive in the UK. Any citizen wishing to enter the UK and claiming right of abode here will have to have either a British citizens' passport or a certificate of entitlement, otherwise s/he will be refused entry and will not be granted a right of appeal. People may only be able to appeal against a deportation order if they have lived in the UK for seven years since they last entered the country.

Spouses Under the immigration rules a spouse is a person from another country who marries a person who is a British citizen, Commonwealth citizen with right or abode, or a person with 'settled' status. Following a decision of the European Court of Human Rights in 1985 that English immigration rules discriminated against women spouses, both men and women seeking to enter the UK as fiancé(e)s or as husbands and wives of men and women **settled** in the UK are permitted to enter the country provided they have obtained entry clearance. The couple have to show that they can accommodate and maintain themselves without recourse to public funds. They also have to show that the primary purpose of the marriage is not to obtain settlement in the UK. A spouse married to a British citizen, once he or she has both 'settled' status and three years' continuous residence in the UK and has during that time remained married, may become a British citizen. Since the Immigration Act 1988 came into force, wives of men who already have a polygamous wife are no longer able to come to the UK on the basis of a right of abode through marriage.

Non-nationals in Britain

EEC nationals are the subjects of the member-states of the European Economic Community – Belgium, Denmark, France, the Federal Republic of Germany, Greece, Portugal, the Republic of Ireland, Italy, Luxembourg, The Netherlands, Spain and the United Kingdom – who generally have the right to look for work and take a job in any of the member-states without the restrictions imposed on aliens. Citizens of the member-states may also use a right of appeal to the European Court of Justice at Luxembourg. There are also a number of reciprocal national health and unemployment benefit services between many of the member-states. A new EEC passport is currently being introduced.

Aliens are people who are not British subjects. They cannot vote at elections, they are subject to certain conditions of entry into the UK and they need work permits if they are employed here. If they gain employment here they are required to register certain particulars with the police.

Both EEC nationals and aliens are subject to UK law in much the same way as ordinary British subjects. However foreign sovereigns and diplomats cannot be sued while they are in office here. This **privilege of diplomatic immunity** is extended to foreign sovereigns, diplomats, ambassadors and to certain members of their families and some employees. This means that these people can escape criminal prosecution and liability in tort. If, for example, you were involved in a car accident with such a person and he was clearly to blame for the accident, you would be unable to sue him in the English courts. A letter to the appropriate embassy, however, may have some effect. In order to reduce the infiltration of terrorists, the Immigration Act 1988 now makes it impossible for embassies and High Commissions to employ staff unless they already have the right to work in the UK.

The right to move in and out of the UK

Provided they hold a current passport, all British citizens may move freely in and out of the country. Certain groups of people who wish to stay in Britain on a temporary basis may enter the country under certain conditions. They may have to get entry clearance which takes the form of either an endorsement stamped in their passport or a letter of consent from the Home Office.

Visitors to Britain Anyone who wishes to visit the UK for an extended holiday, or to stay with relatives or friends or for some other reason, must satisfy the immigration officer that s/he is genuinely seeking entry for the period of the visit as stated and for that period s/he will maintain and accommodate him- or herself and any dependents, or will be maintained and accommodated by relatives and friends. A visitor must show that s/he can pay for his or her return journey. S/he is not allowed to work for money or have recourse to public funds such as income support. Visitors may be admitted for private medical treatment at their own expense provided their illness is not a danger to the public health. Most visitors' period of stay is limited to six months but this can be extended to one year where visitors' rules are being observed and satisfy the immigration officer.

Students from overseas Anyone from overseas who wishes to study in the UK is required to present a current entry clearance. This clearance will be granted if the applicant can show that s/he has been accepted for a course of study at a university, a polytechnic or further education establishment, an independent school or any approved private educational institution. This would include training as a nurse or midwife. Students have to meet the cost of their course and accommodation without taking work and without recourse to public funds. As a general rule an entry clearance is not granted unless the applicant proposes to spend not less than 15 hours a week in organised day-time study. Once the proposed course ends, the student will be required to leave the country unless s/he succeeds in finding work and is granted a work permit.

Work permit holders Anyone with a valid work permit need not get entry clearance, but cannot remain here if the permit is not renewed.

The right to vote

The right to vote is a basic right of any citizen. If you are over 18, British and your name is on the **electoral register** you can vote at

Citizenship and Civil Liberties

general and local elections. The head of the household fills in a form in October every year, giving the names of all adults at the address. The form will arrive at your address addressed to 'The Occupier'. Your name can be included even if you are only 17, but you cannot vote until your eighteenth birthday. You can check the electoral register at main post offices, public libraries and Citizens Advice Bureaux between 28 November and 16 December each year. The right to vote in the UK is also extended to citizens of the Irish Republic who reside in this country. There is a scheme to give a postal or proxy vote to holiday-makers and to other British citizens who are abroad at the time an election takes place.

The right to vote enables you to exercise your democratic right to have a say in who should govern you: it will enable you to:

(i) elect a **Member of Parliament** for your **constituency**;
(ii) elect a **local councillor(s)** to serve in your local authority **ward**;
(iii) elect your **Euro-MP** in the European Parliamentary Elections to serve in the **European Parliament in Brussels**.

Your vote
helps to choose a **Member of Parliament** for your constituency, who goes to

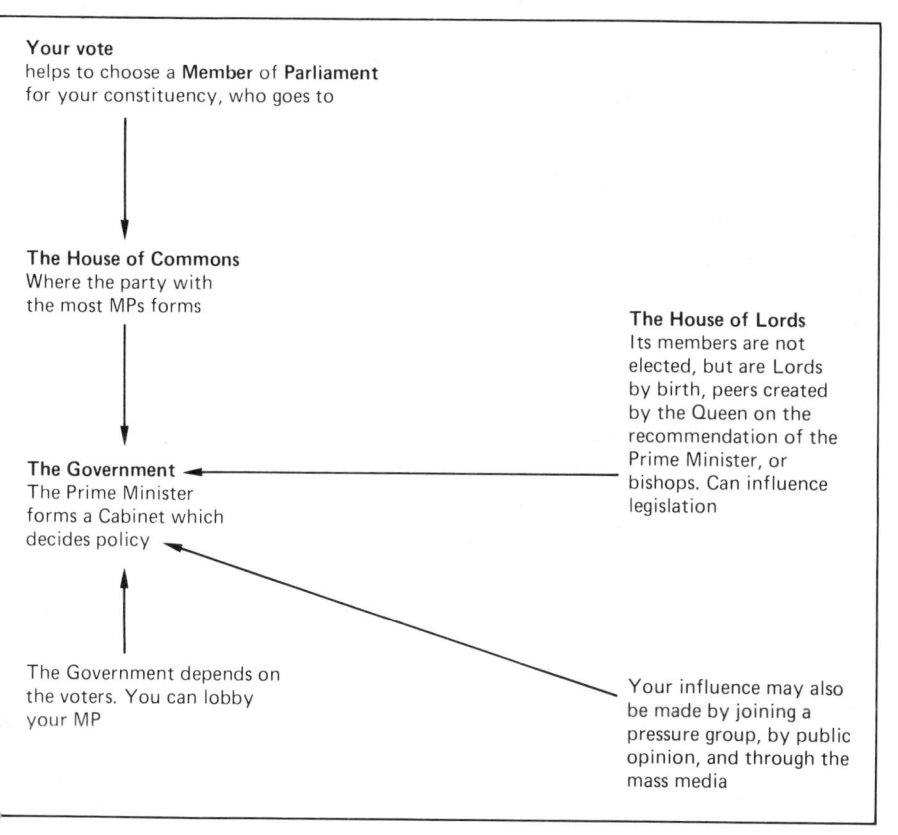

The House of Commons
Where the party with the most MPs forms

The Government
The Prime Minister forms a Cabinet which decides policy

The Government depends on the voters. You can lobby your MP

The House of Lords
Its members are not elected, but are Lords by birth, peers created by the Queen on the recommendation of the Prime Minister, or bishops. Can influence legislation

Your influence may also be made by joining a pressure group, by public opinion, and through the mass media

Figure 8.2 The influence that citizens can have on law-making

Civil Liberties

The UK with its long history of democratic government also allows us as citizens to assume many other fundamental freedoms – freedom of expression, personal freedom, freedom of movement and association, freedom from unlawful imprisonment, freedom from racial and sexual discrimination, freedom of worship and so on. Unlike most other countries, there is no written constitution containing in-built safeguards to the freedom of its subjects. Instead we rely on the existence of the rule of law which establishes certain 'rights' and 'duties'. Liberty or individual freedom is what we do and say when we are not infringing these rights and duties. Or, put another way, a citizen may do as he or she likes unless some legal restriction prevents him or her. These we regard as our **civil liberties**.

The Magna Carta, signed by King John at Runnymede on 15 June 1215, laid down fundamental principles for the government of the realm and bound king and barons alike to maintain them. Its main provisions were that no man should be punished without fair trial, that ancient liberties generally should be preserved and that no demands should be made by an overlord to his vassal (the person under his charge) without the sanction of the great council of the realm.

Today, civil liberties bridge constitutional, civil and criminal law. Consequently, the legal rules governing individual freedoms are varied, often complex and piecemeal. They include: the scope of police powers, the laws relating to detention, defamation, obscenity, censorship, race and sex discrimination, the holding of public meetings and demonstrations, the right to a fair trial and the protection of individual privacy. There have been many moves by British politicians and pressure groups to introduce a **Parliamentary Bill of Human Rights** to help consolidate the law in relation to human rights in the UK, but it is still left to the courts to shape the law through the decisions made in individual cases. Where an individual is unable to get a satisfactory remedy in the UK courts, he or she may take their case to the **European Court of Human Rights** in Strasbourg, but it would be much simpler for British Citizens if the fundamental rights and freedoms guaranteed by the European Convention on Human Rights were encoded into British law. There is a growing fear in the UK that unless human rights are protected by statute the potential for abuse of our basic freedoms could grow as state powers are extended. The European Convention guarantees basic human rights to: life; freedom from slavery; liberty; a fair trial; a respect for private life (which includes data held on computers); freedom of thought and of expression, and freedom of movement. UK cases taken to Strasbourg have resulted in rulings on the *Sunday Times* to publish its findings on the Thalidomide drug and its disabling effect on unborn babies; on equal pension rights for women; on sex discrimination in the immigration rules with regard to husbands of women settled in the UK, among many others.

Now we shall consider the various laws relating to specific civil liberties by way of the following case studies:

Freedom of expression

CASE 1:

Defamation (libel and slander) – official secrets – telephone tapping and surveillance – computerised data banks – the Press Council

Jeff Bigjore was a famous politician and one day, as a back-bencher in the House of Commons, he accused a member of the opposition, Shelley Flight, of being a Fascist and a traitor to her country. He declared that her home telephone had been tapped by the police which revealed she had passed on some official documents to an alien enemy. Also, that there was evidence on a data bank that she had been seen in company with a member of a terrorist gang in a Continental café. This speech caused a national scandal and large sections of Jeff's speech were published in the daily papers the following day. Issues in connection with what Jeff had said were also the subject of comment in many editorial columns. The *Daily Echo* also published alongside the item a feature story on Jeff Bigjore's wife, Olga, alleging that she had had a love affair with an unnamed business man. Both Shelley Flight and Olga Bigjore insisted that the stories about them were untrue. Shelley claimed that the data bank information was false; she admitted to travelling on the Continent but said she had never met up with anyone in a café as alleged. She was also disgusted that her privacy had been threatened by telephone tapping at her home. Olga became particularly frightened when press reporters daily hounded her to get her to reveal the name of her supposed lover, and cameramen intruded into the privacy of her home to take photographs.

Can Shelley sue Jeff and the editors of the newspapers covering her story for defamation of character?

Unfortunately for Shelley she cannot sue Jeff for a defamatory statement made during a Parliamentary debate. Under these circumstances Jeff can rely on the defence of **absolute privilege** which can be raised in **defamation**. This means that in the interests of democratic government anything can be said during parliamentary proceedings however personally damaging the statement may be.

Shelley, herself being a Member of Parliament, has a right of reply in the House of Commons. However, Shelley has no legal redress at all against Jeff. Neither is it likely she would be able to sue the editors of those papers who published Jeff's words for they can rely on the defence of **qualified privilege** which permits **a fair and factual reporting of Parliamentary proceedings**. Similarly, editorial comments may be covered by the defence of **fair comment** which permits newspapers and other mass media to give **an opinion on a matter of public interest**. The defences of **qualified privilege** and **fair comment** will only apply where the statements made were made **without malice** and **in the honest belief that the statement was true**. Shelley could only bring about a successful action if she could show proof of spite or of malice or of improper motive by the editors of the newspapers. Her alternative course of action would be to write a letter to the editor contradicting Jeff's accusation in the hope that it is published in a prominent position. However, if Jeff's accusation is true and Shelley has in fact been giving official documents to an alien enemy, then she could be arrested and prosecuted under the **Official Secrets Act 1911 and 1920**, which make it an offence for anyone to obtain and communicate documents and information which would be harmful to the safety and interest of the state.

Should Shelley officially complain about her telephone being tapped by the police?

To have your telephone tapped would appear to be a gross infringement of personal liberty, but under certain circumstances the government permits this to happen with the authorisation of a government minister. Shelley would have to look at the **Interception of Communications Act 1985** which lays down the grounds under which interception may be authorised. The main grounds are 'the prevention of crime' and 'safeguarding the economic being of the country'. If Shelley is an innocent victim of a telephone tapping and she wishes to complain, she may apply to a special independent tribunal, set up under the Act, which will investigate her complaint.

How can Shelley correct the information in the data bank that she claims is false?

The right of public access to computerised data banks is a contentious area of law. Like the practice of telephone tapping and bugging, this is a fairly recent infringement of civil liberties which has become the subject of legislation. The **Data Protection Act 1984** gives individuals certain rights in relation to personal information about them which is held on computers in both the private and public sectors. Most organisations using computers to hold such information are obliged to notify the **Data Protection Registrar** so that the information may be disclosed to individuals at their request. Shelley, therefore, may be able to approach the Department concerned and obtain a copy of the record relating to her. She, then, could have the inaccuracies corrected or erased. However, there are many records which are exempted for scrutiny under the Act, and Shelley may meet certain difficulties here as files maintained for purposes of national security do not have to be registered. Or, she may discover that the records are contained in manual files and not held on computer. Under the Act data on individuals which is not held on computer does not have to be disclosed.

Can Olga Bigjore sue the editor of the Daily Echo *for defamation of character?*

If as Olga claims, the story by the *Daily Echo* is substantially untrue, she is in a stronger legal position than Shelley Flight to sue the editor for libel or, as the law would put it, for **defamation of character**. First she would have to consider carefully her chance of a successful action as defamation cases can be costly, and no legal aid is available for them. In the trial the question of whether the statement is defamatory or is one of fact has to be decided by a jury, but in practice and as a matter of law, the judge first decides whether the statement is capable of being defamatory; that is, he would have to consider the question: would a reasonable person take the view that the statement is defamatory? Olga would have to prove four points: that the statement was untrue and defamatory and put her reputation in disrepute; that the statement referred to her and no one else; that the statement was published to a third party (in this case the readership of the *Daily Echo*); and that she suffered damage as a result of the publication, such as being 'ridiculed, held in contempt and shunned by right-thinking members of society generally'.

The editor of the *Daily Echo* may try to plead a defence of **fair comment**, which permits a 'fair and accurate' opinion, but this does not normally cover the private lives of public figures. It is more likely that the editor would plead the defence of **justification**, that is, that the material he published was 'substantially true', even though some details are untrue, and it would therefore follow that the statements published would not materially injure the person's reputation. If, however, the story of Olga was substantially invention then she may accept from the editor an **apology**, to be published at the earliest opportunity and a sum of compensation payable through the court. In order for an apology to be successful, the defendant, in an action for libel contained in a newspaper or a periodical, may plead that the publication was made without malice or gross negligence.

Alternatively, the editor could **offer to make amends** where he would have to show that the words he published about Olga were published innocently and that when he published them he did not know they were defamatory. To make such an offer he would have to publish the correction with an apology, and to take steps to notify all those persons to whom he communicated the defamatory matter.

If either the apology or the offer of amends is accepted by Olga then no further action against the editor can be taken. As for being hounded by the press and generally having her privacy disrupted, this is often the penalty for being a public figure. However, it is possible to make a protest to the editor of the newspaper or to the Press Council, a body which is concerned with upholding certain standards of press freedom and reporting.

Defamation

A defamatory statement is one which injures the reputation of a person causing him or her to be hated, ridiculed or held in contempt and shunned and avoided by right-thinking members of society generally. Defamation is generally a **tort** (civil wrong). Defamation cases are tried by judge and jury.

There are two forms of defamation:

1. **Libel** which is a statement made in **permanent** form, i.e. a written or printed statement, a statue, a caricature, a film. *Section 1* of the **Defamation Act** made defamation by broadcasting (radio and television) libel. Although there is no direct authority, it is very likely that statements made on gramophone records, video and sound tapes and software would be treated as libel.

    Libel is treated as actionable **per se**, i.e. without proof of damage.

    Libel may be treated as a crime where the libel is likely to cause a breach of the peace or is obscene.

    Legal aid is not available for defamation.

2. **Slander** which is a statement in a **transitory** (or non-permanent) form, i.e. a spoken statement, or a gesture. Slander is actionable only on **proof of damage,** i.e. an actual financial loss. Unlike libel **it cannot be a crime**. The exceptional cases where slander is actionable without proof of loss concern situations where serious harm is caused to a person's reputation, even by unrecorded words. This occurs in the following instances:

(a) an imputation (false suggestion or assertion) that the plaintiff has been guilty of a criminal offence, punishable by imprisonment;
(b) an imputation that any woman or girl is unchaste;
(c) an imputation that the plaintiff is suffering from a contagious disease, e.g. VD or leprosy;
(d) an imputation that the plaintiff is unfit to be in any job because of dishonesty or incompetence.

Citizenship and Civil Liberties

- **Mere vulgar abuse** – which injures a person's dignity but not his or her reputation is **not** defamation. But an **innuendo** (a hidden meaning or implication) can be defamatory.
- **Proof of defamation** The plaintiff to an action must prove:
  1. that the statement was defamatory;
  2. that the statement referred to him or her and no one else;
  3. that the statement was published to at least one other person.

- **Defences** which may be raised in defamation:

1. **Justification** where the defendant may plead that the alleged defamation is **substantially true,** even though some details may be untrue. If the statement is mostly true, then it follows that the plaintiff's reputation has not been injured by the statement. Section 5 of the **Defamation Act 1952** provides that justification will not fail merely because the truth of **one** of several charges is not established – if, having regard to the other charges, it did no material injury to the plaintiff's reputation.

2. **Absolute privilege** This means that certain statements made in certain places are not actionable. They are:
   (a) statements made in Parliament, or stated in Hansard and Government White Papers;
   (b) statements made in the course of judicial (court) proceedings by a judge, jury, lawyers, parties and witnesses;
   (c) communications which are necessary between Officers of the State on matters of the state;
   (d) communications between a solicitor and client in the course of their professional business.

   Absolute privilege is allowed in these special circumstances where the interests of the state, democracy and justice are paramount. A good illustration of where the defence of absolute privilege was upheld occurred in *Chatterton v. Secretary of State for India (1895)* where a letter from the Secretary of State for India to his Parliamentary Under-Secretary contained certain accusations about Chatterton in answer to a Parliamentary question, and an action for libel failed.

3. **Qualified privilege** Certain statements may be made where the maker of the statement has a social or moral duty to inform another who has a legitimate interest or duty to receive the information. The statement must be made without malice and with an honest belief that the statement is true.

   Examples of qualified privilege is where an employer or teacher passes on a reference to another employer or other person who has a right to receive the information; where statements are made to protect a private interest; where letters of complaint or reports are made to Parliament, government officials, local authorities, the police and other proper bodies; where news media present 'fair and accurate' reports of Parliamentary and other matters of national, international, official or judicial interest. In the case of *Jackson v. Hopperton (1864)* it was ruled that a character reference written by a former employer to a prospective employer concerning the character of Jackson was privileged. And in *Winstanley v. Bampton (1943)* a tradesman complained to a commanding officer about one of his officer's unpaid bills. The court allowed the tradesman's plea of qualified privilege because of common interest in the financial uprightness of HM officers.

4. **Fair comment** A fair comment is an **opinion honestly stated** on a **matter of public interest**. The defendant must be able to prove that his or her remark is honest, relevant and free from malice and improper motive, and is not a distortion of the truth. The statement must not be a comment on a person's moral character. These matters of public interest are: discussions of central and local government; the conduct and speeches of persons who are in public office or generally connected to current affairs; trade unions or the police; works of art, reviews of books, plays, television and radio. The private lives of public figures are not considered to be matters of public interest.

5. **Apology and Offer of Amends**

    Apology **The Libel Act 1843** (amended 1845) provides that, in the case of libel in a newspaper, it is a defence that the defendant apologised and published the apology at the earliest opportunity and paid monies into the court by way of amends. Once the plaintiff has accepted the apology and the sum of compensation, this is the end of the matter.

    Offer of Amends **The Defamation Act 1952** makes available the defence of offer of amends when words have been published **innocently**, that is that the publisher had used reasonable care and did not know of the circumstances and would not have published the words had he or she known they were defamatory.

    An offer of amends does not mean a payment of money, but the defendant is obliged to:
    (a) publish a correction and an apology; and
    (b) take reasonable steps to notify persons to whom s/he sent copies of the offending matter that is alleged to be defamatory to the plaintiff.

If the offer of amends is accepted by the plaintiff, no further proceedings can be taken against the defendant. The defendant, however, may be ordered by the court to pay costs and expenses. If the offer is rejected, the defendant will have to prove that the words were published innocently and that the offer of amends was made without unreasonable delay, and has not been withdrawn.

6. **Consent** It is a defence that the plaintiff gave express or implied consent to the publication of the defamatory material.

- **Remedies** The main legal remedies for defamation are either damages or an injunction, i.e. a court order to do or not to do something.

Official secrets

The **Official Secrets Acts of 1911, 1920 and 1989** make it an offence for anyone to obtain and pass on any information, document or other article of national security, of a secret or confidential nature which could be harmful to the state. The 1920 Act contains wide provisions forbidding the undermining of national security by communicating secret plans and codes to an enemy or foreign power. The more recent 1989 Act, which revises Section 2 of the earlier Act, makes it an offence to disclose, without authority, secret, official or confidential information. The Acts cover persons who are, or have been, members of the security and intelligence service, members of the Royal staff, civil servants, members of the armed forces, police officers and government contractors. These employees in state service are required to sign a declaration in their contract of employment in which they agree not to disclose any official information. *NB* The 1989 Act was not in force at the time of writing.

Telephone tapping and bugging

Over recent years there has been a rapid development in electronically equipped machines of intrusion. Devices for eavesdropping on telephone conversations, for bugging a person's home or office, computer 'hacking' or interception, long-distance telephoto and infra-red camera lenses have obvious detection advantages at times when national security is at risk and for tracking down a violent and dangerous criminal or terrorist. At the same time, there is the disadvantage that a person's privacy may be invaded and that innocent people may find themselves victims of this kind of abuse. Unfortunately the advance of technology has moved more quickly than the law.

The **Interception of Communications Act 1985** regulates all postal and telecommunications systems including mail, telephone, telex, telegrams and electronic transmission of computer information, but it has no control over other forms of technological surveillance such as cameras, radio transmitters, and sophisticated electronic bugging equipment. The Act applies to all three agencies which carry out authorised interceptions: the police, the secret service and the customs. The authorisation for communication interception is made by a government minister, who, before s/he issues a warrant, has to be satisfied that the interception is likely to uncover a serious offence of either a criminal or seditious nature. The grounds of authorisation set down by the Act are:

- the prevention of crime;
- national security; and
- safeguarding the economic well-being of the country.

The Interception of Communications Act was the result of a directive of the **European Court of Human Rights at Strasbourg, 1984**, after the *James Malone* case, in which an antique dealer, suspected of theft, had his premises tapped by the police and had his post intercepted. The European Court defined minimum requirements to be set down by statute: that there should be one single law which allows the surreptitious surveillance of telephone conversations and mail, and that there must be clear rules on where the interception must stop.

Individuals who suspect that their telephone is being illegally bugged or their mail unlawfully intercepted by officials can apply to a special independent tribunal to investigate the matter. If the tribunal finds a warrant has been improperly issued, it will inform the individual and quash the authorisation and order the destruction of any intercepted material. It could also require the government to pay compensation to the victim of the interception. If an interception has been properly authorised, applicants will only be told that there has been no infringement of the Act and will be informed of nothing else. There is no further remedy in the courts.

Computerised data banks

Today it is common practice for organisations – the police, the Inland Revenue, the Department of Social Security, the National Health Service, libraries and many commercial concerns – to keep computerised records on members of the public. The **Data Protection Act 1984** regulates the use of processed information relating to individuals and the provision of services in respect of such information. The aims of the Act are to protect private individuals from the threat of incorrect information held about them on computer and the misuse of such information. Individuals may apply to the **Data Protection Registrar** to inspect a special register of computerised data for any personal information held about them and have it corrected. The request must be in writing and a standard fee is charged. Certain kinds of sensitive information kept on computer by such concerns as the police, the Inland Revenue, doctors and hospitals, and information held for national security by the Foreign and Commonwealth Office, are exempt from scrutiny. (For *The Right to See Police Records* see p. 205 below.) One of

Citizenship and Civil Liberties

the criticisms levelled at the Act is that the protection only applies to computerised data and not to manually held records, such as card indexes, paper files and references.

Some safeguards existed before the 1984 Act, such as the right to request from a credit agency copies of their files on you. Also, under the **Consumer Credit Act 1974** an individual is entitled to have any incorrect information amended. There is also the **Access to Personal Files Act 1987**, which provides access to information held on local authority housing and social services.

The Press Council and personal privacy

The Press Council is a body which was set up in 1953 to safeguard the freedom of the press and to engender a growth of public responsibility and public service among journalists. The Council was also established to receive complaints from the public about the methods used by the press and the general standard of reporting. The Council consists entirely of persons engaged in full-time journalism, and its hearings are held in private. The powers of the Council are limited. It can only discipline its members as it has no legal strength of its own. Many people are of the opinion that it does not go far enough to correct untrue reporting, and many popular public figures, such as actors, politicians and members of the Royal Family, complain of fabricated and sensationalised stories about them.

One big contentious area of press freedom is the degree of intrusion by journalists and press photographers into the private lives of certain public figures, such as members of the Royal Family and members of a family where there is a convicted criminal or someone concerned in a national scandal. Such an example is the publication of a telescopic photograph of the pregnant Princess of Wales who was privately sunbathing on a Caribbean beach.

It has often been argued that an independent press Ombudsman with more legal muscle should replace the Press Council. In 1989, a number of editors of national newspapers, concerned about government interference, agreed on a common voluntary Code of Practice and the establishment of systems of readers' representatives to take up complaints and breaches of the Code. They declared their intention to defend the democratic right of people to a free press, with the readers' representatives safeguarding standards of accuracy, fairness and the conduct of journalists. The powers of the representatives enable them to question journalists and editorial executives and to take prompt action to publish statements of correction and to have their findings published. If a dispute cannot be settled a right of appeal to the Press Council remains. Unfortunately, not all national editors are willing to subscribe to the Code.

CASE 2:

Censorship – broadcasting – films – video cassettes – plays – books

Lucy and Larry had joined Justin and Judy in the college coffee bar and were telling them of their experience of the previous evening when they had been barred from the local cinema which was showing *The Big Bang,* a film about a nuclear-reactor explosion in America. The film had been given an 18 certificate and only people over the age of 18 were admitted. Lucy, who was just 17, declared how stupid the law on censorship was: 'I wasn't admitted to the cinema to see *The Big Bang,*' she told the others. 'But I could have seen the same film last Easter on late-night TV in my own home. Anyone who was prepared to stay up late could have seen it. Also, I can buy the book of the film at any bookshop. I suppose if it were ever written as a play for the theatre, yet another set of rules would apply. Can people be barred from the theatre as they are from the cinema? I don't know. But it does seem to me that the present censorship laws are ridiculously inconsistent.'

Justin said he did not agree with censorship. It was his opinion that artists and others in the business of creating works of art – films, novels, plays on TV programmes – should have absolute freedom to express their thoughts and ideas. 'If Shakespeare had had to worry about not presenting sex and violence in his plays, only half of them would have been written,' he said. 'Look at the way the Victorian novelists were censored; Thomas Hardy had to cut sections out of *Tess of the d'Ubervilles* which were considered then to be indiscreet and blasphemous. Today we accept the full edition as being suitable for schoolchildren to read. Even in this century there was the famous case of D. H. Lawrence's book, *Lady Chatterley's Lover,* which was not allowed to be published unabridged until the court decided in 1961 that it was a work of art. Attitudes change with the times. Also, it's ludicrous that a set of censors should be able to tell the rest of the population what they should see and not see, or read and not read.'

Judy was unhappy with this point of view. 'The one essential weakness of your argument, Justin, is that not everything we see and read is a creative work of art. You know quite well that there's money in soft porn, and that many of the films particularly contain a lot of unnecessary violence, drug-taking and unsavoury sex, and have no artistic merit at all. And, what about the video nasties that people can show in their own homes? I think there must be some laws to protect children and young people from seeing those horrors.'

'But Judy,' butted in Larry, 'research studies show there is no conclusive evidence that children and young people are permanently depraved or corrupted by the violence and soft porn they see on films and on the video. Half of what they see they don't understand anyway. And, don't forget the police have powers to seize pornographic material. Didn't you see them on the news the other evening raiding someone's backstreet factory where porn videos were being produced?'

'I'm not sure their powers go far enough', declared Judy. 'And I agree with Lucy, the censorship laws we have at the moment are silly and inconsistent.'

How far are Lucy and Judy right when they say the laws of censorship are inconsistent?

The laws governing censorship do appear to be very inconsistent. Lucy is right when she says it is possible to see a film in your own home which is barred to audiences under 18 in the cinema, or where the British Board of Film Censors refuses to grant a film a licence. Lucy also wonders whether legal censorship applies to plays. This is another inconsistency. Films shown at the public cinema are censored in a grading system by the **British Board of Film Censors** according to their suitability for adult and young audiences whereas the censorship of plays was abolished in 1968 with the **Theatres Act**, which made it a criminal offence to present an obscene play which 'is likely to corrupt or deprave any member of the audience'. The fundamental difference here is that a film is censored and requires a licence prior to its showing in a public cinema but a theatre play can be publically performed as long as no member of the public contests its presentation under the Theatres Act. Another anomaly is that the Theatres Act covers plays but the definition of 'play' is not extended to sex shows and striptease acts. As for video cassettes for home use, these are subject to the existing **Obscene Publications Acts 1959 and 1964**, which make it an offence to publish any material printed or otherwise which is likely to deprave or corrupt persons who have seen, read, or heard the material. Under the Act the police can obtain a warrant to search premises where they have reason to believe such material exists and magistrates have powers to order the destruction of the material. The **Video Recordings Act 1984** requires video films to be graded as films are.

How far are children and young people protected against obscene material?

When Judy said she felt that children and young people should be protected from films which show scenes of violence, drug taking and other obscenities, she was expressing the view often put forward by parents, teachers, MPs and others. On the other hand, there is also a strong opinion, like the one expressed by Larry, that these things do very little long-term harm to children, who, it is said, are capable of discerning fact from fantasy when they see it. The laws designed to protect children and young people, like the censorship laws in general, are piecemeal and inconsistent in practice. In the public cinema children under the age of 5 are not admitted at all, and then under the ages of 14 and 18 they can be barred from certain categories of films.

Children of any age can be exposed to any TV and radio programme in their own home if their parents permit it. The British Broadcasting Corporation (BBC) and the Independent Broadcasting Association (IBA) operate under different controls but both adopt a general policy not to broadcast programmes that are unsuitable for children during early viewing hours when children are likely to view or hear them. The onus then rests largely with the parents or adults in charge of the children to control what the children see and hear – although they may lodge a complaint with the **Broadcasting Standards Council**.

Publications, such as comics and books, are subject to **The Obscene Publications Acts 1959–1964** and the **Children's and Young Persons (Harmful Publications) Act 1955** which aims to punish people who publish obscene material in words or pictures, which show violence, crimes and cruelty and other horrific things which would be harmful to young minds. 'Obscene publications' applies not only to elements of sexual depravity but also to such behaviour as drug-taking and violence.

Freedom in broadcasting

The British Broadcasting Corporation is incorporated by Royal Charter. This means that the Corporation is granted a Licence from the Home Secretary and is controlled under a Licence and Agreement, which require the publication of certain radio and TV programmes. These programmes include the daily reported (and now twice-weekly televised) account of what is said and done in Parliament. The Licence and Agreement also governs the broadcasting times. The BBC is answerable to the Minister in a number of undertakings, one of which is to ensure that as far as possible programmes should not offend against good taste and decency, or be likely to encourage crime or disorder, or be offensive to public feeling. Also, the Corporation is required to treat controversial subjects such as politics and religion in a balanced and impartial way.

The Independent Broadcasting Authority operates under the **Independent Broadcasting Act 1973 as amended by the Broadcasting Act 1980**, to provide television and sound broadcasting services additional to those of the BBC. The Authority is allowed to contract into interested companies to provide programmes. There is a general statutory duty on the IBA to ensure that the programmes

Citizenship and Civil Liberties

maintain a high standard of content and quality. Also, like the BBC, the IBA is required to maintain a proper balance and a wide ranging variety of subject matter and their programmes must be impartial towards political and industrial controversies. The Acts also provide that nothing is included in the programmes which offends against public decency, or is likely to encourage or incite crime or to lead to disorder, or to be offensive to public feeling.

In 1988 the Home Office set up a **Broadcasting Standards Council** which operates a code to regulate the portrayal of sex and violence on TV, radio and video works. The Council deals with complaints from the public on such matters.

Any person who thinks that he or she has been unfairly treated in broadcasts can make a formal complaint to either the BBC or the IBA. Both organisations have their own procedures to investigate such complaints, which must be a complaint of either unfair treatment or an unwarranted invasion of privacy in the making of the programme. The complaint can be made direct to the **Broadcasting Complaints Commission.** Also the libel laws have effect.

NB There are proposals to change the structure of the Independent TV network, the Independent Broadcasting Authority is to be replaced by the Independent Broadcasting Commission.

Censorship of films

The showing of films relies on a grading indicating their suitability for young and adult audiences. The **British Board of Film Censors** classify and code films into one of four categories: U (for universal viewing); PG (standing for 'parental guidance' where children may only be admitted accompanied by an adult); 15 (for only people of that age and over); and 18 (films for adult viewing only). Children under 5 are not admitted under any circumstances.

The **Cinematagraph Acts of 1909 and 1952** and the **Local Government Act of 1972** require local councils to grant licences to those whom they consider fit to run cinema premises. The local licensing authorites of the council can also decide if a film is suitable for showing in their area. These licensing authorities have powers to grant licences in acordance with guidelines issued by the Home Office. These guidelines provide that no film shall be shown and no poster or advertisement of the film shall be displayed which would offend public taste or decency, or which would be likely to encourage or incite to crime or lead to disorder, or to be offensive to public feeling. A film which has not been passed by the British Board of Film Censors cannot be exhibited without the consent of the licensing body. The criticism often levelled at this arrangement is that the local licensing authorities vary from district to district in their interpretation of the Home Office guidelines, and some permit certain films to be shown while others do not. For example many authorities banned a film called *A Clockwork*

Orange which depicted violent scenes by a teenage gang, even though the Board had given it a certificate. Another criticism is that the British Board of Film Censors decisions depend a great deal on the personal views and bias of those on the Board.

Video recordings

The **Video Recordings Act 1984** covers the supply and possession of videos, in the course of business. A Board of Censors give the videos a classified certificate similar to that for films. The Act makes it a criminal offence to:

- supply in the course of business an unclassified video;
- be in possession of an unclassified video for the purposes of supply;
- mis-label the videos.

The penalty is a heavy maximum fine of £2000.

The exceptions to these rules are videos made for purposes of education; sport; religion and music and video games, unless they show any scenes of perverse sexual activity or gross sexual violence and mutilation to humans or animals.

Freedom of expression in the theatre

The Theatres Act 1968 brought theatre censorship to an end. Instead, it made it a criminal offence to present an obscene play which, when taken as a whole, is likely to corrupt or deprave any member of the audience. Any prosecution brought against a theatre company or group must have the consent of the Attorney General. The defendants must convince the court that the play is for the public good, or that it is performed in the interests of drama, opera, ballet or any other art of literature or learning.

The Act permits plays about the Royal Family and other public figures, famous people recently dead and heads of foreign governments. It also permits plays on religious figures and themes. Anyone who is defamed in the play is protected by the libel laws.

Books and written publications

The Obscene Publications Act 1959 to 1964 provides that an article is obscene if its effect is such as to tend to deprave and corrupt persons who are likely to read, see or hear the matter contained in it. The article, whether it be a book or some other published material, must be 'taken as a whole'. Those charged with the offence can provide a defence if they can show they had not examined the article and had no reasonable cause to suspect that it was obscene. Also the defendant should show proof that the publication of the material is justified as being for the public good on the ground that it is in the interests of science, literature, art or learning or other objects of general concern. The opinion of experts as to the scientific, literary, artistic or other merits can be taken into account.

The Act has been extended so that 'obscene publications' now not only applies to elements of sexual conduct but also to such behaviour as drug taking and violence. Under the Act the police can obtain a search warrant to search premises, stalls and vehicles where they have reasonable belief that the obscene material is kept there for publication or gain. Magistrates can order the destruction of the material.

Police powers and public order

Before we proceed further to discuss the law relating to police powers and public order, it may be necessary to acquaint you with the definitions of certain terms:

- **A summons and a warrant**
  A summons is a document which states the offence with which a person is charged: it normally only relates to minor offences. Signed by the magistrates' clerk, it is sent to the person ordering him or her to appear before the magistrates court on a certain date.
  A warrant is a document signed by a magistrate which orders the police or other arresting agent to arrest a particular offender, to take a person to prison, to search named premises and to seize items on the premises.
- **Arrestable offences** Arrestable offences enable the police to make an arrest at any time without a warrant. Arrestable offences are the more serious offences. They include:
- murder and treason, where the sentence is fixed by law;
- offences which carry a sentence of at least five years' imprisonment, like theft and robbery, rape;
- being in unlawful possession of firearms;
- certain other specified sentences including indecent assault, taking a motor vehicle, driving while unfit or disqualified, going equipped for stealing;
- offences under the Customs and Excise and Official Secrets Acts, and the Prevention of Terrorism Act, and similar offences which cause serious harm to the security of the state or public order; and
- offences which seriously interfere with the administration of justice.

Figure 8.3 The police meet the public

CASE 3:

Police powers of stop, search and seizure away from the police station – road blocks

Nigel and Sue had just come out of a disco at 11 p.m. when the police came up to them and asked for their names and addresses. They then asked Nigel to stand against the wall while they searched his pockets. Also Sue was asked to empty out her handbag. The police did not find anything and let them go home after the search. Nigel and Sue were too scared to say anything at the time, but afterwards wondered what right the police had to stop and search them like that.

Were Nigel and Sue required by law to give their names and addresses to the police?

Yes, the law does require anyone to give their name and address and even their age if stopped by the police and asked to do so, but Nigel and Sue are not obliged to say any more. Under the **Police and Criminal Evidence Act 1984** the police have powers to arrest people who refuse to give their name and address. Anyone who gives a false or unsatisfactory address may be served with a summons.

Citizenship and Civil Liberties

searching Nigel and Sue, or anyone else, a police officer must first identify him- or herself by giving his or her name and the police station to which he or she belongs. Officers in plain clothes are required to provide documentary evidence of their identity.

Had the police a legal right to stop and search Nigel and Sue?

A police officer has no general right to search anyone, but, when a search takes place, he or she should state the reason for the search and the grounds for carrying it out. The right to search a person in the street must depend upon whether the police have reasonable grounds for suspecting that the person is in possession of drugs, firearms, offensive weapons, burglary tools and goods that have been stolen or unlawfully obtained. It is difficult for Nigel and Sue to judge whether the police who searched them had 'reasonable suspicion' or not, as police officers will make their decision based on the circumstances as they see them. For example, there might have been a tip-off to the police that drugs were being passed around at the disco that night, which could possibly constitute a 'reasonable suspicion' for searching them as they did. To refuse a search might have made matters worse. The mere fact that the police found nothing on Nigel and Sue does not, of itself, mean that they were not justified in carrying out the search. The Act requires the police to record all occasions 'when practical' in which the police stop and search, so if Nigel and Sue really feel strongly about the justification for the search then they should notify the Chief Superintendent of the police station to which the officers belong.

Could the police who stopped Nigel and Sue have asked them to remove some of their clothing?

Suspects may be required to remove some of their clothing during a street search but in a public place this cannot go beyond the removal of an outer coat, jacket or gloves. If a further removal of clothing is required, then the suspect has to be taken to a police van or police station and searched there but only by and in front of persons of the same sex.

Could the police have searched the homes of Nigel and Sue?

This would have depended on the kind of evidence they were looking for, and whether they had arrested or were about to arrest either Nigel or Sue. Normally the police need a magistrate's warrant to enter private premises if they convince the magistrate that they would find evidence there of substantial value to their investigations. They could not have entered their homes without a warrant unless they had had 'reasonable grounds' that they would have found evidence related to an arrestable offence.

Police powers of stop, search and seizure outside the police station

Police powers are generally regulated by the **Police and Criminal Evidence Act 1984**, which has the force of law, and a **Police Code of Practice,** which does not have the force of law, but if not followed, it may still form the basis for a complaint against the police.

- **'Reasonable suspicion'** A person or a vehicle may be stopped and searched for stolen or 'prohibitive articles' such as drugs, offensive weapons, burglary tools and stolen goods if the officer has grounds for 'reasonable suspicion' that the person or vehicle has any of these items. Before searching anyone, the police officer must make his or her name and the police station made known to the person and state the purpose and grounds for carrying out the search. He or she may use 'reasonable force' to ensure that the person complies with the request to stop and be searched. A police officer, who stops a vehicle in connection with a traffic or road tax offence or under reasonable suspicion, must be in uniform. The Police Code of Practice makes it clear that race, colour or sex in themselves must not be grounds for a search. A person may be stopped and searched in any place to which the public normally has access at that time, or in a garden or yard of a private house if the police officer believes that the person should not be there. If an unattended vehicle is searched, a notice must be left stating that the vehicle has been searched and that the registered owner of the vehicle may obtain a record of the search within twelve months.

- **Removal of clothing** Suspects in the search are only required to remove certain items of outer clothing such as a coat, jacket and gloves, but not headgear. The purpose of this provision is to avoid embarrassment to religious groups such as Sikhs. The removal of headgear and other clothing should be made out of public view, in a police van or at a police station and should only be done by and in the presence of persons of the same sex.

- **Road blocks** The power to set up road blocks enables the police to stop all vehicles or a selection of vehicles, such as heavy goods vehicles, as opposed to the stopping and searching of one vehicle. A senior police officer of the rank of superintendent or above has powers to authorise a road block in an emergency and on suspicion of a serious arrestable offence for up to seven days. Road blocks may be put into operation when a violent criminal, terrorist or escaped prisoner is known to be at large. Records must be kept of all road blocks and road checks.

- **Search and seizure in the home and other premises** Normally, the police do not have the right to enter private premises unless they have either a magistrate's or judge's warrant to enter, to carry out a search and seize anything they reasonably believe is there which

Citizenship and Civil Liberties

will assist their criminal investigations. However, there are some circumstances when the police may enter premises without a warrant. **Entry without a warrant** may apply, where the occupier consents, to seize someone who is 'unlawfully at large'; to make an arrest of a person suspected of an arrestable offence whom they suspect is on the premises and to seize any property owned or controlled by the suspect in connection with the offence, and when it is necessary to save life and limb or prevent serious damage to property.

Entry with a magistrate's warrant can only take place when the magistrate is satisfied that there are reasonable grounds for believing that an arrestable or serious arrestable offence has been committed and that there is on the premises material of substantial value to the investigation of the offence. However, once lawfully on the premises the officer may seize any permissible evidence of any offence if he or she believes it may otherwise be concealed, lost or destroyed. **A judge's warrant** is required when the evidence is not 'permissible' under a magistrate's warrant. This covers confidential personal material such as medical and social worker's records, correspondence between a lawyer and client, and records relating to the person's occupation and spiritual counselling. It also includes journalistic material.

As with other types of search, the officer must identify him or herself, produce the warrant if there is one, make records of the search and of the items seized, and is permitted to use 'reasonable force' to make an entry and search the premises.

The Prevention of Terrorism (Temporary Provisions) Act 1989

The Act was first introduced after the bombings by the IRA in Birmingham in 1976 and is renewable annually with the aim of preventing acts of terrorism. The Act enables the Secretary of State to prescribe certain organisations concerned with terrorism and to exclude certain people from Great Britain or the UK, and to set up port controls. The Act also forbids the wearing of any item of dress, or the carrying or display of any article in a public place which is identified with support for the IRA and the Irish National Liberation Army. The Act has been amended to include all terrorists who attempt to operate in the UK. Under the Act the police are given extended powers:

- to search premises and seize items of evidence, by force if necessary, with a warrant, but without one in a case of great emergency, where immediate action is necessary;
- to stop and search without a warrant anyone suspected of being involved in terrorism;
- to detain persons suspected of being involved in terrorism for up to 48 hours. The period can be extended by the Secretary of State by a further 5 days, making 7 days in all.

The Criminal Law Act 1967 This Act makes it an offence:

- to impede the apprehension or prosecution of a person who has committed an arrestable offence;
- not to disclose information which might be of material assistance in securing the prosecution of a person who has committed an arrestable offence;
- to knowingly waste police time, i.e. 'to cause any wasteful employment of the police by knowingly making to any person a false report tending to show that an offence has been committed, or to give rise to apprehension for the safety of persons or property, or tending to show that he has information material to any police enquiry'.

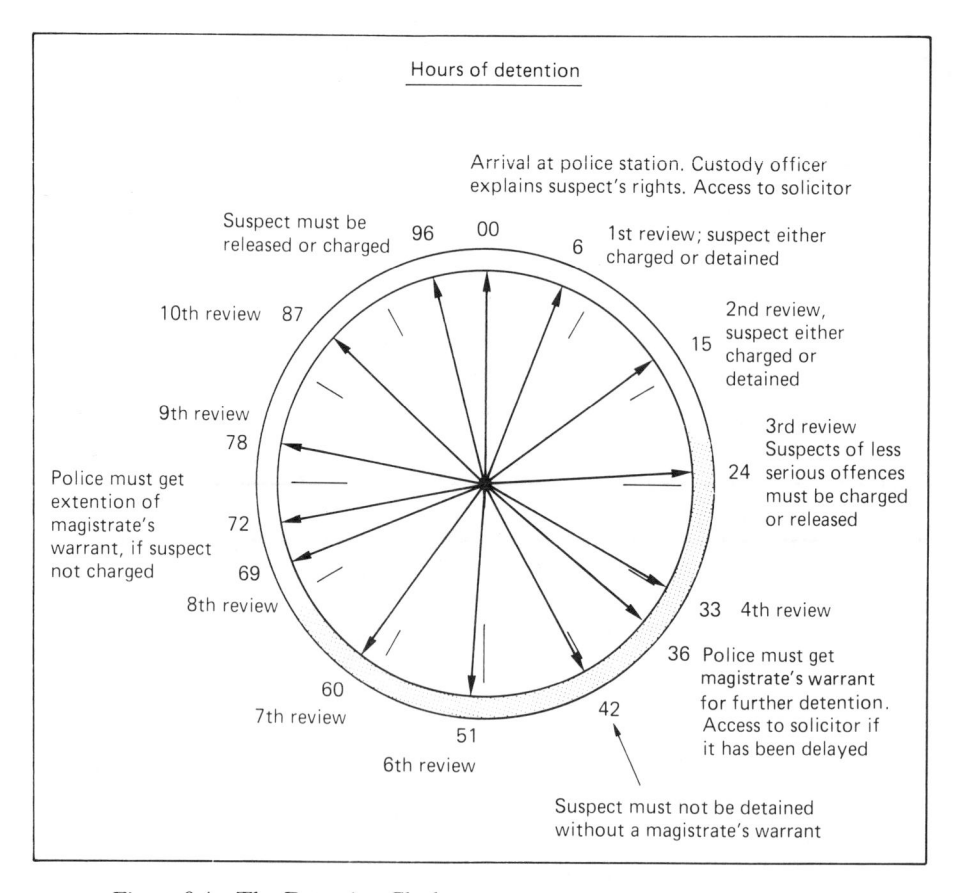

Figure 8.4 The Detention Clock

CASE 4:

Police powers on arrest and at the police station – habeas corpus – public order – meetings and processions – freedom of association

Martin was on his way home after a visit to the Model Railway Exhibition when his curiosity was aroused by a procession of demonstrators. The group then came to a square and stopped and gathered together for a public meeting. The meeting appeared to be concerned about some refugees who, the speakers claimed, had been badly treated on entry to the country. Suddenly a group of yobbos came out of a side street and set upon the group of demonstrators. Some of the demonstrators fled, the group running towards where Martin was standing. Anxious not to get involved, he turned tail and darted towards a side-street. Suddenly he found himself in the arms of a tall policeman and immediately taken with some of the demonstrators and their attackers to the police station. Despite his protestations of innocence, Martin was arrested and detained at the police station for eighteen hours for questioning. Later he was charged with obstructing the highway and for disorderly behaviour under the Public Order Act 1986. Others were charged with causing an affray.

Have the police the right to detain Martin for as long as eighteen hours?

The police have the right to detain Martin for questioning without charge for up to 24 hours, and this can be a day longer if the arrest takes place on a Saturday. Reviews have to be made of the detention not later than six hours after the detention, then at every nine hours by an officer of at least the rank of inspector. However, the **Police and Criminal Evidence Act 1984** (often referred to as **PACE**) also makes it possible for a suspect to be detained for longer periods of 36 an even 96 hours if he or she has been arrested for a serious arrestable offence. Further detention after 36 hours has to be authorised by a magistrate's warrant. Since Martin was arrested for ordinary, not serious, arrestable offences, this is unlikely to happen to him. The custody officer, who is responsible for ensuring that all suspects are treated in accordance with PACE and the Police Codes of Practice, must decide whether there is enough evidence to charge Martin with the offence or offences for which he has been arrested. If there is insufficient evidence, then Martin should be released without charge after 24 hours. Unfortunately, Martin was charged for obstructing the highway and for disorderly conduct. He is then likely to be released on bail, provided he undertakes to appear before the magistrates' court, or the juvenile court if Martin is under 17, the next day. Some of the yobbos charged with affray may not be granted police bail if the custody officer has 'reasonable grounds' for not temporarily releasing them.

What other rights does Martin have at the police station?

First, on his arrest he should have been told of the reasons for his arrest and properly cautioned. The detention code states that suspects on arrival should be informed by the station custody officer of their rights to consult a solicitor as soon as is practical and to have someone, such as their own solicitor, relative or friend, informed of their arrest. If Martin is a juvenile then a parent or an equally responsible adult, such as a teacher or social worker, should be informed at the earliest possible moment that he has been arrested, and be present when Martin is interviewed or asked to sign a written statement. In addition to these rights, Martin should be shown the Codes of Practice and informed about his eligibility for legal aid. He could be required to undergo a body search if the police suspect he has an offensive weapon on him. A detailed record of his detention, known as a custody record, must be kept and either Martin or his solicitor may request copies of this. Martin may decide not to make a statement to the police until his solicitor or a duty solicitor – a solicitor who is available on duty at the police station – is present. This may be a wise move in Martin's case as the solicitor may be able to convince the police that Martin was an innocent bystander – he may discover that Martin still has his ticket stub for the Model Railway Exhibition, or find someone who would stand witness to his not being associated with either group of demonstrators, and thereby secure Martin's immediate discharge. If, at this point, the police are not prepared to drop the charge against Martin, then it is most likely that the Crown Prosecution Service lawyer, who examines the police documents in order to prosecute in court, may see no reason to proceed with the case.

If Martin is innocent and detained against his will can he apply for a writ of habeas corpus *to secure his release?*

Habeas corpus only operates where the detainer has no jurisdiction to detain the person and it is generally assumed that, once a person is arrested on grounds that are reasonable, this is a lawful detention. Even if Martin had not been arrested but merely detained for questioning he would still have had to convince his lawyer that he was being wrongfully imprisoned. It is seldom that a lawyer will seek a writ of *habeas corpus* during this period of detention as the courts have a long reputation for not granting these writs against the police. If the detention continued longer than the lawful duration, then Martin

Citizenship and Civil Liberties

might be able to rely on securing his release upon a writ of *habeas corpus*.

Is there not in Britain a fundamental right to demonstrate and hold a public meeting wherever we like, free from interference?

It is generally assumed that law-abiding citizens can go about their lawful business without interference either from other individuals or from the state. However, there is no basic right for an individual to hold a public meeting or to hold a demonstration anywhere they please. Under the **Public Order Act 1986** the police have no powers to ban public assemblies. However, they may impose certain controls over assemblies of 20 or more persons held in the open air if the assembly is likely to result in public disorder, serious damage to property or serious disruption to the life of the community. They also have powers to control the place and time of demonstrations for the same reasons. People who gather for open-air meetings on the public highway may be held guilty of obstruction if they block the passage of passers-by and the police have powers to arrest them without a warrant. Because the demonstrators were caught up in an affray, an offence of public disorder committed by one or more persons, it is possible for them to be arrested under the provisions of the Public Order Act. To protect themselves from unprovoked attack by other groups, the organisers should have informed the police of their demonstration in advance and have arranged for some police protection.

Police powers at the police station

Anyone attending a police station voluntarily, not under arrest, is free to leave at any time. The person may simply be 'helping the police with their enquiries'. If the police wish to detain a person against his or her will, they must arrest him or her.

Arrest To arrest a person is temporarily to take away his or her liberty so that s/he is available to answer an alleged or suspected offence. In the majority of cases the arrest is carried out by a police officer but it may also be carried out by a private citizen:

- **A police officer may arrest with a magistrate's or judge's warrant or without a warrant for arrestable offences** (see p. 195 above). Under the **Police and Criminal Evidence Act 1984**, the police may also make an arrest if a person fails to give his or her name and address or is suspected of giving a false or unsatisfactory address. Except in the more serious offences, the police normally use summonses rather than arrest.

- **A private citizen may make an arrest without a warrant** when he or she reasonably suspects a person of committing an offence. This would include the right of a store detective to arrest a person for shoplifting. If the person arrested brings an action for unlawful arrest, it is up to the arrester to prove that the arrest was lawful. Anyone who arrests privately must hand the alleged offender over to the police as soon as is reasonably possible. If he or she doesn't do this he or she may be liable in the tort of trespass to the person for a false imprisonment.

Detention   The custody officer at the police station is responsible for ensuring that the suspect is treated in accordance with the Police and Criminal Evidence Act and the Police Codes of Practice and for keeping a custody record for each suspect. The custody officer must do the following.

- Tell suspects of their rights under the 1984 Act and Code, and advise them of their right to legal aid.
- Allow suspects to consult a solicitor as soon as is 'practicable'. A suspect may choose a solicitor from a given list, use his or her own solicitor, or use his or her statutory right to consult with the duty solicitor who takes a turn on a 24-hour rota system at the police station. A police officer of at least superintendent's rank may authorise a delay in access to a solicitor during the first 36 hours if the officer has reasonable grounds for believing access to a solicitor would hinder the police in gaining evidence for a serious arrestable offence or might lead to other persons being harmed.
- Allow the arrested person to contact one relative, friend or another person known to him or her, who is likely to take an interest in his or her welfare. In the case of children and young persons under 17, the police should take all practicable steps to ensure that the person responsible for the youngster's welfare is informed that he or she has been arrested and where he or she is being detained. The person should also be present when the youngster is interviewed and required to make a statement.

A person may be detained without charge for a maximum of 24 hours for a minor offence, for 36 hours for an ordinary arrestable offence, and for a maximum of 96 hours on a serious arrestable offence, with reviews at regular intervals (see Figure 8.3 The Detention Clock). Under the Prevention of Terrorism Act, a person may be detained for as much as a week.

Police bail   Bail is where a person is granted temporary freedom provided he or she promises to appear at court on a fixed date and pay a certain sum if the promise is broken. A suspect must be considered for bail if he or she is to be held longer than 24 hours after being taken into custody and before being brought before the magistrates' court.

Citizenship and Civil Liberties

Evidence Suspects are required by the police to make a statement and sign it, usually in the presence of a solicitor. Police interviews are very often recorded on a tape-recorder and can be reproduced in court during a trial. Other evidence may be obtained in a number of ways:

- **Witnesses** may come forward to make a statement and be prepared to give evidence in court.
- **Body searches** can be carried out by a person of the same sex. Nobody of the opposite sex should be present. The police may seize any article found on the suspect if they have reasonable grounds to believe that it is evidence of any offence or that the item may interfere with acquiring evidence, cause injury to a person, damage property or be used as a means of escape. Intimate body searches are permitted for weapons, such as razor blades, or hard drugs. Police can carry out searches for weapons but doctors and nurses must carry out searches for drugs. Non-intimate body samples, like hairs or nail cuttings, may not be taken without the suspect's written consent unless they are relevant to a serious arrestable offence. The taking of intimate body samples, like blood, semen or saliva, require both the written consent of the suspect and the authorisation of a senior police officer of at least superintendent rank, and they must be taken only by a registered medical practitioner if the samples are relevant to a serious arrestable offence.
- **Fingerprints** may only be taken with the suspect's written consent, or, if the suspect is a child, with the parent's or guardian's consent. However, there are some serious circumstances where the police may take a suspect's fingerprints without his or her consent and use 'reasonable force' if necessary. Records of fingerprints must be destroyed if the person is cleared or is found innocent of the offence.
- **Photographs** cannot normally be taken without the suspect's consent, unless the person has been convicted of an offence which has to be recorded in the police national records, or unless the police need pictures, taken at times of riots at football matches and in the streets, to make certain arrests.

Right to see police records Under the **Data Protection Act of 1984** a person has a right to see information held about her/him on computer. This applies to information held on the Police National Computer and that held by local police forces. By obtaining a form from the local police station, the person has a right to order access to some computer records.

The information held by the police is divided into many different categories. There is a fee of £10 to check each category. More than one category can be checked at the same time. The categories include: convictions from 1981, fingerprints, disqualified drivers, wanted or missing persons, a vehicle index including registration numbers, owners, stolen or suspect vehicles, public order, adult cautions, crime pattern analysis, and a criminal names index. This includes the names of those convicted and acts as an index to further information held by local forces.

The police can refuse to disclose certain material Special branch files are usually exempted from the **Data Protection Act** on grounds of national security, and some police information is also exempt on the grounds that disclosure will impede the prevention or detection of crime and the prosecution of offenders. Each refusal is dealt with on a case by case basis and a right of appeal exists.

Habeas Corpus This is perhaps the most famous symbol of British liberty. It originated in the Magna Carta of 1265 and was later given statutory authority by the *Habeas Corpus Acts of 1679 and 1816*. The phrase 'habeas corpus' means 'have you the body', and a writ of *habeas corpus* can secure the release of any individual who has been unlawfully imprisoned or detained. The application may be made to the High Court, and the writ orders the person responsible for the imprisonment to bring the detained person before the court to justify the imprisonment. If the detention is found to be unjustified then the court will order the release of the prisoner. *Habeas corpus* only operates where the detainer has no jurisdiction to detain the person. Some examples where the writ has succeeded are where some Polish seamen were freed from their ship in the Thames because they feared political reprisals if they returned to Poland, and where a patient in a mental hospital was illegally kept there by the hospital authorities.

Lay-visitors scheme This is a scheme encouraged by PACE which enables members of the community to go into local police stations and to observe, comment and report upon the conditions under which detainees are kept. Lay visitors have to be persons of good character; they visit the station in pairs and may arrive unannounced to inspect the cells, the charge areas, detention rooms and medical rooms, but they may not interrupt interviews in progress. The visitors, who sign an undertaking of confidentiality, may talk to detainees and examine their custody records with the detainees' permission. The purpose of the scheme is to secure a greater public understanding in the way police work and to guard against police malpractice. Unfortunately, not all districts have got around to appointing lay visitors.

For **Police Complaints Authority** see Chapter 10.

Other citizens' rights

Freedom to hold a public meeting or a procession

There is no statutory right of assembly either in the Public Order Acts of 1936 or 1986 or elsewhere. Nor does the common law specify the right to

Citizenship and Civil Liberties

demonstrate or to hold a public meeting. Members of the public are only free to meet and demonstrate where they are not breaking the law. Public meetings held in parks and other open spaces and controlled and regulated by specific local authority by-law, and even meetings held in those open-air strongholds of free speech, Speakers' Corner and Tower Hill in London, are controlled and regulated by the Department of Environment.

The Highways Acts make unlawful any obstruction of the passer-by.

Meeting halls which are owned or given a licence by the local authority and hired out are also governed by local by-laws. Some local authorities exercise a discretion not to let their halls to any group, such as the National Front, from their halls.

There is no strict legal requirement regarding holding **a procession**, except that it must pass along the Queen's Highway in a reasonable manner and allow free passage. It is an arrestable offence wilfully to obstruct a free passage along a highway without lawful excuse. **The Public Order Acts 1936 and 1986** permit a chief officer of police to divert the route of a procession where he expects public disorder to erupt, for example, to avoid a politically or racially sensitive area.

Freedom of movement It is generally assumed that any law-abiding citizen may move around the UK without interference from other individuals or the state. The original tort of trespass, introduced after the Norman Conquest, was aimed at protecting the land, goods and person of the king and his free subjects from unlawful interference. Today many of our laws relating to the use and enjoyment of our land and property and individual movement, as well as protection against theft, assault and battery and other offences against property and person, are rooted in these early laws. Nonetheless, there are restrictions imposed upon our movement and places where we are not permitted to go. The civil law requires us not to trespass on to private property without the permission of the occupier to be there. People such as postmen and women, refuse collectors and other visitors are assumed to have the occupier's permission to go on to the land. The criminal law requires us not to enter certain places designated as military restricted areas, such as airfields and Ministry of Defence property, nor to loiter near these places to take photographs. Also, only authorised persons are admitted to government restricted areas such as top security and nuclear research establishments. There are the Road Traffic Acts, the Police and Criminal Evidence Act 1984 and the Public Order Acts of 1936 and 1986 which confer certain powers on the police to stop us and our vehicles in the street and to create road blocks on the public highway and to deter groups of trespassers.

Public order

The Public Order Act 1986 empowers the police to have control over public assemblies of twenty or more persons held in the open air where there is the likelihood that the assembly may result in public disorder, serious damage to property, serious disruption to the life of the community, or the intimidation of others. Picketing in large numbers, open-air concerts, assemblies involved in racial intimidation are all covered by the Act.

- Offences under the 1986 Act, aimed at dealing with disorderly conduct in public places, are:

Riot – where twelve or more persons use or threaten to use violence for a common purpose in a way which would put reasonable persons in fear of their safety. Maximum penalty: 10 years' imprisonment.

Violent disorder – where three or more persons are gathered together to form a violent disorder. Maximum penalty: 5 years' imprisonment.

Affray – where an affray, i.e. unlawful fighting or a display of force, but without actual violence, is committed by one or more persons. Maximum penalty: 3 years.

Threatening behaviour – where threatening, abusive or insulting words or behaviour are used with the intention to cause another person fear of violence or to provoke the violence of another. A summary offence, i.e. triable only in the magistrates' court.

Disorderly conduct – where threatening, abusive, insulting or disorderly (non-violent) behaviour is used within the sight or sound of a person who is likely to be alarmed, harassed or distressed by it. A summary offence.

The Act also aims to control football hooliganism and the incitement to racial hatred:

- **Football matches** The 1986 Act makes changes to public order law to tackle the problem of hooliganism at football matches. The Act makes it possible to exclude troublemakers and to prohibit them from attending future football matches; it also controls the presence of alcohol at sporting events and imposes restrictions on articles such as smoke-bombs being taken into the grounds. The Act allows photographs to be taken for the purpose of identifying troublemakers.
- **Incitement of racial hatred** It is an offence to intentionally incite racial hatred by threatening, abusive or insulting words or behaviour. The Act encompasses verbal and written materials which are broadcast or relayed by way of plays, shows, tapes, videos or in other similar ways. To possess such materials is also an offence and the police may search for and seize such material.

Citizenship and Civil Liberties

Freedom of association

There is no general restriction of association imposed upon citizens of the UK. We are free to associate with whomever we wish, whether it be a social, political, business or a trade union association or gathering providing the reason for the association is a legal one. Any association, such as a secret society with an illegal purpose, is not permitted. It is also unlawful if two or more people get together with the intention to commit a crime. This is referred to as **conspiracy** in criminal law.

Religious freedom   One of our fundamental rights is freedom of worship. There is no compulsory state religion, and minority faiths are accepted as part of our multi-racial society, and it is generally illegal to discriminate against a person because of a religious belief. However, the Queen, as Monarch, must be a member of the Church of England. It is a legal provision in the **Education Reform Act 1988** to require pupils in all state schools to take part in daily collective worship and to receive religious education. Although the Act puts an emphasis on Christianity, it also says: 'such Christian and other religious denominations as, in the opinion of the (local) authority will appropriately reflect the principal religious traditions in the area'. Church of England schools are exempt from this latter provision.

Racial and sexual discrimination   The Race Relations Act 1976 and the Sex Discrimination Act 1975 seek to outlaw unjustifiable discrimination on the grounds of race or sex. This is dealt with in Chapter 4.

The National Council for Civil Liberties (NCCL) is a campaigning, watchdog and help organisation whose aim is to defend people's rights and liberties. It deals with hundreds of cases a year where it is alleged there has been a misuse of the law or of legal powers given to certain bodies such as the police, immigration officials, local authorities and civil servants, which have led to unfair and inhumane treatment or to racial harassment of innocent people.

Exercises and assignments

1. Explain what is meant by (a) nationality, (b) domicile, and (c) diplomatic immunity.
2. Explain the differences between (a) a British citizen and a British Overseas citizen, and (b) an EEC national and an alien.
3. How would the law apply in the following situations?
    (a) Mohammed Ullah arrives at London Airport to attend the wedding of his niece at the invitation of his brother. He

intends to stay with his relatives in London for three months. He is refused entry and told to return to Pakistan.
- (b) Emma, who is a British Overseas citizen, wants to marry Malik, an Austrian, and the pair hope to settle in Britain.
- (c) Leroy is a Jamaican who would like to come to England to study engineering for three years. He secretly hopes that once he is in the UK he will be allowed to stay and apply for British citizenship.
- (d) Sadie's family have moved house to another area of Britain. She is 18 and wonders whether she will be able to vote at the next General Election.
- (e) Matthew was stopped and searched in the street and the police found in his jacket pocket some bicarbonate of soda which he was taking in water in place of indigestion tablets. He was promptly arrested and charged with being in illegal possession of a dangerous drug.
- (f) Bill, a former member of the Communist Party, wants to arrange a demonstration march and meeting to protest against nuclear weaponry. When making a telephone call to a fellow demonstrator, he heard clicking noises on the line and suspected that his telephone was being tapped.
- (g) Rosi-Lee, a well-known folk singer, read a story about herself in the *Daily Echo*, which she knew to be distorted and exaggerated.
- (h) Linda was offered a job subject to an acceptable character reference from her last school. Two weeks later the manager of the company wrote saying that he was now unable to offer her the job. Linda is convinced the reference had been untruthful and unfair.
- (i) Ingrid went to see a new play. She came away outraged by the display of sex and violence she had witnessed on the stage.
4. Imagine that you are Rosi-Lee, the folk singer in question 3(g) above. Write a **letter** of complaint to the Press Council about the exaggerated and distorted story in the *Daily Echo*.
5. *A debate or class discussion*
   Motion 'All laws governing censorship should be abolished'
   Make use of the information given in this chapter and other sources such as newspaper articles, journals and library books on civil liberties, for this exercise.
6. As a group activity **formulate a Bill of Rights** for the United Kingdom.

GCSE course work assignments

7. Consider the question of police powers. Perhaps prior to writing up your course work you could carry out an opinion poll in your school or college on such matters as: stop and search, the treatment of detainees, and possible ways of quelling riotous criminal behaviour, for example, by the use of plastic bullets, water cannon and tear gas.
8. Consider, with current examples, the various ways whereby members of the general public and the mass media may influence the laws of Parliament.
9. Discuss the rights and wrongs of the immigration and nationality laws.

Other assignments

10. Find out the names of (a) your Member of Parliament, (b) your local ward councillor(s), and (c) your Euro-MP.
11. Get a copy of a map of your district, or draw one, and mark on it in distinguishing colours the boundaries of (a) the parliamentary constituency in which you live, and (b) the wards of your local authority. (This information can be obtained from your Town Hall or Civic Centre, from any public libraries, or from your school or college library.)
12. Write a letter to your MP requesting a class or group visit to the Houses of Parliament.

Suggested outings

Following assignment 12 arrangements could be made to visit the Houses of Parliament where distance, time and resources permit. Alternatively a visit could be made to the local Council Chamber, or to listen to a local council meeting one evening. Visit the local police station, or invite as a guest speaker the Police Community Liaison Officer, or some other officer.

9 Crime and Punishment

Figure 9.1 A view of Leicester prison

Crime and Punishment

Elements of a crime

Crime, its prevention and the treatment of the perpetrators of crime by way of punishment is a continuing problem for all societies. Some statistics claim that in the UK a crime is committed every minute. These statistics cover all types of crime, serious crime such as murder, rape and robbery and less serious crime such as petty theft, causing a public affray and motoring offences. A large proportion of the less serious crimes are committed by youths between the ages of 14 and 21. Whatever the degree of seriousness, crime is regarded as a threat to the peace and stability of the realm. It is for this reason that, within the law of the land, the police are employed to track down offenders, the courts have been created to give the alleged offender a fair trial before magistrates and judges and juries, and, on the basis of proof of guilt, the judiciary decide how to punish the offender.

What, then, is a crime? How does a criminal court decide on whether an accused person is guilty or innocent? And who, in the eyes of the law, is capable of committing a crime?

A crime is an offence committed against the state, for which an accused person is put on trial in a criminal court to establish his/her guilt or innocence. The law presumes the innocence of a person until guilt is established. If guilt is established **beyond all reasonable doubt**, then the state will punish the convicted person.

In the majority of cases, a person cannot be found guilty of a crime unless the court establishes the presence of **two elements:**

- the *actus reus* – a wrongful act; and
- the *mens rea* – a guilty state of mind.

An *actus reus* is more than just a physical act: it also includes the circumstances surrounding the act and the consequences of the accused's conduct: for example, in the case of a stabbing incident, the court will want to know whether the accused person had a knife or similar implement, whether s/he was seen at a certain time and place flourishing it before the victim in the case. The accused's conduct must be voluntary, that is, not performed unconsciously by someone who was, for example, sleepwalking in a trance, having an epileptic fit or being attacked by a swarm of bees at the time the offence was committed. (See below under, *General defences*.) An **omission to act** may also be regarded as an *actus*; for example, where a baby is left to starve to death by its parents.

A *mens rea* is the guilty state of mind of the person before and at the time of committing the *actus reus*. The court has to decide: did the accused **intend** the crime to take place, or was the accused **reckless** as to the consequences of it having taken place. For example, a man may either set out with the deliberate intention to kill or steal; or he may set light to a building disregarding the fact that the act of arson may cause the death of anyone inside. Another form of *mens rea* is **gross negligence**, which is often applied to cases of unlawful and dangerous driving causing the death to another. Where a death or injury of a person is caused by an accident, and there is no intention whatever to harm that person, there is no *mens rea* present, and therefore no crime has been committed, unless, of course the accused has infringed some other regulation under, for example, the Road Traffic Acts.

Crimes of strict liability

These are crimes for which no *mens rea* is required for proof of blame, but where the accused can be assumed guilty for having committed the element of *actus reas*. Statutory liability offences include: road traffic offences, such as travelling over the speed limit or ignoring red traffic lights; offences under the **Health and Safety at Work Act**, and offences committed under the **Food Act 1984, Trade Descriptions Act 1968,** and similar legislation.

Criminal liability

Minors It is generally assumed that a child under 10 years is incapable of committing any crime. Children between the ages of 10 and 14 years are capable of committing a crime but only where it can be shown that the child knew s/he was doing something morally and gravely wrong; only then can s/he be convicted. Young people over 14 are liable for criminal offences in the same way as an adult. It is often the case that a person under 17, who has committed an offence, is taken into care under the Children's and Young Persons Act 1969 rather than have a prosecution brought against him or her.

Corporations Corporations may be convicted for crime as if they were a person. There are certain crimes they cannot commit, like murder, rape or bigamy. These offences, however, may be committed by individual persons within the company, and they would be brought to trial in the normal way. In certain instances managers of a corporation can be vicariously liable for the acts of its employees, particularly where the corporation appears to have sanctioned the offence, e.g. by knowingly allowing an employee to drive a defective lorry or operate fraudulent practices.

Crime and Punishment 215

Parties to crime

The law divides those who take part in a crime into two main categories:

- The **principal** is the chief perpetrator of the crime. It is possible to have more than one principal if his/her role is more that than of secondary party.

- **Secondary parties**, are those who assist in any way to bring about a crime by **aiding and abetting** the principals(s); i.e. assisting them at the time of the offence by **counselling** them, i.e. giving them advice or encouragement or, procuring for them, i.e. providing them with tools or other items for the commission of the crime. The general rule is that their liability is the same as that of the principal, providing the *actus reus* and *mens rea* can be shown to exist.

Problem-solving exercises on crimes

In this section you may either work on your own or in class groups.

In the following exercises you are required to do what police, lawyers and judges and juries are often required to do, that is, to establish which offences have been committed, whether any of the accused persons are capable of raising a defence to establish his or her innocence, and, where guilt is proven, to decide what the appropriate punishment should be.

There are three stages to work through:

1. Read the following case-studies, then read through the list of **specific crimes** given below to establish which crimes may have been committed. Begin by making a list of the people involved and then sort out any offences for which each one may be prosecuted or summonsed.
2. Once you have established your list of alleged offenders and specific crimes, read through the list of **general defences** to a crime to establish any possible defences that the individuals might raise in court. Then say whether you think they are guilty or not guilty.
3. For those individuals whom you consider guilty, decide what you think the **statutory or correct punishment** should be. Here your own views on punishment may be at variance with either those penalties which are laid down by statute or with those of your

fellow students. To assist you with this question look for news cuttings on sentencing or visit your local magistrates' court.

NB Before attempting these questions you may find it helpful if, first, you work through the progress test at the end of this chapter.

CASE 1:
D, E, J and P got together to plan to steal some jewellery from K's house. It was agreed between them that, because P was only 15 years old, he should be the lookout. When the four of them arrived at K's house, E and J forced open a window at the rear of the house and took some cash and jewellery. D went to the side of the house and saw a scooter standing in front of a garage; he called to P, the lookout, to jump on the back and they drove off. As they reached a bend in the road, D suffered a blackout causing the scooter to swerve. P was thrown off and suffered severe injuries. In the mean time, E and J set light to the garage in K's garden, the blaze of which spread to a neighbour's workshop.

CASE 2:
X, Y and Z went to the Drover's Arms in X's car for a drink. Unknown to X, Y laced X's alcohol-free drink with some potent alcohol. During the evening Z, who is subnormal, met an old friend and bought some drugs from him and took some. When a rival gang turned up at the Drover's Arms, Y and Z got themselves involved in a fight, in which Y caused severe bleeding to B, and Z stabbed A with a knife he had been carrying. A had to be taken to hospital. X was so disgusted with the behaviour of Y and Z that he drove off on his own. On the way home X nearly knocked down a pedestrian and was arrested by the police on a charge of being in charge of a motor vehicle with excess alcohol in his bloodstream. One month later, A died as a result of the knife wounds he had received from Z.

Specific crimes

Crimes can be described under four headings: unlawful homicide; non-fatal offences against the person; theft; and criminal damage to property.

1 Unlawful homicide

Homicide is the killing of one human being by another. The act of killing may be lawful in such circumstances as in time of war or when

Crime and Punishment 217

a person successfully pleads self-defence. Homicide becomes unlawful when a person commits murder, infanticide or manslaughter, or causes the death of another by reckless driving:

- **Murder** is defined as unlawful killing with malice aforethought. The prosecution must prove that the death took place within one year and a day after the day of the attack. Malice aforethought describes the necessary intention, or *mens rea* to kill or to cause grevious bodily harm. Recklessness is not sufficient.
  Maximum penalty Life, although in some cases a judge may recommend a minimum number of years to be served.
- **Infanticide** is the unlawful killing of a child of under 12 months, committed by the mother. It must be shown that she committed the offence while in a state of mental disturbance brought about by giving birth.
  Maximum penalty (as for manslaughter).
- **Manslaughter** is unlawful homicide without malice aforethought. The law makes a distinction between voluntary and involuntary manslaughter:
  Voluntary manslaughter occurs when a person has committed an act of murder but successfully pleads a specific defence, such as diminished responsibility, or provocation, i.e. loss of self-control in a situation in which a reasonable man would have acted in the same way.
  Involuntary manslaughter occurs when an unlawful killing of a human being takes place, but without malice aforethought. Examples of involuntary manslaughter are: gross negligence, illustrated in the case of *Andrews v. DPP* (1937) in which a motorist driving on the wrong side of the road late at night killed another road user; and also in such instances where another's death is caused by an unlawful act which would not normally kill or cause serious bodily harm, such as throwing missiles at a moving train and killing the guard.
  Maximum penalty: Life, but sentences may be reduced according to the circumstances surrounding the killing.
- **Suicide** Since the **Suicide Act 1961**, a person who attempts to kill him or herself cannot be convicted of a crime. However, it is a criminal offence to aid, abet, counsel or procure the suicide of another. Hence a suicide pact, where two or more persons agree to their own or each other's killing, is a crime. Survivors of a suicide pact are likely to be charged with voluntary manslaughter.
- **Causing death by reckless driving** The **Road Traffic Act 1972 (S.1)** makes reckless driving, which creates a risk of causing personal injury or substantial damage to property, an offence. The penalty depending on the circumstances, can be severe. The

court must order disqualification for a period of not less than two years. Where the reckless driving causes the death of another, the offence is punishable by imprisonment of up to five years and/or a fine.

2. Non-fatal offences against the person

- **Assault and battery** At common law there are two basic offences of assault and battery. The two are often taken together to mean actual violence. However, an assault does not necessarily require the touching of a person: it is enough to show that the offence was sufficiently threatening to put another in real fear of immediate and unlawful personal application of force, whereas a battery is the actual application of force. So, to corner another person and threaten him/her with a clenched fist, or to spit on him/her, could amount to an assault; punching or slapping him/her would be a battery. (In the civil law of torts, assault and battery are trespass to the person.) **Common assault** is also a crime under the **Offences Against the Persons Act 1861 (S24)**. The Act requires the prosecution to establish that the victim was put in fear of immediate and unlawful violence. To prove battery the prosecution must prove that the accused intentionally or recklessly inflicted unlawful personal violence on the victim.

  The **Offences Against the Persons Act 1861** also provides for other more serious crimes:

- *S47* makes **assault causing actual bodily harm** an offence, which is punishable by up to five years' imprisonment. The prosecution must show that the outer and inner skin of the victim were cut.
- *S20* makes **unlawful malicious wounding** or the infliction of any grevious bodily harm, with or without a weapon or instrument, an offence. The maximum penalty is five years' imprisonment.
- *S18* makes it an offence to unlawfully and maliciously wound or **cause grievous bodily harm (gbh)** to any person with the intent to resist or prevent the lawful arrest or detention of a person. The maximum penalty is life.
- Under *sections 20 and 18* the wounding must be more than bruising or scratching: bleeding from the broken skin appears to be necessary for these offences.
- **Rape** Under the **Sexual Offences Act 1956** the offence of rape occurs when a man has unlawful sexual intercourse with a woman without her consent. The law in Scotland makes it possible for a husband to rape his wife; however, under English law, a husband can only commit rape against his wife if they are

Crime and Punishment 219

legally separated. Nonetheless, a husband can be charged with assault or causing bodily harm if he uses violence to get her to have intercourse with him. A woman who forces a man to have unlawful intercourse with her may be charged with indecent assault.

NB Consent as a defence to an offence of assault, battery or harm against a person is permitted for lawful activities, such as having a haircut or dental treatment, or agreeing to an operation performed by a hospital surgeon. Even when you walk down a crowded street, ride on a bus full of people or engage in rough sporting activities, you consent, by implication, to other people bumping or knocking into you. However, if the touching becomes unacceptably hostile, violent or outside the rules of the sport, then a criminal offence may have occurred.

3 Theft and related offences

The two **Theft Acts of 1968 and 1978** set out many offences against property.

- **Theft Act 1968,** *S1* states: 'A person is guilty of theft if he dishonestly appropriates property belonging to another with the intention of permanently depriving the other of it.' *Maximum penalty:* Ten years.

  The *actus reus* of **theft** is the 'appropriation of property belonging to another'. 'Appropriation' is more than taking the property, more precisely it is interpreted as the person treating the property as if it belonged to him/her. However, 'appropriation' of itself may not be a criminal wrong; for example, you may treat a friend's bicycle or book as if it were yours in the belief that s/he would not mind if s/he knew you had it. It is therefore necessary to establish not only the *actus reus* but also the *mens rea* for proof of theft; that is, the 'dishonest intention to permanently deprive the owner of his property'. If a person assumes ownership of a consignment of video tapes and then sells them to the unsuspecting rightful owner, then there has been an intention to deprive him/her permanently – by the assumption of ownership by the dishonest person – of the value of goods which should have been his/hers.

  'Property' covers money, goods, domestic animals, and any item that can be owned, including, in certain circumstances, land. It is not theft to pick wild mushrooms, flowers, fruit or foliage or trees growing wild, provided the picking is not done for sale, or other commercial purposes. It is also an offence to dishonestly divert or waste electricity (*S13*).

- **Robbery** *S8(1)* of the 1968 Act provides that: 'A person is guilty of robbery if he steals and immediately before or at the time of doing so, and in order to do so, he uses force on any person in fear of being then and there subjected to force.' This is saying that theft by use of force amounts to robbery. The force, or putting the victim in fear of it, can happen before or at the time of the act of theft. The force does not necessarily have to be applied to the victim of the theft; it can be directed at anyone who happens to be with the victim at the time of the theft. So, someone who stole from a bank manager and coshed a cashier to do so will be guilty of robbery. *Maximum penalty:* Life.

- **Burglary** *S9* of the 1968 Act makes a person guilty of burglary when s/he either, (a) enters a building, or part of a building, as a trespasser with intent to commit an offence of theft, inflict grievous bodily harm, rape or unlawful damage, or (b) having entered a building as a trespasser, steals or attempts to steal anything in the building or inflicts or attempts to inflict grievous bodily harm upon any person in the building. The crime of burglary, therefore, connects the offence of theft with breaking and entering or unlawful trespass. Generally, a 'person entering a building' can refer to any part of the body, such as in a case where someone breaks a shop window with his fist and puts his hand over the sill to steal jewellery inside the shop. A 'part of a building' may mean a floor area in a department store where the till is kept and which is out of bounds to the customers (*R v. Walkington 1979*). *Maximum penalty:* Fourteen years' imprisonment.

- **Aggravated burglary**, defined under *S10* is burglary with the additional offence of carrying or using any firearm, offensive weapon or explosive, real or imitation. *Maximum penalty:* Life.

- **Taking a conveyance** *S12* of the 1968 Act makes it an offence to take a conveyance without the consent of the owner or to drive or travel in the conveyance knowing it to have been taken without the owner's consent. This offence is commonly known as 'joy riding'. A 'conveyance' includes anything which carries people on land, sea or air. *Maximum penalty:* Three years. When the conveyance is a bicycle there is a maximum fine of £50.

  NB Under S25, anyone who is guilty for **going equipped to steal** is subject to a maximum penalty of three years' imprisonment.

- **Blackmail** *S21* of the 1968 Act makes a person guilty of blackmail if, with a view to make a profit, he makes an unwarranted demand with menaces. 'Menaces' may be threats of violence, or threatening actions of an unpleasant kind. *Maximum penalty:* Fourteen years' imprisonment.

- **Handling stolen goods** It is an offence under *S22* of the 1968 Act to dishonestly receive, keep, remove or dispose of goods, or arrange any of these actions, knowing or believing the goods to be stolen. 'Belief' has to be something stronger than 'mere suspicion'.

- **Theft by deception** These offences are acts whereby a person thieves or causes loss to another by dishonest deception. The deception can be by word or conduct. Both the 1968 and 1978 Acts state a number of these offences:

Theft Act 1968
S15 It is an offence **to obtain property by deception**, for example, where a delivery man picks up a crate of oranges from a wholesaler and deliberately does not deliver them to the retailer who has purchased them (*R. v. Skipp 1975*), or, when someone test-drives a car with the intention of not returning it to its rightful owner.

S16 It is an offence **to obtain pecuniary advantage by deception**, such as where a person gains money by making a false claim to an insurance company, or deceives a bank manager into providing him with a bank overdraft on the false information that he is expecting a large cheque in a month's time.

Theft Act 1978
The 1978 Act has revised two offences of deception (formerly in the 1968 Act) and created a new offence of making off without payment:

S1 It is an offence **to obtain services by deception**, for example, in cases where a person allows a hairdresser to cut his hair, travels on a bus, or stays at a hotel, fully intending not to pay for the service.

S2 makes it an offence **to evade a liability, or financial obligation, by deception**. Examples of this offence are: where a landlady to whom rent is owed is persuaded to allow the tenant to stay on by a false story that the tenant is coming into some money when, in fact, he has no intention of paying her, or, when someone falsely tells a newsagent that he has paid his bill already and the newsagent accepts that his staff have made a mistake.

S3 makes it an arrestable offence for a person **to make off without having paid** for goods or a service with the deliberate intention to avoid payment. Such situations are when an on-the-spot payment is expected. It is therefore an offence when someone drives away from a self-service petrol station without having paid, or when a person leaves a restaurant and avoids paying for a meal he has just eaten there.

4 Criminal damages

The **Criminal Damage Act 1971 S1.** It is an offence to unlawfully destroy or damage property belonging to another, either intentionally or recklessly. *Maximum penalty:* Ten years.

S1(2) makes it an aggravated offence to unlawfully destroy or damage property with the intention of endangering the life of another. For this offence the property can belong either to another or to the offender himself. For damage or destruction to property by fire the charge is arson. For both these offences the *maximum penalty* is life.

Attempt/conspiracy/incitement

The **Criminal Attempts Act 1981** says that a person is guilty if he attempts to commit a criminal offence. The attempt must be more than an act of 'mere preparation' to commit the offence, even if it becomes impossible to carry it out. (The intention, or *mens rea*, is still present.) The law regards an attempt to commit a crime as seriously as committing the crime itself.

Under the **Criminal Law Act 1977**, it is an offence to conspire to commit a crime, i.e. for two or more people to agree on a course of conduct which involves bringing about a crime by one or more of them. It is also an offence at common law to incite (persuade, urge or encourage) another person to commit a crime. A casual bystander is unlikely to be viewed as one who incites unless he shouts words of encouragement.

Other offences

Under-age drinking The **Licensing Acts** make it an offence for those licensed to sell alcohol to sell alcohol to someone under 18 and for anyone under 18 attempting to buy it. To sell alcohol unlawfully is normally an offence of strict liability. The licensee may produce a defence of having exercised all due diligence to prevent an offence being committed or who had no reason to suspect that the person concerned was under 18. The Licensing Act 1988 permits public houses and clubs to open for the sale of alcoholic drinks between 11am and 11pm.

Drugs The **Misuse of Drugs Act 1971** makes it an offence to unlawfully produce, supply or offer to supply a controlled drug. A 'controlled drug' is one which may be used and supplied legitimately by doctors, dentists, hospitals and pharmacists. Anyone who traffics drugs or is a 'drug pusher' commits an offence under the Act. It is also an offence where someone knowingly allows his or her premises to be used for the production or use of drugs. These offences are dealt with very severely by the courts. Even someone who possesses a substance, unaware that what he or she is carrying is a controlled drug, may be found guilty of an offence, unless s/he can prove that s/he had no suspicion or reasonable grounds for suspicion that what s/he had in his possession was a controlled drug.

Penalties for drug offences range from heavy fines to several years' imprisonment. Those who have become addicted to drugs may be sent to a detoxification centre.

Road traffic offences

Road traffic offences are many and various: they range from parking on a double yellow line to causing death by dangerous driving. They apply to all who drive a mechanically propelled vehicle, including motorbikes, to drivers who are experienced and learners. Offences prescribed under the **Road Traffic Acts** are often regarded as offences of strict liability. The penalties range from a parking ticket to years of imprisonment. There is also a penalty points system for various offences: generally a driver who acquires 12 penalty points in a period of 3 years will lose his or her licence for at least 6 months.

The law states that all drivers must have:

- **A road fund licence** for the current year. This is proof of road tax having been paid for a vehicle kept, parked or used on the road – and this includes an 'old banger' that needs mechanical attention before it will go. *Penalty*: Unpaid duty plus fine of twice the unpaid duty.
- A current **MoT (Ministry of Transport) test certificate** for vehicles of three years old and over. The test requires the vehicle to be roadworthy on the day of the test. A current MoT certificate is not regarded as proof by the courts that the vehicle is roadworthy for the ongoing year from the day of the test. The test covers steering, brakes, lights, tyres, seat-belts, exhaust, washers, wipers, body and suspension. *Penalty:* £10 fine or more if 3 months overdue.
- **Registration Document**, or 'log book' which shows who is the registered keeper (not necessarily the owner) of the vehicle. When a car is sold the DVLC (Driver and Vehicle Licensing Centre) at Swansea must be told immediately by both the buyer and seller of the vehicle. There is a £50 fine for failure to register change of ownership.
- **Insurance** Parliament requires all drivers to be insured so that anyone who suffers personal injury or damage to car or motorbike, property and possessions through the driver's negligence

should be able to recover damages. There are two standard types of insurance policy, one for comprehensive cover, and one for third party, fire and theft, which excludes the negligent driver's own claim for damages. Insurance companies require insured drivers to report all incidents of damage and theft even if they have no intention of making a claim. To claim may mean increased payments because of loss of a no-claim bonus. Failure to produce insurance cover can mean £15 fine and an endorsement. To use a car without insurance is an offence, the penalty for which is £100 fine, endorsement and even disqualification at the court's discretion: even if a car is left jacked up on a road and is not being driven, it is regarded as a moveable vehicle.

Table 9.1 lists some common traffic offences and their penalties. The offences of causing death by dangerous driving and driving and taking away a motor vehicle have been dealt with above.

Table 9.1 Some road traffic offences and their penalties

Offence	*Typical penalty*	*Penalty points*
Reckless driving	Large fine; endorsement; 6 months' disqualification	Yes
Careless driving, driving without the due care and attention of a reasonable and prudent driver	Fine; endorsement	2–5
Driving with alcohol in blood or urine above limit	Large fine; endorsement; 1–3 years' disqualification	Yes
Failure to provide a specimen of blood or urine	Fine; endorsement, 18 months'; disqualification	Yes
In charge of a vehicle while unfit through drink/drugs	Fine; endorsement; 6 months' disqualification	Yes
Driving while disqualified	Large fine, but more likely imprisonment; endorsement	6
Failing to stop at or to report an accident	Large fine; endorsement; perhaps disqualification	4–9
Exceeding speed limit	Fine for every mile per hour above the limit; endorsement	3
Disobeying traffic directions	Fine; endorsement	3
Parking in a dangerous position	Fine; endorsement	3

Offence	Typical penalty	Penalty points
Driving without L-plates	Fine; endorsement	2
Provisional licence holder not accompanied by a qualified driver	Fine; endorsement; possible disqualification	2
Not wearing a seat belt Children must always wear a belt even in the back seat	Fine	
Riding a motorbike on footpath	Large fine; endorsement	

General defences

When the accused person raises a defence in a court of law, s/he is, in effect, attempting to establish his/her innocence by showing the jury that the *mens rea*, and sometimes, the *actus reus*, did not exist nor could have been present, at the time of the alleged offence. There are a number of defences s/he may rely on:

- **Accident** There can be no conviction for an offence which was the result of something beyond the control of the accused, or which was the unexpected consequence of a lawful act, e.g. where a person out shooting pheasants fires a gun causing the bullet to bounce off a tree and injure a bystander.
- **Intoxication** The general rule is that a person who commits an offence while under the influence of drink or drugs cannot raise a defence of intoxication; however, if it can be shown that his/her mind was so affected by the drink or drugs so as not to form the *mens rea* of *specific intent* (crimes of specific intent are most likely to be murder, or theft, and do not include offences which were committed recklessly or carelessly), then the defence could stand. Self-induced intoxication destroys the defence.
- **Insanity** The rules relating to a successful defence of insanity were established in 1843 after a decision in the case of Daniel M'Naghten, who shot and killed a man he mistook to be Robert Peel, the Prime Minister. M'Naghton was found to be insane, and **the M'Naghton rules** were established by the House of Lords. It must clearly be proved that at the time of committing the act, the party accused was labouring under such a defect of reason, from 'disease of the mind', as not to know 'the nature and quality of the act' he was doing, or, if he did know it, that he did not know that what he was doing was wrong.

When the accused is found insane, the Criminal Law Procedure (Insanity) Act 1964 provides that a verdict of 'not guilty by reason of sanity' shall be returned. The accused is then detained 'during Her Majesty's pleasure', although a right of appeal is possible.

- **Automatism** This is applicable to cases where a person commits an offence while undergoing a spasm, an uncontrollable reflex muscle action, or convulsion. The automatism may be 'sane', such as in a case where a man during a horrifying dream killed his wife believing her to be an enemy in a war; or 'insane' – there the M'Naghton rules apply.
- **Diminished responsibility** This defence may only be raised in cases of murder, and, today, is more likely to be used in place of the defence of insanity. **The Homicide Act 1957** S2(1) states that to plead 'diminished responsibility', the prosecution must show that the accused was 'suffering from such an abnormality of mind . . . as substantially impaired his mental responsibility for his acts and omissions in doing or being party to the killing'. An 'abnormality of mind' can mean anyone whose mind has not developed in some way through a physical or mental illness, injury or some inherited condition. Psychiatric evidence is normally required as proof.
- **Duress** The accused may claim that his act was not a voluntary one because another person threatened him or his family with serious injury or death, causing him to commit the offence. Duress will not be accepted as a defence if the accused had the opportunity to escape from the threat. Threats to damage an accused's property do not provide a defence.
- **Self-defence** The **Criminal Law Act** (S3) provides 'A person may use force as is reasonable in the circumstances in the prevention of crime.' The crime may relate to the person or property of the accused. 'Reasonable in the circumstances' generally means that the force used to prevent the crime must not be stronger than, or exceed, the force used to perpetrate the crime, e.g. it would be unreasonable to fire a shotgun at the legs of an unarmed burglar. A person who is provoked into committing an offence against his or her will, may also plead self-defence.
- **Necessity** There is no general defence of necessity, although necessity may be upheld in cases of self-defence or prevention of violent crime. It cannot be used for self-preservation, such as in the case of *R. V. Dudley and Stephens (1884)* in which two shipwrecked sailors killed and ate a cabin boy after being adrift in a small boat without food for three weeks.
- **Mistake** A mistake of law is no defence since it is generally presumed that 'ignorance of the law is no excuse'. However, in

certain instances a person may claim that, had s/he known the true facts, a crime would not have been committed; for example, where a man could honestly show that he would not have had unlawful sexual intercourse with a girl had he known that she was under the age of consent. Mistake when pleaded must be reasonable.

Criminal punishments

In the preceding pages some penalties for specific crimes and road traffic offences have already been mentioned. Now, we examine particular punishments which society imposes on offenders.

Capital punishment

The death penalty can be imposed on persons of 18 and over if they carry out the offences of treason or piracy with violence. Today, there is considerable opposition to the death penalty and it is very unlikely to be put into practice in peacetime.

Imprisonment

- **Prisons** The length of time a man or woman is kept in prison may vary from a life sentence for murder, rape and robbery to a short sentence for a first-time offender of a misdemeanour. It will depend on the nature of the offence and circumstances surrounding the commission of the offence. A fixed-term sentence is where the number of years has been prescribed by Parliament, but such sentences are capable of being reduced by remission for good behaviour by the Parole Board. The offence the prisoner has committed, his or her age, medical and social reports may determine the kind of prison he or she is sent to: the serious offender is likely to be sent to somewhere like Wormwood Scrubbs, Wandsworth, Leeds, Birmingham, Durham – for both men and women, or Holloway – for women only; offenders under 21 are likely to go to a Young Offender Institution and the mentally-ill offender to somewhere like Broadmoor. Many of these prisons are grossly overcrowded, and some of the older prisons are without adequate toilet facilities and are very unhygienic.
- **Remand Centres** hold people who either have been charged and are awaiting trial but have not been granted bail, or have been convicted and are awaiting sentence.
- **Open prisons** have no physical barrier to prevent prisoners from escaping. They only hold prisoners who are first offenders and

are unlikely to escape or who are believed to be a low-security risk. It is possible for well-behaved prisoners who have served part of a long sentence in a secure prison to be transferred to an open prison to complete their sentence.
- **Young Offender Institutions (YOIs)** In 1989 the YOI replaced the former Youth Custody Centres and Detention Centres. They are for young males of between the ages of 14 and 21 who are required to serve a sentence. The YOIs are divided internally into units separating out offenders according to age and the severity of their sentence. The majority of YOIs are closed prisons although a few are open. The aim of YOIs is to train young offenders so that they can leave prison equipped with some job skills in the hope they won't re-offend.

Suspended sentences

A court which passes a sentence of imprisonment for a term of no more than two years may order the sentence either to be suspended or partially suspended, and the offender may be put in the charge of a probation officer. The suspended part of the sentence will not be served by the offender unless he or she commits another offence during the period of suspension. Then, he or she will be required to serve both the new and the suspended sentence.

Absolute or conditional discharge

Discharges only apply to offences for which the penalty is not fixed by law.

- An **absolute discharge** is where a person is proved guilty of an offence but the court take the view that the circumstances of the case are such that it would not be right to impose any punishment.
- A **conditional discharge** is where the guilty offender may go free provided he or she does not re-offend within a stated period, which must not exceed three years. If the person does re-offend during the conditional period, then he or she will be punished for both offences.

Fines

A fine, by far the most common form of punishment, may be imposed by the courts for any offence other than murder. The amount of the fine is – within the maximum set down – related to the gravity of the crime. Sometimes magistrates will take into consideration the financial circumstances of the offender. It is possible to pay a fine in instalments. Not to pay on time constitutes a further offence, the penalty for which may be a further fine or imprisonment.

Probation

Except where the sentence is fixed by law, the court may consider it would be in the best interests of the offender to make a probation order rather than send him or her to prison. A person who is the subject of a probation order must be 17 or over and have expressed a willingness to comply with the order. He or she must report regularly to his or her probation officer. Probation officers may help offenders and their families in a number of ways, even to the extent of helping them to find employment or to claim any welfare benefits to which they are entitled. Some probation officers run workshops for young offenders in their care.

Community Service Orders (CSOs)

A CSO is an alternative way of dealing with offenders who would otherwise have to serve a short-term sentence. The offender is required to perform within 12 months between 40 and 240 hours of unpaid work for the benefit of the community. The work may consist of decorating church halls or old people's homes, gardening for disabled or elderly people, or conservation projects, like clearing canals, planting trees and assisting at archaeological sites. The CSO is dependent on suitable work being available.

Juveniles

Juvenile offenders, who must be over 10 years of age, who have offended for the first or even second time, may be dealt with by way of a caution at a juvenile bureau in preference to prosecution at the juvenile court. The caution is an oral warning by a uniformed police inspector or juvenile liaison officer about his or her conduct and about the possibility of a future prosecution. The young person must have committed the offence and agree to the caution. The juvenile's parent or guardian must also agree that the caution be administered to the juvenile. If the juvenile becomes involved in future court hearings, the caution will be taken into account. Juveniles who continue to offend will either be put into local authority care by way of a supervision order, or may still live at their home, or they may be placed either with a foster parent or in a community residential home. If over 14, the young person may be sent to a Young Offender Institution.

Theories of punishment

When defendants are sentenced following a conviction in a criminal trial they are being punished by the state for an offence they have committed. There are a number of views on how and why society should make the guilty pay for their wrongdoing. One reason for punishing offenders is to deter them – and others who may be inclined to commit a crime – from committing similar offences. Courts sometimes pass unusually severe sentences on offenders in the hope of making an example of them. This happened when a man was imprisoned for ten years for holding acid-house parties where hard drugs were openly pedalled. Many prison inmates are dangerous and are kept imprisoned to protect the general public from harm. The imprisonment of offenders often causes many problems: there is the problem of overcrowding with prisoners sharing a cell meant for one person; there is also the problem of the person who is imprisoned for the first time being taught 'how to be a criminal' by professional crooks while he is inside.

Many liberally minded people would like to see more punishments aimed at reforming the personality and character of the offender. This is generally the purpose behind community service orders, probation orders and occupational training in both community and prison workshops, but staff shortages often mean that these schemes are not always as successful as they might be. Even where the conditions and staffing are adequate, many offenders still do not seem to respond to these schemes as a chance to make good. For severe cases of criminal behaviour, such as where a man has pathological tendencies to kill, to rape women or to sexually abuse children, medical and psychiatric treatment may be used and sometimes group therapy methods for other kinds of persistent offenders.

The rehabilitation of offenders who have spent long spells in prison is also important as released men and women must be taught and helped to fit back into their family circle, into a job and into society to become normal citizens again. The **Rehabilitation of Offenders Act 1974** enables an ex-prisoner's criminal record to be wiped clear after a certain number of trouble-free years: the number of years depends on the length of sentence the person has served; for example, for sentences under 6 months, the period before rehabilitation is 7 years, for sentences over 6 months and under two-and-a-half-years, the period would be 10 years and for a fine 5 years.

Victims of crime

The criminal law, the courts and the mass media generally pay a great deal of attention to criminals and criminal behaviour, but not to the victims of crime.

Crime and Punishment 231

The most likely way to assist the victim has been to pay him or her compensation through the **Criminal Injuries Compensation Board**. The Board is made up of lawyers and lay-people to consider claims, submitted by post on a prescribed form, made by those who have suffered injury caused by an offender and those who had become injured through assisting the police to capture an offender. The award is discretionary and is assessed according to the seriousness of the injury and its future effect to the victim. The criminal courts also have powers to grant compensation on a victim who makes a claim in court once the accused has been convicted.

Since the mid-1980s the **Victim Support Scheme**, a charitable organisation, has been established in many districts to provide a counselling service for all victims of both minor and serious crimes. Also, many Rape Crisis Suites and Centres have been created throughout the country by both the police and voluntary services to help victims of rape. There are also centres for battered women.

Exercises and assignments

Progress test

1. In the majority of cases, a person cannot be found guilty of an offence unless the court establishes two elements of a crime.
   (a) What are these elements?
   (b) Describe the two elements.
2. What is meant by 'a crime of strict liability'?
3. At what age is a person capable of committing a crime?
4. Is suicide a criminal offence?
5. Explain the differences between the following:
   (a) the principal to a crime, and a secondary party to a crime;
   (b) a homicide and an infanticide;
   (c) a murder and a manslaughter;
   (d) causing 'actual bodily harm', and 'grievous bodily harm';
   (e) a 'conspiracy to commit a crime', and an 'incitement to a crime';
   (f) a burglary, and a robbery;
   (g) a driver's road fund licence, and a registration document.
6. In the following, has a crime been committed? If so, which?
   (a) Joe knocks Ben out in a boxing contest.
   (b) Sara drives recklessly in the fog and kills a pedestrian.
   (c) Anoop clenches his fist at Marcel in anger. Marcel believes he is joking and scoffs at him.
   (d) Dan, suffering a hallucination, knocks down Ann and grabs her gold pendant.
   (e) Tracey takes Edwin's motorbike, rides it 20 miles to the coast

and leaves it there knowing there is a good chance that the police will find it and return it to Edwin.
   (f) Fred collects some antiques from Rupert's shop to deliver to a collector in Sheffield. He decides to keep them for his own use, until the time is right to sell them and make a profit.
   (g) Fiona allowed a hairdresser, Jasper, to style her hair not intending to pay him.
   (h) Harry set fire to Bessie's shed by accident.
   (i) Bert sells alcoholic drinks to Kashaf when Kashaf shows him a card showing the bearer to be 18 years of age. In fact, Kashaf is 17 years old and the card belongs to his older brother.
   (j) Lennie, who is disqualified from driving and has lost his licence, sits with Sue, a learner driver to give her some driving practice.
7. What are the maximum penalties or punishments for the following offences:
   (a) murder,
   (b) a battery;
   (c) a driver failing to report an accident;
   (d) a driver is in charge of a vehicle while unfit through drink;
   (e) an attempted rape;
   (f) theft;
   (g) burglary with the use of a firearm;
   (h) using a car without insurance cover.

Suggested GCSE coursework assignments

8. Examine the way juveniles are dealt with by the police and the courts. Take into account the increase in crime among young people. Try to speak to someone from the Juvenile Bureau.
9. Examine the question of imprisonment and ways of reducing the number of inmates in overcrowded prisons. What do you think are suitable alternative methods of punishment?
10. Consider the position of the victims of crime: the kind of compensation they might receive, the role of local Victim Support Schemes. Is it a good idea for the offender to meet the victim to see the effect of his wrongdoing?
11. Study this extract and then answer questions (a) to (e) which follow:

> A devoted wife who killed her husband after years of drunken beatings wept as she was placed on probation by an Old Bailey judge yesterday. Mrs Valerie Flood pleaded not guilty to murdering her husband but guilty of manslaughter on grounds of provocation.

Crime and Punishment

The judge accepted the plea and said he would show mercy because of the exceptional circumstances. The court heard that Maurice Flood was a devoted husband and father when sober, but during heavy drinking bouts he became violent. Mrs Flood was frequently beaten, hit with hammers, cut with a machete and burnt with cigarette ends. Mrs Flood finally snapped and stabbed her husband six times after he had tried to strangle her.

(Adapted from the *Daily Telegraph* 12 November 1986)

(a) What is meant by probation? (2)
(b) Why do you think this case was heard at the Old Bailey? (3)
(c) What is the Common Law definition of murder? (4)
(d) What constitutes 'provocation'? (6)
(e) Does the leniency exercised by the court in a case like this lessen the seriousness of the crime of murder? (10)

(from LEAG June 1988 Examination Paper)

Suggested visits The Magistrates' Court; The Crown Court.

Suggested speakers A Magistrate; a Probation Officer; a Victim Support worker; a member of the Juvenile Bureau.

10 Ways of Seeking a Remedy

Out-of-court solutions – legal and quasi-legal services – the courts – legal personnel – legal remedies

In Chapter 9 we saw how the state deals with criminal offenders by way of punishment. In this chapter we shall look at the way individuals may seek a legal solution.

Once it has been established that you have a legal problem requiring a remedy, you have to decide what is the best, cheapest and quickest way to resolve it. The majority of **civil** disputes, among individuals, firms, companies, tenants, landlords, government departments and other organisations, are settled out of court, sometimes even as late as at the doors of the court-room itself on the day the action is due to commence. In fact it is a wise policy to avoid court action if you possibly can. Court actions can be slow and are often costly, and after you have waited for months and even years and paid lawyers and court fees, you may find you gain far less than you had hoped. There is also the risk that you will lose your case and have to pay your own costs and those of the other party. Even if you win your case and are awarded compensation, this is not the same as receiving the money. Often – especially in court cases – the losers do not pay up, simply because they have no money or realisable assets, or maybe because they are cunning and experienced dodgers who dishonestly avoid payment indefinitely. The onus is then on you, the creditor, to enforce the judgement through the court – this means that you will have to take further steps to retrieve the money and this will cost you additional fees and can leave you even more out-of-pocket than you were before.

This chapter sets out to give the various steps that should be taken to resolve different types of problem. Part I is about seeking a remedy without going to a court or a tribunal. Part II describes the courts, their jurisdiction and procedures and some of the personnel you are likely to meet there. The various appeal procedures are also explained in both sections. The majority of the addresses of the organisations

Figure 10.1 Seeking advice from local agencies

mentioned in these sections can be found in the telephone directory or at your Town Hall, the public library, a Citizens Advice Bureau and other advice agencies.

PART I. Seeking a solution out of court

Table 10.1   First steps to solving problems out of Court

Type of problem	First steps to a solution	
Consumer complaints	*Step 1*	*If Step 1 fails, then Step II*
Faulty goods/services	Dealer/servicer	Write to managing director or head office
Adulterated food/drink commodities affecting health	Environmental Health Officer at local Council and manufacturer (if he is to blame)	
False trade description, weight, measure, unfair practices	Trading Standards Department of local Council	
Gas/Electricity	Gas or Electricity Boards	Gas or Electricity Consumer Consultative Councils (address on the bills)
Post Office, poor service or lost post	Post Office	Post Office Users Council (address at your post office)
Buying by post	Write to trader	Write to trade association, or Advertisement Manager of the newspaper, journal.
Holidays	Tour operator or hotel proprietor	ABTA (Ass. of British Travel Agents) if holiday organiser is a member, or CAB
Insurance	Insurance broker or company	Association of British Insurers, or the Insurance Ombudsman
Employment		
Matter of dismissal, redundancy, health and safety, discrimination, etc.	Employer's grievance procedure (if any)	Application for Industrial Tribunal on form IT1

Ways of Seeking a Remedy 237

Type of problem	First steps to a solution	
Employment *cont*		
Breach of contractual terms and conditions	Employer's grievance procedure (if any)	County court or High Court
Failure to give statement of terms and conditions, wage slips	Employer's grievance procedure (if any)	Department of Employment and Industrial Tribunal
Low-wage-earners protection and conditions (wages for over-21s)	Employer's grievance procedure (if any)	Wages Councils, Department of Employment (shops, hairdressers, catering, hotels, tailors, etc.)
Apprenticeships – terms and wages	Employer and/or trade union	National Joint Council (with trade union backing) (if employer is a member) or county court.
Youth Training Schemes	Employer or approved training organisation	Careers Officer or Training Commission
Income Tax	Employer or Inland Revenue (the local office can help with general enquiries)	Inland Revenue Appeal Tribunal
National Insurance	Employer	DSS
Housing		
Landlord/tenant contracts	Other party to the contract	County court or Tenancy Relations Officer (local authority)
No rent book	Landlord	Rent Assessment Committee
Community Charge	Local authority	Magistrates' court
Housing benefit	Local authority	Social Security Appeal Tribunal
Mortgages	Creditor	County court or High Court
Neighbour nuisance	Neighbour (talk or letter)	Solicitor's letter or county court, Public Environmental Officer (local authority), for noisy parties the Police

Type of problem	First steps to a solution	
Family		
Divorce or separation	CAB and/or solicitor	County court or High Court (Family Division)
Maintenance, Judicial separation	CAB and/or solicitor	Magistrates' (Domestic) court or County court
Benefits		
Social security	Social Security Office	Adjudicating Officer Social Security Appeal Tribunal, then Social Security Commissioners on point of law only
Social fund	Social Fund Officer	Adjudicating Officer Social Security Appeal Tribunal, then Social Security Commissioners on point of law only

If after taking these first steps you have still not been successful in seeking a remedy to your problem, then you may find you will have to resort to one of the following:

- a trade association conciliation and arbitration service if you have not already taken this step (see below)
- the county court, if your claim is for a sum under £5000, or the High Court
- a tribunal, if you have not already done this; an Employment Appeal Tribunal or the Social Security Commissioner (see Part II of this chapter)
- for complaints about catalogue mail order write to The Mail Order Traders' Association, 507 Corn Exchange Building, Fenwick Street, Liverpool L5 7RA; and for complaints about books and records; write to The Mail Order Publishers' Authority, 1 New Burlington Street, London W1X 1FD. The trader must be a member.

A particular complaint or grievance may also be dealt with by any of the following:

Ways of Seeking a Remedy

- **Member of Parliament** *(MP)* Your elected MP will deal with any complaint concerning a matter between you and any of the state departments. He is also concerned with local matters. Most MPs run regular 'surgeries' to hear constituents' problems at first hand. Lists of these are available at your town hall, public library, CAB and at the local party headquarters. Also you can write to your MP by addressing your letter to the House of Commons, London.

- **Ward councillors(s)** Like the MP your ward councillor can be contacted on any matter concerning the local authority and you. Names and addresses of your local councillors can be had from the town hall, public library and CAB.

- **Ombudsman** An Ombudsman is an independent figure who can investigate **cases of maladministration causing injustice**. There are various types of Ombudsmen:

    Parliamentary Ombudsman – if you have a complaint against any central government department, you can ask your MP to send it to the Ombudsman.

    Local Ombudsman – if you feel you have a complaint about the administration of the local council or Water Authority. You must first complain to your ward councillor or the Water Authority before the Ombudsman can help you.

    Health Service Ombudsman – if you feel you have been let down by any part of the National Health Service or that you have been treated unjustly through bad administration, your complaint must be made to the local health authority before you can approach the Ombudsman.

Today, all kinds of associations outside the public sector, such as those overseeing the banks, insurance companies and building societies, also have an official Ombudsman to investigate customer's complaints. The role of the Ombudsman is limited to investigating bad administration, such as long delays, wrong and misguided advice, poor service, bias, letters not being properly dealt with, failure to follow proper procedures, etc. (A leaflet entitled *Which Ombudsman?* is available from town halls, CAB and the Central Office of Information.)

- **Office of Fair Trading** The Office of Fair Trading is a government agency whose job is to safeguard against unfair trading practices, protecting both consumers and businessmen. The Director General of Fair Trading works very closely with the local **Trading Standards Departments** to encourage members of trade organisations to draw up and abide by Codes of Practice to raise standards of service and to deal with complaints; to keep a look-out for and to take to court traders who persistently commit offences or break their obligations to customers, and to check on the fitness of traders who provide credit or hire goods to individuals and issue licences. The Director General also has a duty to keep an eye on monopolies, mergers and restrictive trade practices. The Office of Fair Trading does not take up people's complaints about such things as faulty goods or services.

- **Trade Association Arbitration** Codes of Practice are rules drawn up by trade associations and other organisations for their member traders and industrialists to follow. The codes aim to improve standards of service and to provide the customer with low-cost independent conciliation and arbitration schemes. With arbitration, both sides put their case to an independent person, who considers the evidence and then decides who is right. If you choose this form of arbitration you cannot then go to court as well. Arbitration under Codes of Practice is generally a cheaper and more effective way of getting a consumer dispute settled out of court, but it is only available if the trader you have dealt with is a member of a trade association. Trade association members usually indicate their membership on their printed notepaper and invoices, etc. Alternatively there are various leaflets issued by the Office of Fair Trading which publish trade association addresses (available from your local Trading Standards Department or from a CAB). The products and services which are covered so far include: buying by post; cars; electrical goods; furniture; launderers and dry cleaners; funerals; package holidays; photography; the Post Office and buying from doorstep sales-people and at parties.

- **Sex and Race Discrimination** Complaints can be referred to the Equal Opportunities Commission (Overseas House, Quay Street, Manchester M3 3HN) or the Commission for Racial Equality (Elliot House, 10–12 Allington Street, London SW1E 5EH), or contact your local Community Relations Officer.

- **Police** The Police Complaints Authority will investigate complaints made about the police. Or you may contact your MP.
  There are basically three kinds of complaint which can be made against the police:
  1. Those investigated under the supervision of the Police Complaints Authority. Police officers from a different area to the one where the complaint is made conduct the investigation. If the complaints are justified, the Police Complaints Authority have powers to discipline the officers.
  2. Alleged criminal offences by the police can be investigated by the Director of Public Prosecutions (DPP). The Police Com-

plaints Authority have powers to discipline the offending police officers.
3. Police officers can face a disciplinary investigation for alleged racial discrimination, under both the Police and Criminal Evidence Act 1984 and the Public Order Act 1986.

Many people are of the opinion that complaints against the police should be investigated by a more independent body of people than the Police Complaints Authority.

Community and Police Liaison Groups The setting up a means of liaison and cooperation between local citizens and their local police force is a requirement of the Police and Criminal Evidence Act. The objects of the groups, which work better in some areas than others, are to work towards a good relationship between the police and the community and to agree solutions to local problems where policing is a factor. The groups involve themselves in crime prevention and in maintaining a peaceful environment. They are prepared to listen to complaints about policing and policing methods in the area, but not about individual cases.

Getting advice and assistance

During any stage of resolving a dispute you may want to turn to someone or to some organisation for expert help or information. Where there is a legal problem you may need representation either in court or at a tribunal. If you are unsure of what to do, the wisest course of action is to seek advice immediately – the sooner the better. All too often people do not seek help until it is too late to help them effectively.

Where to go? Here are some agencies who may be able to help you:

Citizens Advice Bureau (CAB) A great deal has been said in this book about the CAB. This is because the CAB is a nationwide service available to most people. There are just over 900 bureaux scattered around the country and each bureau offers a free, impartial and confidential service to anyone seeking information, advice or help with any kind of problem. It is a good starting point for assessing the nature of your problem and your chances of a successful outcome. If you are told you have no case legally then this advice may save you a great deal of time, money and exasperation spent in pursuing a worthless action. If, on the other hand, it is thought you have a genuine case to pursue, then the CAB worker can help you in a number of ways, either by assisting you in fighting your own case, dealing with it him- or herself or by referring you to an expert such as a solicitor, a DSS officer, or social worker, or some other appropriate specialist.

The CAB worker may be a paid worker but it is more likely that s/he will be one of the 90 per cent of volunteer workers in the country. Paid or not, the worker is highly trained to deal with the generalities of a wide variety of problems and information – consumer, employment, housing, legal, taxes, social security, nationality and immigration, family and many personal matters. She or he may assist with form-filling, letter-writing and looking up information, or may act as negotiator between the disputing parties, or simply be a listener to those who have no one else with whom to talk over matters that have been worrying them. The National Association of Citizens Advice Bureaux ensures a high standard of up-to-date advice-giving from its workers, and each bureau possesses a wide variety of published leaflets on practically any topic of concern and these are available to the general public. The aims of the CAB also ensure that 'individuals do not suffer through ignorance of their rights and responsibilities or of the services available; or through an inability to express their needs effectively' and 'to exercise a responsible influence on the development of social policies and services, both locally and nationally'.

Other advice-giving agencies Local authorities and other organisations such as churches, charities and self-help groups may provide local advice and information centres, but these will vary from area to area. Ask at your Town Hall or Civic Centre or your public library. You may find you have certain specialist agencies in your area such as a Consumer Advice Centre, a Consumer Protection Department, a Housing Advice Centre or Housing Aid Centre, Citizens Rights Agency, and so on. There are also national organisations such as the Child Poverty Action Group, and Shelter whose concern is homelessness. These services are more specialised than the CAB and in some cases can provide legal representation for clients at county court and tribunals.

Solicitors

Lawyers in this country are divided into two professions – **barristers** and **solicitors** (see Figure 10.2). This is unlike most countries where there is one profession of lawyers who deal with all aspects of legal work. The barrister's work is mostly concerned with representing people in court and with matters connected with court representation. More will be said about barristers and their role in the courts in the second half of this chapter. Here we are concerned with the solicitor

Ways of Seeking a Remedy 243

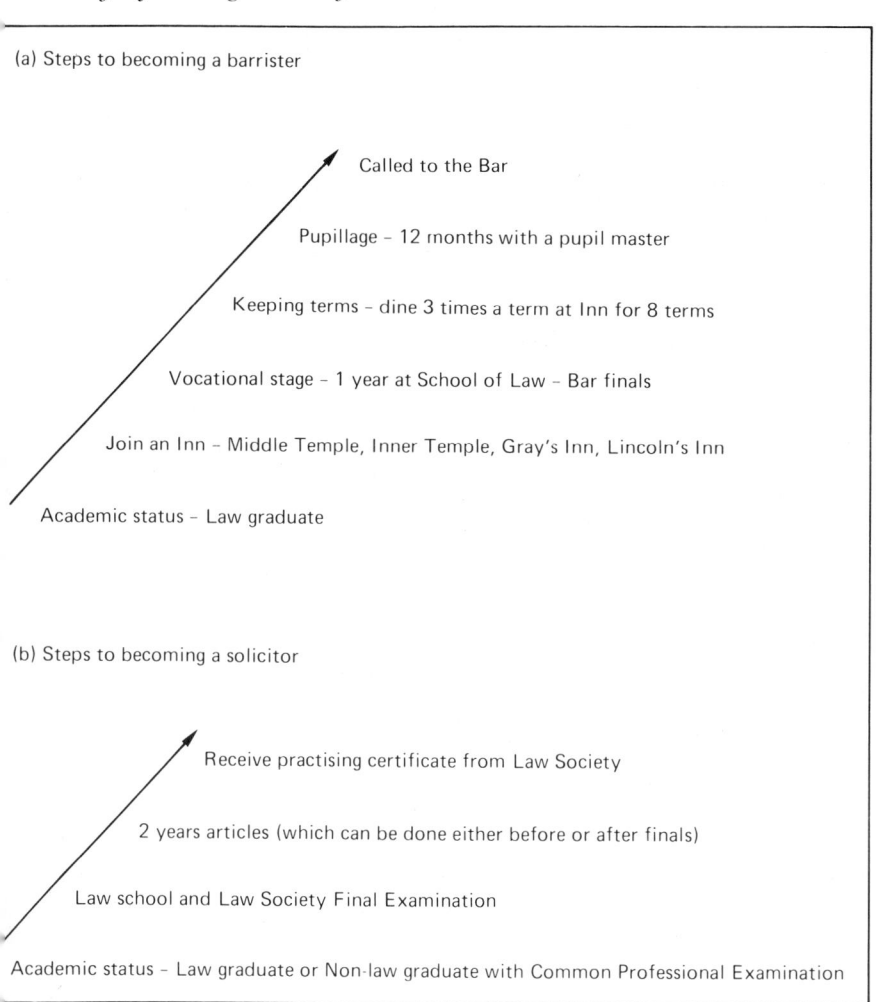

(a) Steps to becoming a barrister

　　　　　　　　　Called to the Bar
　　　　　　　Pupillage – 12 months with a pupil master
　　　　　Keeping terms – dine 3 times a term at Inn for 8 terms
　　　Vocational stage – 1 year at School of Law – Bar finals
　　Join an Inn – Middle Temple, Inner Temple, Gray's Inn, Lincoln's Inn
Academic status – Law graduate

(b) Steps to becoming a solicitor

　　　Receive practising certificate from Law Society
　　2 years articles (which can be done either before or after finals)
　Law school and Law Society Final Examination
Academic status – Law graduate or Non-law graduate with Common Professional Examination

Figure 10.2 Two separate ways of training lawyers

to whom you will have to go in the first instance once you realise that only a solicitor will be able to assist you. A solicitor has a dual role; a large part of his work takes place in his office where he may give legal advice and assistance, assist clients with the drafting of a will, with the buying and selling of property, with matrimonial matters and with a preparation of any legal or court documents; the other part of his work takes place in the magistrates' and county courts, where he can represent a client at either a criminal or civil trial or hearing. Solicitors cannot normally represent a person in the higher courts – they are required to hand over the case to a barrister. The only time a solicitor may appear in the higher courts is where there is a case on appeal from the magistrates' court to the Crown Court, or in an uncontested civil case on appeal in the High Court or Court of

Appeal. At the time of writing proposals are afoot to extend the right of audience of solicitors in the High Courts. Unlike a barrister, a solicitor does not wear a wig and gown.

All practising solicitors must be members of the **Law Society** which sets the codes of practice and educational qualifications for its members. It also has powers to investigate complaints against solicitors and if necessary discipline them. The Law Society has also set up an independent Solicitors Complaints Bureau to which members of the public may lodge a complaint if they are not satisfied with the service or behaviour of their solicitor.

When you need a solicitor, make an appointment to see him or her, enquire how much you will be charged and also whether you are eligible for financial assistance under the Legal Aid scheme. Also, remember that you are the solicitor's client and that **the solicitor acts on your instructions** even though he is likely to give you some helpful professional advice. So, if you do not want him to continue with your case or to handle it in a particular way, say so. Solicitors' fees can be high and many people on low incomes are deterred from seeking a solicitor for this reason. There are, however, some schemes available to aid the poorer members of the public:

Legal Advice and Assistance Scheme This scheme is commonly known as the **Green Form Scheme**. It was introduced as part of the Legal Aid provisions to assist financially those on low incomes seeking any sort of practical help from a solicitor except for the making of a will – although clients over 70 and those who are 'substantially' disabled are given assistance – and conveyancing, unless it is part of a divorce or separation settlement, and court representation. One criticism of this scheme is that the qualifying financial limits are too low. You only qualify for free legal advice and assistance if you are receiving income support or you are receiving a **disposable income** (or take-home pay) which is not much above this level. After that clients have to pay a contribution based on their income – this is set out on a scale and the highest limit is still proportionately low average earnings. You are also assessed on your **disposable capital** (what you have saved) such as the value of your savings and valuable possessions, excluding the value of your house, furniture, clothes and the tools of your trade. The qualifying rates are raised annually. (Leaflets giving the rates are available from CAB, the Law Society, or the Central Office of Information.) At the time of writing the Green Form is about to be reformed by the Lord Chancellor. (See Table 10.2.)

Assistance By Way Of Representation (ABWOR). This is an off-shoot of the Legal Advice and Assistance Scheme; however, the disposable capital limits are higher than those required under the

Table 10.2 *The Legal Aid Scheme*

Legal Aid and Assistance Scheme
Green Form Scheme
Civil and criminal work
Non-litigious work done by a solicitor
Not normally for wills and conveyancing; not defamation
Application to the solicitor
Means-tested

Legal Aid for Civil Court representation
1. Means-tested
2. Case must be considered worthy of legal aid by the Legal Aid Area Office
3. Exceptions:
   (a) Tribunals except:
       Employment Appeal Tribunals
       Land Tribunals
       Mental Health Review Tribunals
   (b) Defamation suits
   (c) County Court: arbitration, undefended divorce and judicial separation suits
   (d) Coroner's Courts
4. Application normally through a solicitor to the Legal Aid Area Office

Legal Aid for Criminal Court Representation
1. Means-tested
2. For serious offences
3. For less serious offences only 'where it is in the interests of justice'. Court discretion: e.g. where the accused is likely to go to prison or lose his/her job, or where there are substantial questions of law to be argued, or where the accused cannot understand the proceedings because s/he does not speak English very well or is mentally ill.
4. Application to trial court

Note: The scheme, Assistance by Way of Representation (ABWOR), has not been included in this table. For details see pp. 244-5

Green Form Scheme. The assistance covers the cost of a solicitor preparing a client's case and representing the client in most civil cases in the magistrates' court for separation, maintenance, custody, affiliation and defended adoption proceedings. It may also be given to parents and some children in care proceedings in juvenile courts. ABWOR is also available to patients before Mental Review Tribunals and to prisoners facing disciplinary charges before boards of visitors. The solicitor has to decide whether it is reasonable to grant ABWOR to the client, although the final decision to grant or refuse the assistance rests with the Legal Aid Office.

Solicitor's fixed-fee interview Many solicitors operating the Legal Aid Scheme offer a fixed-fee interview, currently for £5 (+ VAT). Some may not charge at all, others may charge more. The interview will not last for more than half an hour and it will not extend beyond the giving of advice. This service has the advantage of being able to ascertain with the solicitor whether you should pursue your intended legal action or not. If you decide to take action, then for anything the solicitor does for you in connection with your case you will have to pay his fees or apply through him for financial help under the Green Form Scheme. The names of solicitors who operate the fixed-fee interview are in the Law Society Solicitors Regional Directory, a reference book which is found at public libraries, town hall information services, magistrates' and county courts and the CAB.

Community or Neighbourhood Law Centres These centres are staffed by salaried full-time and part-time solicitors and their aim is to give free advice, assistance and representation to people in the area. Most law centres are situated in inner-city deprived areas to act for people who would not normally go to a conventional solicitor in a high street practice. The work done in these centres is generally limited to employment, housing and welfare law cases and criminal law cases for youngsters under 18, so as not to take business away from the conventional solicitors. The law centres must be approved by the Lord Chancellor and are given a waiver to advertise by the Law Society. They are usually housed in a shop and provide both a walk-in service and an appointments system. The service is free and confidential, and the atmosphere of a law centre is generally informal and friendly.

CAB legal services Some CABx provide a legal service similar to that of the law centres. They may have paid or honorary solicitors on their staff who give their services free and who will represent clients either in court or at a tribunal.

Part II Going to court:
The courts

Today's court system largely came into being with the **Judicature Acts 1873–5** when a massive reorganisation of the courts was carried out in England and Wales. There have been some smaller changes since then, for instance the introduction of the small claims court and

Ways of Seeking a Remedy

the merging of the former Assizes and Quarter Sessions to create the Crown Court, both of which took place in 1971.

Every court exercises **jurisdiction**, a term which has two meanings: it can signify the geographical area in which the court is permitted to operate and it also refers to the power of the court to hear particular proceedings. The courts operate as a hierarchical system of 'inferior' and 'superior' and as 'first instance' and 'appeal' courts (see Figure 10.3). 'Inferior' courts, such as the county court and the magistrates' courts are local courts with local jurisdiction, whereas the 'superior' courts, such as the High Court, the Crown Court and the Court of Appeal, are more centralised with wider

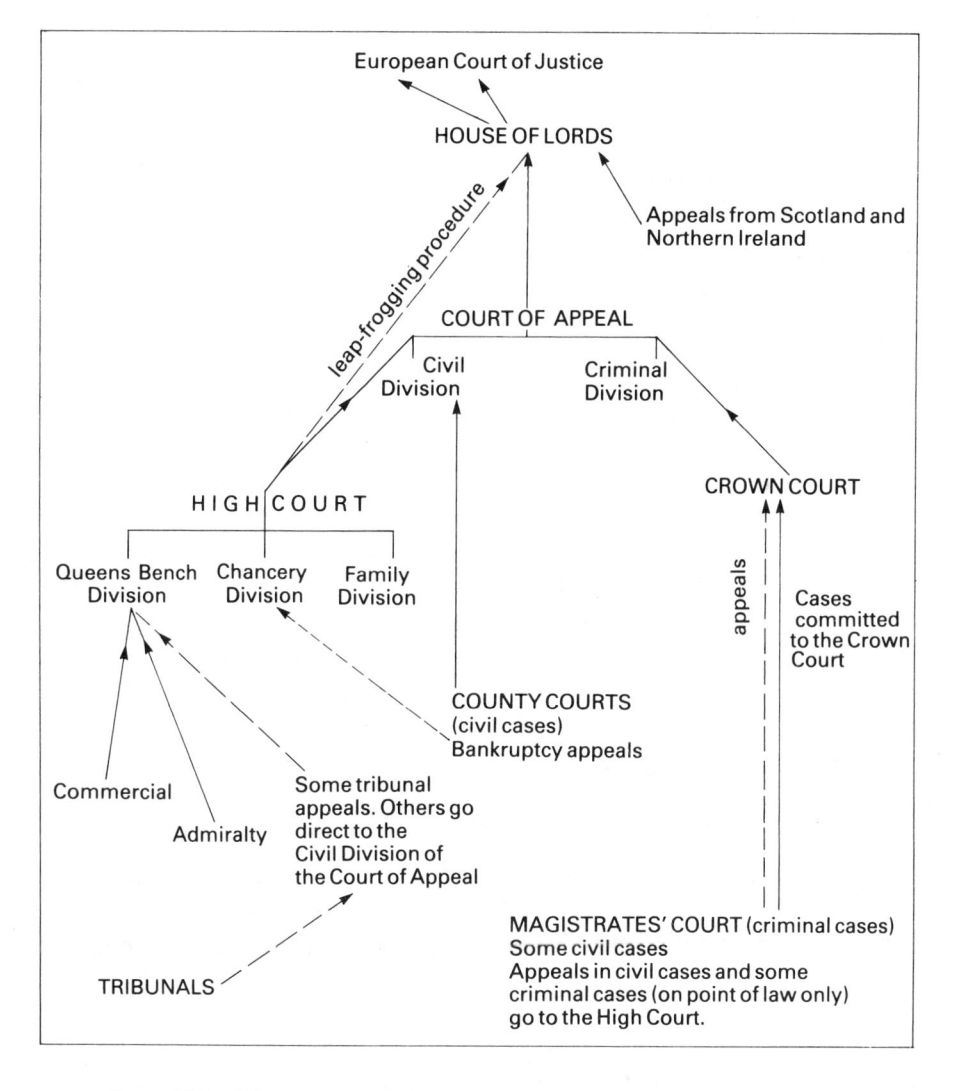

Figure 10.3 The structure of the courts in England and Wales

jurisdiction. A 'first instance' court is one which tries a case the first time. 'Appeal courts' hear appeals of aggrieved parties who get their cases or sentence of a lower court reconsidered by a superior court. The court's permission is required before an appeal can be registered. The House of Lords is the final court of appeal for the United Kingdom. Certain further appeals can be heard in the European Court of Justice, and individual appeals in connection with human rights issues can be taken to the European Court of Human Rights. Tribunals, although separate from the main court system, provide an ultimate right of appeal either to the High Court or to the Court of Appeal (Civil Division).

Legal time limits

Some actions have to be taken to court within a certain time. Most time limits are covered by statute particular to the subject area in which they arise. If a time limit is not covered by a particular statute, it is mainly dealt with under the provisions of the **Limitation Act 1980**. The general rules are:

Court action for personal injury	3 years
Court action arising from contract or agreements to pay money	6 years
Court action arising from disputes over land	12 years
Time period for prosecution for minor criminal offences, e.g. Road Traffic offences, which can be tried in the magistrates' court	6 months
Other criminal offences	Forever

In the following pages, the courts, their procedures and the respective roles of the judges, arbitrators, the lay-judiciary, barristers or counsel, will be explained. We shall begin at the lower end of the civil, then criminal, systems with the inferior courts and then proceed to the superior courts.

The civil action

Bringing a case

In a civil action one party, the **plaintiff, sues** another, the **defendant**, for an alleged breach of the civil law. The parties are referred to as *Brown v. Smith* and they are given a 'Plaint Number' for easy reference. In the case of an appeal against a decision the parties are referred to as the **appellant** and the **respondent**. The civil action, unlike a criminal case, is a private action between two or more parties who might be individuals, companies or other organisations. They come to court to seek a **remedy**, the most common being

Figure 10.4 A county court

damages – a sum of money assessed as compensation. Other remedies include various forms of injunctions and court orders and decrees of specific performance, i.e. to get someone to fulfil their part of a contractual agreement.

Court representation and Legal Aid

In some actions such as county court small claims and undefended divorce suits, the services of either a solicitor or a barrister are unnecessary and financial help given through the Legal Aid Scheme is not available for these proceedings. Neither is it available for the majority of tribunal hearings. The idea is that the proceedings have been made simple enough for litigants to conduct their own cases. For most other actions the services of a barrister may be necessary.

Barristers

A barrister does not have immediate contact with members of the general public. You have to go first to a solicitor, who (once proceedings have been instituted) will find a barrister to represent you in court. The main role of a barrister is advocacy – that is, to argue the case as **counsel**, either for the plaintiff (the prosecution in criminal cases) or the defendant, in court on the basis of the evidence you and your solicitors have supplied to him.

Barristers belong to one of the four Inns of Court, i.e. Lincolns Inn, Grays Inn, the Inner Temple and the Middle Temple. A person wishing to become a barrister must apply to one of these Inns, and after serving his or her pupillage there, will be called to the Bar. The principal governing and disciplinary body of the Bar is the **Senate of the Inns of Court and the Bar**. Longstanding and successful barristers can apply to the Lord Chancellor to be appointed Queen's Counsel (QC). This is often referred to as 'taking the silk' because unlike other barristers they wear a silk gown instead of a gown made of stuff. A barrister may also be appointed a judge in any of the courts.

Legal Aid (civil)

This is likely to be the next step of financial aid for those who have not managed to resolve their problem with a solicitor under the Legal Advice and Assistance Scheme, or Green Form Scheme (see p. 244). Civil Legal Aid can provide financial assistance for all work leading up to and including court proceedings and representation by lawyers, either solicitors or barristers (counsel). Civil Legal Aid is available for actions in all civil courts up to the House of Lords, for Employment Appeal Tribunals, Land Tribunals and, in some cases, the Restrictive Practices Court. Other certain proceedings are covered by the

Assistance by Way of Representation Scheme (see pp. 244–5). Civil Legal Aid is not available for: small claims arbitration, proceedings before the majority of tribunals, a coroner's court, or for cases involving undefended divorce or defamation. Although it is likely to be the barrister who will represent you in court, it is your solicitor who puts forward your application to the local Legal Aid Office. The qualifying conditions of disposable income are similar to those for Legal Advice and Assistance. The level of disposable capital allowed is higher. The one snag is that if you win a compensation claim you will have to pay back into the Legal Aid Fund the cost of your assistance.

The county court

The **County Courts Act 1845** set up a network of 400 courts to administer **civil** disputes **locally** and **cheaply** where the amounts of money in dispute were small. In 1971 the **Small Claims Act** set up within the county court a system of cheap justice to deal with the very small claims of individual citizens, shopkeepers, businessmen and traders, made either against each other or against a large company or organisation. Today, the county court, often referred to as the small claims court, deals with over 90 per cent of all civil actions. These actions include not only claims over money, but also other matters relating to land and property, cases of undefended divorce and the adoption of infants. Before you take your case to a county court make sure you choose the right court. The action must be taken to the county court in the district where the defendant resides or carries on his business, or where the cause of action arose. The exception to this rule is that undefended divorce may been instituted in any county court.

The jurisdiction of the county court

- Actions in contract and tort (excluding defamation) concerning sums of money up to £5000, e.g. hire-purchase debts, non-payment of rent, claims against sellers of faulty goods, or against someone who has provided a faulty service, etc.
- The recovery of possession of land (e.g. eviction orders, etc.) and disputes over the right of ownership.
- Matters concerning trusts, mortgages, the administration of estates, the dissolution of partnerships, certain bankruptcy cases, subject to the limit of £30 000.
- Probate, the settling of disputes over the estate of someone who has died, where the net value of the estate is less than £15 000.

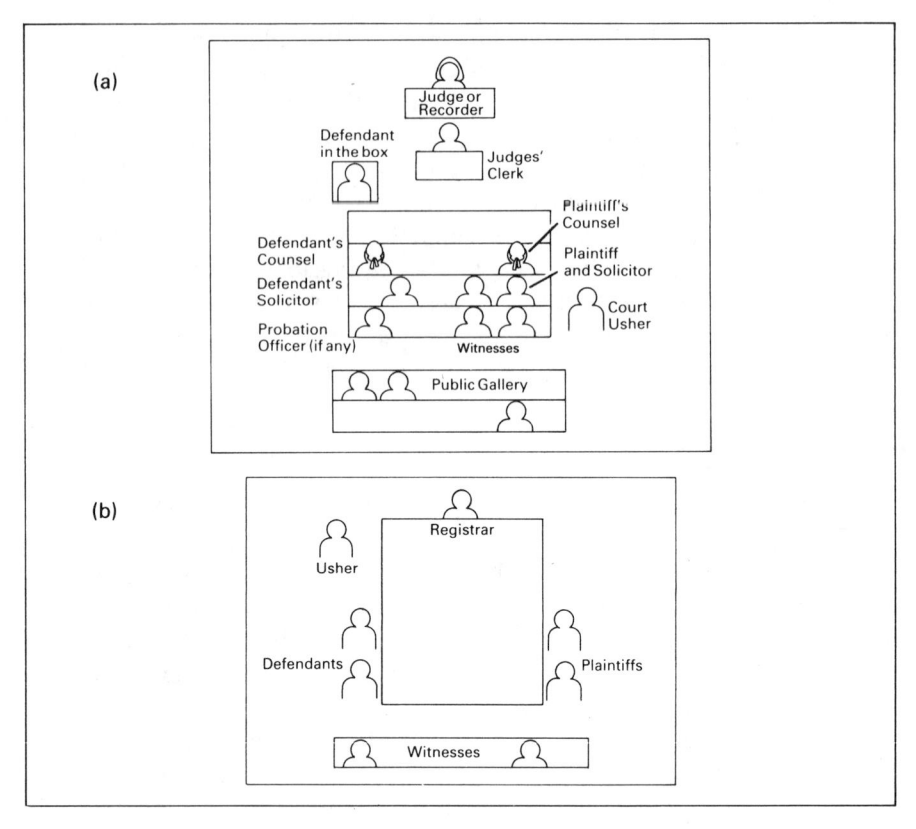

Figure 10.5 The county court (a) a plan of the main court (b) a plan of the arbitration proceedings

The jurisdiction of many county courts also includes:
- Family proceedings, such as the adoption of infants, undefended divorce and settlement of property in separation cases. ALWAYS HEARD IN PRIVATE.

Where the financial limits are higher than those mentioned above, the case must be taken to the High Court unless the parties agree to be heard in the county court. The majority of claims not exceeding £500 can be dealt with separately in **arbitration** (see below).

The proceedings

The next thing you must consider is which type of proceedings you use:
- *Arbitration* If your claim is for **£500 or less**, you may use the quicker and inexpensive **Small Claims Arbitration Court** where you only pay the cost of the court expenses, roughly 10 per cent of

Ways of Seeking a Remedy 253

the claim if you lose the case. Arbitration is presided over by the court **Registrar**, a civil servant appointed by the Lord Chancellor who must be a solicitor of at least seven years standing. The proceedings are held in private, are informal and like a structured conversation. The Registrar will have to read all the documentary evidence in advance, he will listen to what both parties have to say and make an on-the-spot judgement which is enforceable. There is no right of appeal except on a point of law or a perverse decision.

- *Main court* Where your claim is for **more than £500 or your action fits into any of the other categories of the court's jurisdiction**, then your case may be heard in the main **open court** before a **Circuit Judge**, a barrister or solicitor of at least ten years standing, or a **Recorder**, who is a part-time judge. The open court proceedings take the form of trial with the parties and witnesses being examined and cross-examined by counsel (barristers). However it is the general practice of the civil courts to endeavour to settle the case out of court by bringing the contending parties together in private before the Registrar or an expert arbitrator in a

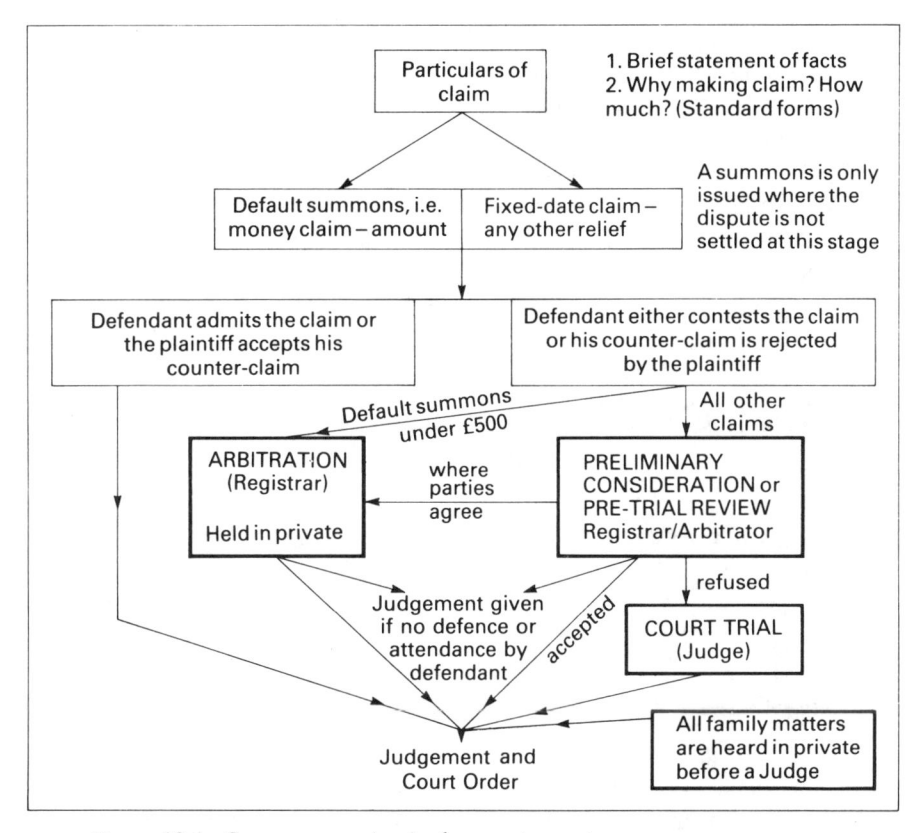

Figure 10.6 Steps to an action in the county court

pre-trial or preliminary consideration. Where no settlement can be reached at this stage, the case then comes before the open court.

The way to institute proceedings in the first place is to go to the county court and fill in a form which is appropriate to your case. Various standard forms are available. A copy of your claim or case will be sent to the other party, who will either defend it or admit to it, or make a counter-claim against you. Even at this stage the court officials will try to get the parties to settle without coming before either the Registrar or a Judge. If the matter cannot be settled then the proceedings will go ahead either in arbitration or in the main court.

There is a right of appeal to the Court of Appeal but not for arbitration cases.

The magistrates' court (civil)

Although the magistrates' court is essentially a criminal court, it has some civil jurisdiction, it can grant licences for the serving of alcoholic drinks and for betting and deal with unpaid community charges, unpaid TV licences and gas and electricity bills where a public authority has issued a summons. There is also the **domestic court** where the magistrates hear disputes between husbands and wives over maintenance orders; orders for care and control of children and can grant judicial separation orders. Also linked to the magistrates' court is the **juvenile court**. This is where a special panel of magistrates deal not only with young offenders but also with those children and young people who are in need of care, protection and control, or who are in some kind of moral danger. In both the domestic and the juvenile courts the proceedings are held in private.

The High Court of Justice

The High Court is part of the Supreme Court of Judicature and is situated in The Strand in London. It consists of the Queen's Bench Division, the Chancery Division, and the Family Division. To each of these courts a High Court or *puisne* judge sits alone to hear a case. In certain cases such as defamation, in the Queen's Bench Division, a jury can be called. Each of these three courts has its own **divisional** court for appeals. Two or three judges will sit where a case is on appeal.

- *The Queen's Bench* This is the largest and busiest of the three courts. It is presided over by the Lord Chief Justice. The first-instance jurisdiction of the court covers mainly those cases of contract and tort which cannot be heard in the county court. They

Ways of Seeking a Remedy

are usually over complex issues involving large sums and huge compensation awards. The count also deals with commercial claims and Admiralty matters, and has a supervisory role over the activities of the lower courts and tribunals, making sure they do not usurp their legal powers and that decisions are taken in a proper manner.

The **Divisional Court of the Queen's Bench Division** hears appeals from certain tribunals, from commercial arbitrations, the Solicitors' Disciplinary Tribunal and other such institutions. It may also hear appeals of criminal cases from the magistrates' court and from the appellate section of the Crown Court.

- *The Chancery Division* The first instance jurisdiction of Chancery covers the administration of estates of dead people; trusts; mortgages; bankruptcy; the winding-up of companies, and landlord-and-tenant disputes which are not dealt with in the county court. In theory, the Division is presided over by the Lord Chancellor, but in practice it is the Vice Chancellor who presides.

  The **Divisional Court of the Chancery Division** hears appeals on Inland Revenue cases, bankruptcy and land registration cases from the county court.

- *The Family Division* Presided over by the President of the Family Division this court's first instance jurisdiction covers cases concerning marriage, defended divorce, legitimacy, wardship, adoption, guardianship, domestic violence, and disputes over family property.

  The **Divisional Court of the Family Division** deals with appeals on family matters from the lower courts.

High Court proceedings The plaintiff can obtain a **writ** from the Central Office of the Supreme Court in London or from the district registry and then serves it on the defendant. The writ outlines the claim and the remedy being sought. Once the defendant has acknowledged the writ, the **pleadings** are delivered by one party to the other. The pleadings are drafted by the counsel and consist of a detailed account of the particulars of the claim. The defence will also set down his or her version and confirm or deny any allegation made against him or her. This can be a lengthy process. Once the pleadings are exchanged, evidence has to be prepared before the trial can begin. As with the county court proceedings, many of these cases are settled out of court before they reach the stage of a trial.

Should the case come to trial, the proceedings are opened with the disputed issues being outlined by the plaintiff's counsel to the judge. Then, beginning with the plaintiff, both parties and their respective witnesses are examined and cross-examined. Once the case has been presented by both sides, the judge will decide the case on both law and matter of fact and deliver his judgement. Sometimes this is not done immediately, the judge may take time to consider the outcome and deliver his judgement later.

High Court Judges or *puisne* judges are usually appointed from practising barristers of at least ten years' standing.

Masters in the High Court are effectively deputy judges who decide many preliminary matters, ensuring that the pleadings are complete and that the case is ready for trial by the judge. This private pre-trial work is called 'sitting in chambers'.

Court of Appeal (Civil Division)

This court hears appeals from the High Court and the county courts, the Restrictive Practices Court, the Employment Appeal Tribunal and other tribunals. The Court has the power to uphold or reverse the decision of a lower court. On rare occasions it can order a new trial where new evidence has come to light, which, if it had been available at the time the case was tried, would have affected the lower court's decision. The Lord Chancellor, the Lord Chief Justice, the Master of the Rolls and the President of the Family Division, are all *ex officio* judges of the court. Normally three to five Lord Justices of Appeal sit to hear the appeal. These may include the Master of the Rolls who presides over the Court.

The criminal courts and their procedures

A criminal offence is regarded as a public wrong which is punishable by the state. So we say the prosecution is **brought by the Crown** and cases are referred to as *R. v. Brown, R.* standing for *Regina* (meaning Queen) or *Rex* (meaning King), and 'Brown' being the name of the accused. The majority of cases are brought before the courts by the police. Customs and Excise, the Director of Public Prosecutions, and some agencies like the trading standards departments and the DSS, may also initiate proceedings. In rare circumstances a private individual may bring another individual to trial. The criminal law in this country assumes that an accused person is innocent until proved guilty 'beyond all reasonable doubt' in a properly conducted trial before a court of law. The majority of criminal trials are open to the public and all the courts have a public gallery where anyone can go and observe the proceedings. A person who is found guilty of an offence is convicted by the court and punished according to the seriousness of the crime and the motive for doing it. (See Chapter 9

Ways of Seeking a Remedy

Crime and Punishment for criminal penalties.) All criminal cases are initially heard in the magistrates' court.

The magistrates' court

There are over 900 magistrates' courts in England and Wales and over 98 per cent of all criminal prosecutions are dealt with by magistrates. The offence must have taken place in the district in which the court is situated, that is, within its own **petty sessional division**. The less serious, or **summary** offences such as those relating to traffic, drunken and disorderly behaviour, etc., are tried summarily by the magistrates. There is no jury. The more serious charges, or **indictable** offences such as murder, robbery, rape, blackmail, are committed to the Crown Court for trial by judge and jury. Some offences can be tried either way. These include theft, criminal assault and dangerous driving, and the accused is asked by the Magistrates' Clerk to state his or her preference for trial in the magistrates' court or the Crown Court. (See Figures 10.7 and 10.8.)

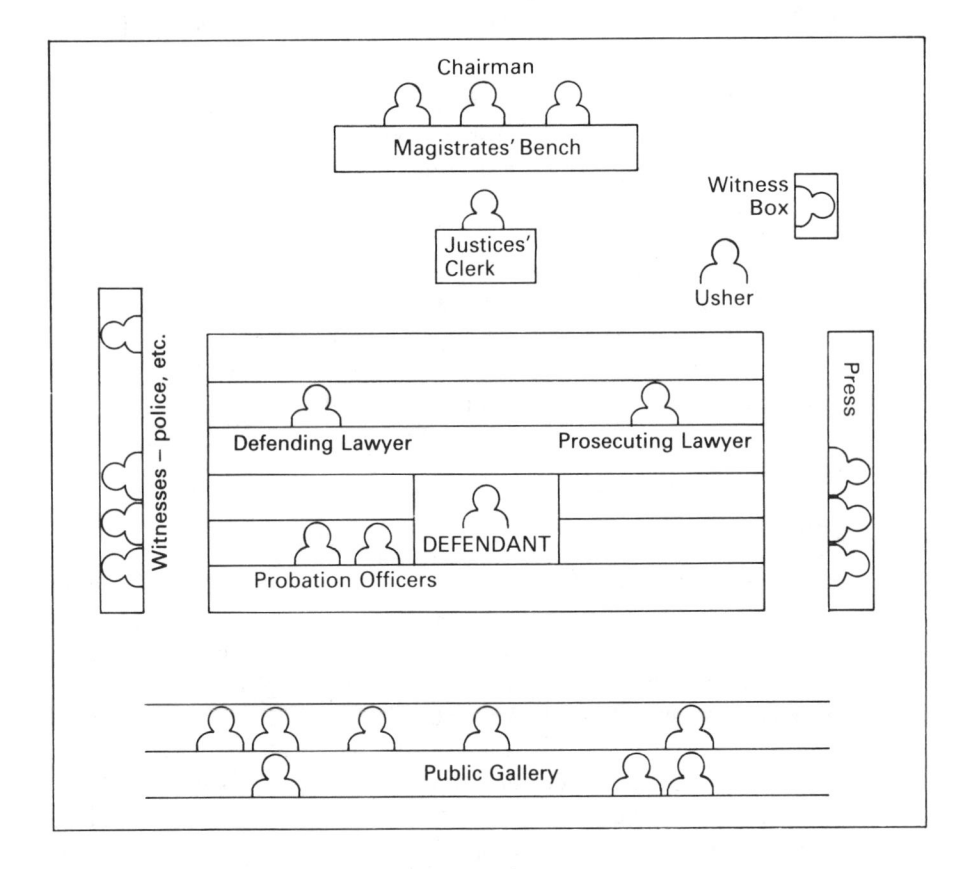

Figure 10.7 Plan of a typical magistrate's court

The magistrates Apart from the stipendary magistrates in the large cities, the magistrates or Justices of the Peace (JPs) are unpaid, dedicated citizens who are appointed by the Lord Chancellor for their personal qualities and integrity and for the useful work they have done for the community. They are part-time and come from different walks of life; they may be doctors, teachers, businessmen, trade unionists, factory workers, Citizens Advice Bureaux workers and so on. The only money they receive is out-of-pocket expenses. The only qualification is that they must live within 15 miles of the court in which they sit. In court, magistrates sit on the bench, usually three at a time although there may be any number from two to seven. A special panel of magistrates, of which there must be at least one man and one woman, sits in the juvenile court the proceedings of which are held in private. Where a case from the magistrates' court appears at the Crown Court the magistrates can sit with a Circuit Judge or Recorder in the Crown Court. Out of court, the magistrates issue warrants for arrest and deal with applications for criminal legal aid. In addition to these duties there are the duties of civil jurisdiction (see p. 254), and they also frequently make themselves available to the general public to countersign such documents as passport applications.

A stipendary magistrate sits alone on the bench in the courts of the cities and some large boroughs. He or she is a full-time paid magistrate who is a lawyer of at least seven years' standing.

Lay-magistrates, those who are unpaid and who are not legally qualified, are often criticised for the amateurish way they administer justice and for their strictness or leniency in sentencing offenders. Different magistrates' courts throughout the country vary considerably in their granting of legal aid and bail – despite the statutory guidelines. On the other hand, they give an invaluable service by providing cheap and speedy justice at a local level.

Other personnel to be found in the magistrates' court

The Clerk to the Magistrates is legally qualified, being a barrister or solicitor of at least five years' standing. He or she is a court official who sits in court immediately below the magistrates' bench. The duties of the Clerk are to advise the magistrates on points of law, procedure and sentencing, but he or she is never allowed to make the judgements – this is left to the magistrates. The Clerk also makes a record of evidence and prepares statements sworn on oath by witnesses as in those cases sent to trial at the Crown Court and does administrative work such as preparing summonses and warrants and collecting fines.

The Crown Prosecution Service (CPS) is a team of lawyers who conduct the prosecutions in the magistrates' court and Crown Court. The police provide the CPS lawyer with details of their evidence and charges against the accused.

- **Probation officers** are specially trained workers who help offenders in various ways before and after the trial. They help with personal problems, arranging social and psychiatric reports for the mitigating circumstances which are revealed to the court between the verdict and the conviction, and generally helping past offenders to become rehabilitated into the community. There is usually a probation officer on duty at the courts who will see anyone and answer their queries. They cannot, however, advise anyone on legal matters.

- **Duty solicitors** The Police and Criminal Evidence Act requires all magistrates' courts to have a rota of solicitors to be on duty at the courts to help an accused person who has not had access to a solicitor before his or her trial.

The Crown Court

The Crown Court is the court where the accused is tried by judge and jury, the jurisdiction mostly being serious trials of the first instance. The Crown Court was created in 1971 by the merger of the assizes and quarter sessions, and it forms part of the Supreme Court of Judicature. Although there are about ninety courts in six circuits in England and Wales, sitting in three tiers according to the seriousness of the cases they try, we refer to them collectively as the **Crown Court** as if they were one entity. Although the jurisdiction of the Crown Court is essentially criminal trials in the first instance, there are a number of designated courts which try both criminal and civil cases before a circuit judge. In the Crown Court there is a hierarchy of judges – High Court judges, circuit judges and recorders – who with a jury, preside over different categories of cases according to their seriousness. These cases are divided into four classes:

- **Class 1** Cases of treason, murder, rape, genocide, offences under the Official Secrets Act 1911, and incitement, conspiracy or attempts at any of these, are tried by a High Court judge.
- **Class 2** Cases of manslaughter, infanticide, various sexual offences other than rape, sedition, piracy, offences under the Geneva Conventions Act 1975 and incitement, conspiracy or attempts at any of these – are tried by a circuit judge or recorder.

- **Class 3** Indictable offences which are not classified in Classes 1, 2 and 4 – are tried by any category of judge.

- **Class 4** Cases such as robbery, causing grievous bodily harm or causing death by reckless driving, and mostly those cases where the accused from a magistrates' court has elected to be tried by judge and jury in the Crown Court – are tried by a circuit judge or recorder.

The Crown Court also deals with appeals from the magistrates' court and the juvenile courts by way of re-hearing the facts of the case. There is no jury for appeals, only for original hearings.

The jury in criminal cases A jury in the Crown Court consists of twelve persons of either sex and from all walks of life provided that their names are on the Electoral Register. Anyone between the ages of 18 and 65 (to be changed to 70) who has lived in Britain for five years or more becomes liable for jury service. Some categories of people are not allowed to serve. These are peers, judges, MPs, clergymen, lawyers, medical practitioners, members of HM Forces and police officers. Ex-prisoners are disqualified from serving on a jury, and mentally-ill persons and people who cannot speak or understand the English language are not eligible. Other members of the public may be excused if they have a very good reason such as a death in the family or a small child who cannot be left unattended. Jurors receive payments for travelling, subsistence and financial loss within certain limits.

Juries have to be sworn in and are on oath to 'well and truly try the case and give a true verdict according to the evidence'. The defendant has a right to challenge the jury and to ask any jurors to stand down for a **justifiable cause**. Others will be empanelled to take their places. Juries are required to retire from the court-room to consider their verdict in private. No record is made of their deliberations. The majority verdict of a jury must be at least ten. If for any reason the numbers become reduced, for example by the illness or death of a jury member during the trial, then the majority verdict must be nine out of ten. Where a jury fails to agree they may either be sent back to reconsider the case or a new jury may be sworn in and the case starts again.

The **civil jury** is now a rarity although the Administration of Justice (Miscellaneous Provisions) Act 1933 provides that a civil court may have discretion to use a jury and that a jury may be ordered on the application of either party in cases of defamation, malicious prosecution, false imprisonment and cases of fraud.

Ways of Seeking a Remedy

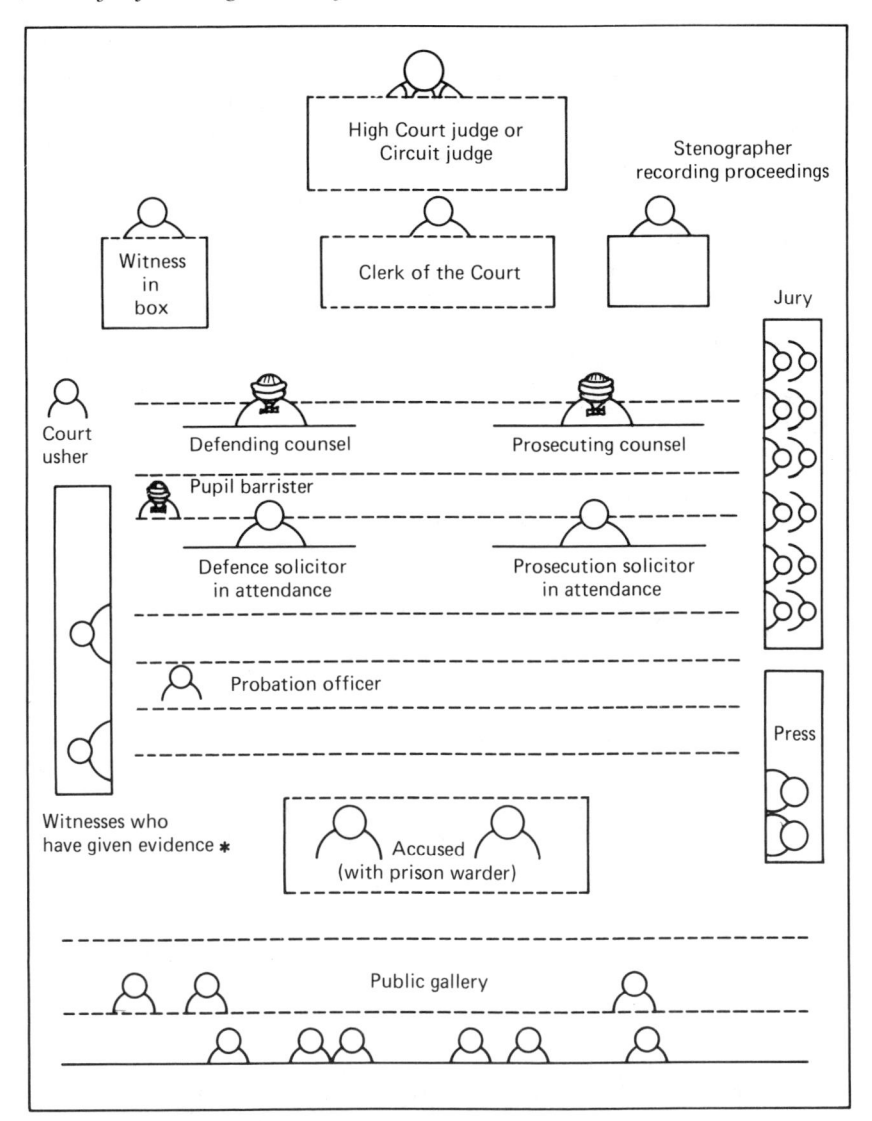

*Witnesses who have not given evidence remain outside the courtroom until called

Figure 10.8 The Crown Court trial

The criminal trial

The parties to a trial are referred to as the **prosecution** and the **defendant**, the latter being the accused person. The case may be tried summarily in the magistrates' court or committed to the Crown Court or it may be **put on remand** – this means put back to another date while evidence is being sought, or the accused is given time to consult a solicitor.

An accused person who might otherwise be held in custody can be **released on bail** if the hearing is adjourned, or if he or she is committed for trial or sentence. This means that he or she is released on condition that he or she presents his or herself at the court when required to do so. The court may refuse bail where the accused has failed to turn up in court or has jumped bail and is likely to do so again, where there are substantial grounds for believing he or she would abscond, commit an offence or obstruct the course of justice or where it can be shown he or she would be in danger or would be likely to endanger others once released. The prosecution's objections to bail will be considered by the magistrates, and the magistrates must give their reasons for not granting bail.

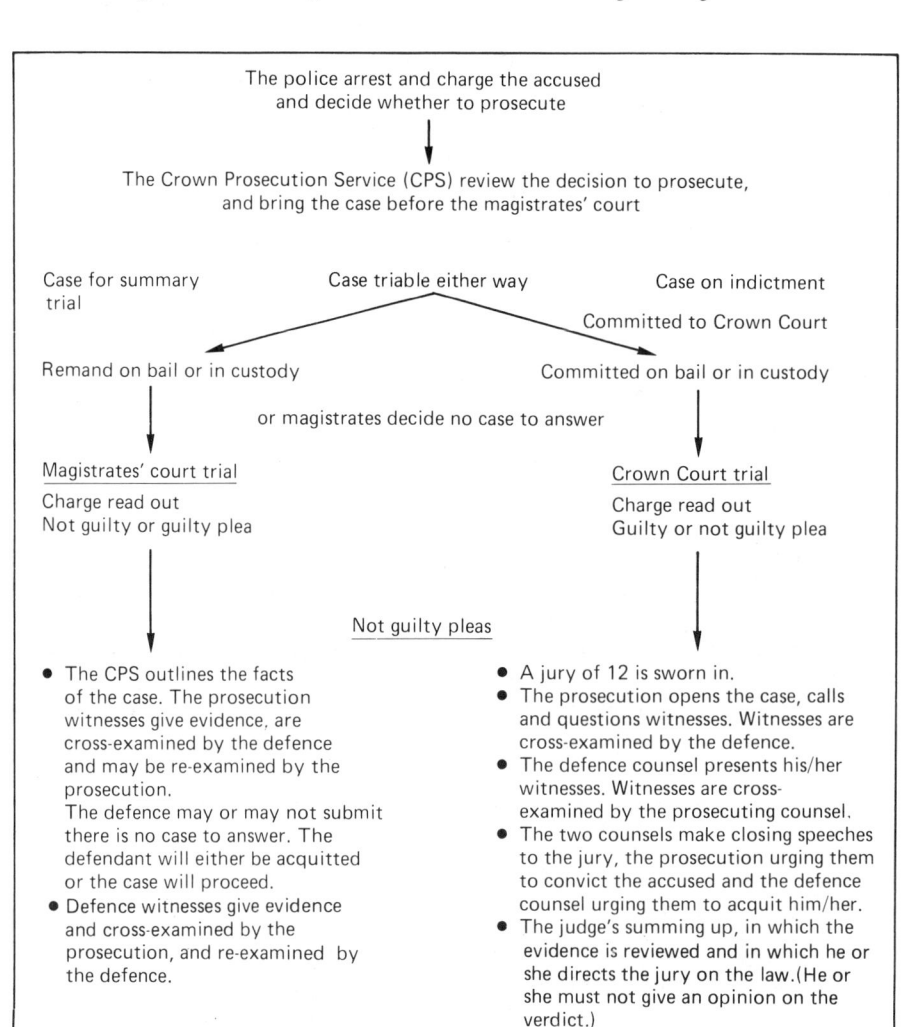

The police arrest and charge the accused
and decide whether to prosecute

↓

The Crown Prosecution Service (CPS) review the decision to prosecute,
and bring the case before the magistrates' court

Case for summary trial	Case triable either way	Case on indictment
		Committed to Crown Court
Remand on bail or in custody		Committed on bail or in custody

or magistrates decide no case to answer

Magistrates' court trial	Crown Court trial
Charge read out	Charge read out
Not guilty or guilty plea	Guilty or not guilty plea

Not guilty pleas

- The CPS outlines the facts of the case. The prosecution witnesses give evidence, are cross-examined by the defence and may be re-examined by the prosecution. The defence may or may not submit there is no case to answer. The defendant will either be acquitted or the case will proceed.
- Defence witnesses give evidence and cross-examined by the prosecution, and re-examined by the defence.

- The prosecution, and then the defence, make final speeches.

- A jury of 12 is sworn in.
- The prosecution opens the case, calls and questions witnesses. Witnesses are cross-examined by the defence.
- The defence counsel presents his/her witnesses. Witnesses are cross-examined by the prosecuting counsel.
- The two counsels make closing speeches to the jury, the prosecution urging them to convict the accused and the defence counsel urging them to acquit him/her.
- The judge's summing up, in which the evidence is reviewed and in which he or she directs the jury on the law.(He or she must not give an opinion on the verdict.)
- The jury retires to consider the verdict. They must reach a majority verdict.
- The jury return – give verdict.

Ways of Seeking a Remedy 263

- Magistrates retire and return to give their verdict. The case is either dismissed or proved.

Guilty pleas
- CPS give evidence of defendant's past record and of any previous convictions. The defence can ask for other offences to be taken into consideration: a speech may be made in mitigation – giving social, medical or other reasons for the defendant's behaviour and asking for them to be taken into consideration.
- Prosecution can ask for costs and compensation order.
- The defendant can call character witnesses. The magistrates may ask for social enquiry reports from a probation officer or social worker.
- The magistrates pass sentence and, where appropriate make orders for costs and compensation. The highest penalties magistrates can impose is 6 months imprisonment for each offence or a maximum fine of £2000.
- Right of appeal to the Crown Court, or, where a point of law is involved, to the Divisional Court of the Queen's Bench Division of the High Court.

- The defendant is either acquitted and is free to leave the court, or is found guilty and is convicted.
- Details of the prisoner's criminal record are given. A plea in mitigation is made by the counsel asking for a lenient punishment.
- The judge pronounces the sentence.

- Right of appeal to the Court of Appeal, Criminal Division.

Figure 10.9 Steps in a criminal action

Court of Appeal (Criminal Division)

This is a particularly interesting court to visit (in the Strand, London). Appeals can be made by the defendant against the severity of the sentence, the decision of the jury, or on a point of law. The judges are the Lord Chief Justice, the Lords Justice of Appeal, and judges of the Queen's Bench Division. Usually three sit. The court may dismiss the appeal or allow it and may order a conviction made in a lower court to be quashed; it may or may not increase the sentence made in a lower court. The court also has powers to order a new trial.

The House of Lords

This is the final court of appeal in the UK for most cases. The court hears appeals of cases both civil and criminal which must be a matter of general public importance. There is no right of appeal; permission must be granted either from the House of Lords itself or from the Court of Appeal. The court also hears appeals from the superior appellate courts of Scotland and Northern Ireland. The **Administration of Justice Act 1969** also provides for appeals direct from the High Court in civil cases by what is termed the 'leap-frog' procedure. The case must be certified by the High Court Judge as being one of public importance. The Law Lords usually sit in fives although it has been known for three or even seven to sit at one time. The Lord Chancellor is the nominal head of the House of Lords appeal jurisdiction, and may sometimes sit himself. The Law Lords may uphold the decision of the previous court or reverse it, or, in rare cases, overrule a previous decision when deciding a present case. The final judgement is based on a majority decision.

- The **Lord Chancellor** has both a political and a judicial role. He is head of the Judiciary and presides over the House of Lords when it sits as a court of appeal. He also presides over the House of Lords when proposed legislation is being heard there. He is Speaker of the House of Lords and a member of the Cabinet. He is appointed by the Queen on the advice of the Prime Minister and advises on the appointment of the High Court and Circuit Judges, Recorders and lay magistrates.
- The **Attorney General** is a Law Officer and head of the English Bar. He is appointed by the Prime Minister. He may prosecute in important and difficult criminal cases and give his consent to certain criminal proceedings where corrupt practices, offences against the Official Secrets Act, the Public Order Act, etc. are involved. He also advises the Cabinet and Government departments on important legal matters. The **Solicitor-General** is deputy to the Attorney General and has similar duties and may deputise for him.

Legal aid for criminal offences

If you do have the misfortune to be charged with a criminal offence and you need financial help to pay for the services of a solicitor you can apply for legal aid. You can first seek an appointment with a solicitor under the Legal Advice and Assistance (Green Form) Scheme or the Fixed-fee interview. But **once you have been charged with a criminal offence** and during any of the time up to the hearing of your case, you can apply for criminal legal aid. It is advisable to apply as early as possible as this will give the solicitor more time to prepare your case. The legal aid will also cover court representation by the solicitor and, if you have to go to the Crown Court, the services of a barrister. Legal aid, however, is not available to everyone. You will have to satisfy the court that you will need help to pay the costs of employing a solicitor and this decision will rest on your disposable income and whether your savings are less than

Ways of Seeking a Remedy 265

£3000. Even then you may have to pay a contribution towards costs when the court asks you. The court will also have to look at the seriousness of your case. Legal aid can be refused if your case is related to a minor or less serious offence, or does not satisfy the 'interests of justice', for example where you are not likely to be sent to prison or lose your job if you are found guilty. Accused people who are in danger of not understanding the proceedings because of a mental or language disability are likely to be granted legal aid 'in the interests of justice'. If you want legal aid you have to apply to the magistrates' court and your legal aid can be extended for the higher courts where necessary. Application forms are obtainable from the magistrates' court or from your solicitor. The solicitor may help you fill in the form. If the court refuses you legal aid you may re-apply to a special committee but not if the court has decided your means are above the statutory limit. However, if your case is committed to the Crown Court and legal aid has been refused by the magistrates, you may make another another application to the Crown Court (see Table 10.2).

The Coroner's Court

The role of this court is to **investigate the cause** of any sudden or unexplained death. Every county has to appoint one or more coroners, who are experienced doctors or lawyers, to do this. In the majority of cases the coroner is able to ascertain that a death was due to a natural cause. The coroner's task is merely one of enquiry into how the death occurred and to establish particulars which have to be registered by the Registrar of Deaths. The inquest does not attempt to put a person on trial – this is the role of the criminal courts. Where the circumstances of the death are suspicious, the coroner sends his evidence to the Director of Public Prosecutions. In certain cases, where the death was caused by an industrial disease or occurred in prison, a jury must be summoned by the coroner. From seven to eleven jurors are summoned to attend and they can give a majority verdict when no more than two disagree. The jury is not expected to view the body.

Tribunals

Tribunals – or **administrative tribunals** to give these forms of hearing their full name – are a good example of how contemporary legislation has tried to bring to ordinary people a form of inexpensive legal protection together with speedy, informal and just hearing. Tribunals are many and various, there are different tribunals for different types of dispute, the jurisdiction of each tribunal being governed by a number of related statutes covering matters such as rent control, land valuation, mental health reviews, industrial and employment disputes, social security appeals and many more. Tribunals give the individual a chance to contest a department of state, an employer or some large state or similar administrative body, without incurring a great deal of expense and time. **Legal aid is not available for legal representation at most tribunals** (see Table 10.2). It is usually assumed that the litigants can speak for themselves and need not use a solicitor. This however is not always the case, so money to pay for representation may have to be found, unless the services of a CAB or Law Centre solicitor or trained representative, or trade-union representative, can be acquired.

Each type of tribunal operates its own policies and procedures and is independent of other tribunals and of the lower courts. The Queen's Bench Division of the High Court exercises a supervisory role over the tribunals making sure that they do not step outside the powers given to them. There is also an ultimate right of appeal from tribunals to either the High Court or the Civil Division of the Court of Appeal.

Examples of tribunals are the Rent Assessment Committees, the Lands Tribunal, the Mental Health Review Tribunal, the Social Security Appeal Tribunal, the Industrial Tribunal and the Employment Appeal Tribunal. There are many more. The most commonly used is the Industrial Tribunal.

The Industrial Tribunal

Much of the Industrial Tribunal's business falls under the **Industrial Training Act 1971** and **Employment Protection (Consolidation) Act 1978**. It also falls under the **Equal Pay Act 1970, Health and Safety at Work Act 1974, Sex Discrimination Act 1975, Race Relations Act 1976**, the **Employment Acts**, and various other Acts under which compensation may be awarded. It generally deals with claims against employers for statutory rights given to employees under these Acts, although an employer may also make a claim against an employee. Matters concerning an employee's contractual rights, usually to money claims, are dealt with by the county court.

Each tribunal has a panel of **arbitrators** (*not* judges) consisting of a legally qualified chairman, who is a lawyer of not less than seven years' standing, and two lay-members from each side of industry. The chairman is appointed by the Lord Chancellor and the lay-members by the Secretary of State for Employment. The person bringing the case is referred to as the **applicant** and the other party as the **respondent**.

Ways of Seeking a Remedy

The procedure

1. Where individuals think they have a case for an industrial tribunal they must first fill in a form IT1 (see Figure 4.6) which is obtainable from the Employment Office, Jobcentre or CAB with an explanatory leaflet which will state where to send it and the time-limits in which the application must be made. The form must be filled in with the precise details of the grievance.
2. A copy of the application will be sent to the other party, usually the employer, who is required to fill in another form giving his reply to the application.
3. The documents are received by the central office, where they are examined to ensure their validity and that the application is appropriate to the business of the tribunal. The documents are then sent to the regional office. In most cases the documents are sent to the officer of the Advisory, Conciliation and Arbitration Service (ACAS). The officer tries to get the disputing parties together to settle the matter at this stage. He may also advise the applicant on the advisability of pursuing the claim, but he cannot compel him to drop it.
4. If the claim cannot be settled at the ACAS stage, the application goes to the area Industrial Tribunal and the parties and any legal representatives they choose to have will be called to attend at a certain date.

(The layout of a tribunal is shown in Figure 10.10.)

The hearing The average time of a hearing is one day. The hearing is open to the public and the proceedings are orderly, simple and flexible, with a degree of informality. Generally they follow the following format:

1. The parties and witnesses are sworn.
2. The respondent (e.g. the employer) generally presents the case, calls his witnesses and questions them.
3. The respondent and his witnesses can be questioned by both the arbitrators and the applicant (the employee).
4. The applicant and his witnesses go through the same procedure.
5. At the chairman's discretion, the parties may go out of the room to make their own settlement at any time before the judgement is given. This would settle the case.
6. If no settlement is reached during the proceedings, then the chairman after consultation with the other two arbitrators will give an on-the-spot decision. The decision will be either:
    (a) to reinstate the applicant in his original job (if dismissed); or
    (b) to direct the employer to re-engage the applicant in a different position in the firm or company; or

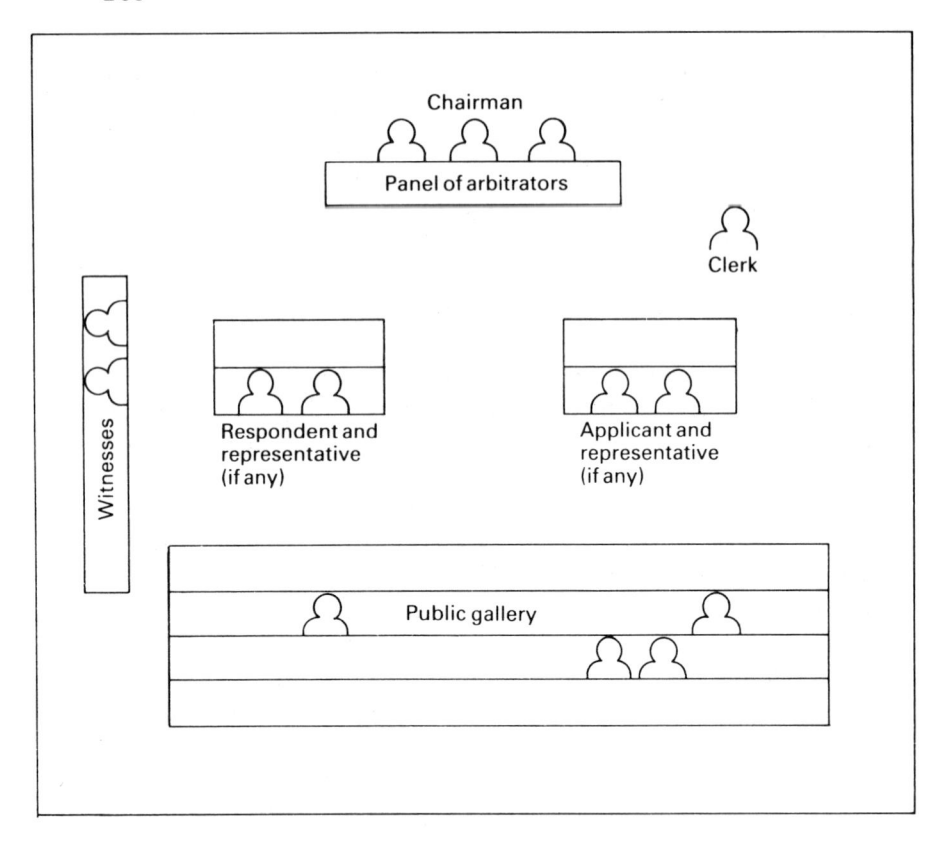

Figure 10.10 Plan of an industrial tribunal

(c) to award compensation, to the applicant if he wins the case; or
(d) to find that there is no case to answer and the applicant has lost the case.

There is a right of appeal to the **Employment Appeal Tribunal**, before a judge and two lay-members from both sides of industry. Legal aid is available at this stage, and a further appeal would go to the **Civil Division of the Court of Appeal**.

The Courts of Europe

The Courts of Europe can make certain rulings which can affect and change the law in the UK and the other member-states.

The European Court of Justice

The European Court of Justice is situated in Luxembourg and acts as a kind of referee between individual organisations, member-states

Ways of Seeking a Remedy 269

and the Council of Europe and the European Commission in the event of a dispute, in respect of EEC law. When the UK joined the European Community in 1972 it acceded to the provisions of the Treaty of Paris (1951) which established the European Coal and Steel Community and the two Treaties of Rome (1957). Thus the UK came under the legislative rules drawn up by the European Commission and agreed by the Council of Ministers which is made up of representatives of the member-states. The effect on English law has been that the House of Lords must refer any matter connected with a point of EEC law for a preliminary ruling on interpretation, and the lower courts may also refer a case to the European Court for a preliminary ruling. The Court does not enforce its rulings but refers the case back to the courts of the member-state and then the member-state applies the ruling through its own laws. The judges and advocates-general at the Court are judges from the different member-states on a six-year appointment. They elect a President to serve a three-year term.

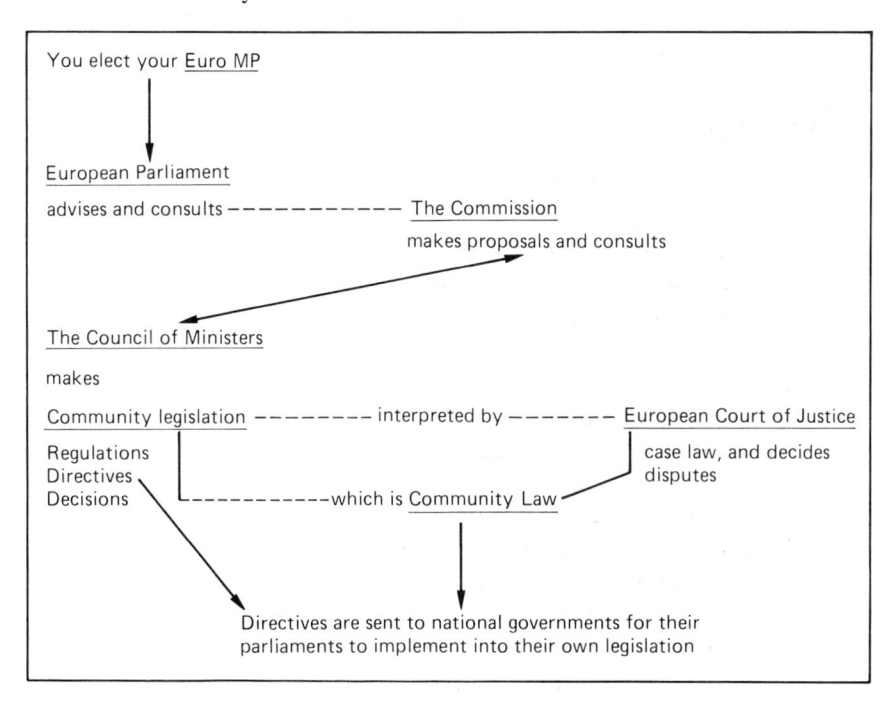

```
You elect your Euro MP
        │
        ▼
European Parliament
advises and consults ----------- The Commission
                                 makes proposals and consults

The Council of Ministers
makes
Community legislation -------- interpreted by ------- European Court of Justice
Regulations                                           case law, and decides
Directives                                            disputes
Decisions            ----------which is Community Law

            Directives are sent to national governments for their
            parliaments to implement into their own legislation
```

Figure 10.11 Decisions made in the European Community can affect the law in the UK

The European Court of Human Rights

The European Court of Human Rights is situated in Strasbourg and receives complaints of breaches of the **Convention for the Protec-**

tion of **Human Rights and Fundamental Freedoms (1950)** which seeks to protect the human rights set out in the UN **Universal Declaration of Human Rights (1948)** which laid down standards for all peoples and nations to observe, and claimed that all human beings were born free, and equal in dignity and rights. The Declaration sets out all the rights and freedoms to which all are entitled 'regardless of race, colour, sex, language, religion, political or other opinion, national or social origin, property, birth, or other status'. The rights include the right to life, to the prohibition of torture, inhumane treatment and forced labour, to the protection of freedom of thought, conscience and expression and to respect for family and private life. In Europe seventeen of the twenty-one member-states recognise the right of individual petition. Applications are made by letter to the secretariat to the Convention or through the member-government and the complainant must show that he or she is a 'victim' under the provisions of the Convention. The Court's rulings are referred back to the state concerned and, although the state is expected to change its own law accordingly, the rules of the Convention are not an enforceable code.

Exercises

1. Where would you *first* go to put right the following disputes:
   (a) a faulty camera?
   (b) a badly serviced car?
   (c) a complaint about a holiday?
   (d) holiday entitlement at work?
   (e) income support?
   (f) an alleged racial inequality?
   (g) housing benefit?
   (h) an unfair trade practice?
   (i) the purchase of a loaf of bread with a nail in it?
   (j) national insurance payments?
2. To which court or tribunal would you go:
   (a) to claim a debt of under £500?
   (b) to claim unfair treatment at work on the ground of unequal pay?
   (c) to get a licence to sell alcohol?
   (d) to be made a ward of court?
   (e) to be tried on a summary offence?
   (f) to sue for an undefended divorce?
   (g) to sue in a contested divorce case?
   (h) to be tried by judge and jury on an indictable offence?
   (i) to settle a dispute over a complex bankruptcy matter?
   (j) to sue someone in breach of contract for the sum of £4000?

(k) to take a case on a human rights issue?
  (l) to claim damages for a personal injuries where the amount is over £5000?
  (m) to arrange a simple adoption?
  (n) to appeal against the decision of an Industrial Tribunal?
  (o) to settle a dispute over a company contract worth £180 000?
  (p) to be sued for unpaid rent?
3. Briefly explain the role of:
  (a) the arbitrator at the county court;
  (b) a High Court judge;
  (c) the magistrates;
  (d) The Crown Prosecution Service;
  (e) the tribunal arbitrators;
  (f) the Lord Chancellor.
4. Describe the work of barristers and solicitors.
5. Who can serve on a jury?

Essays

1. In what ways can people on low incomes acquire inexpensive justice? In your answer make reference to the Legal Aid Scheme and to the alternative help, advice and conciliation services.
2. Compare the jurisdiction and procedures of any TWO of the following courts: county court, coroner's court, Industrial Tribunal, magistrates' court.

Assignments

1. Try to obtain copies of a court form or the tribunal form IT1 (see Figure 4.6) and fill in the details of an imaginary case. Follow this by a mock trial using the procedure explained in this chapter.
2. Pay a visit to your local magistrates' court and write a newspaper article on what you observe there.
   Other suggested court visits: Industrial Tribunal; County Court (by arrangement with the Clerk's office); Royal Courts of Justice, London.

Suggested GCSE assignments

3. Many people are of the opinion that the legal profession should not be divided into solicitors and barristers and would like to see the two professions merged. This is called *fusion*. With reference to newspapers, journals and textbooks, examine the advantages and disadvantages of fusion.

4. Consider the usefulness or dangers of using lay-people, i.e. magistrates and juries, in the courts. Collect news-cuttings and make court visits to help you with this assignment.
5. Generally speaking High Court actions are slow, very costly and deter many ordinary people from pursuing a claim. The Lord Chancellor is seeking reforms, or changes, to the system. Consider what some of these changes might be.
6. Try to find examples of cases which were heard either in the European Court of Justice or the Court of Human Rights and subsequently led to a change in the law in the UK. Likely areas are discrimination against women and human rights issues.

Update on YTS

NB At the time of going to print the government intends to replace YTS with Youth Training (YT), which will enable young people to work, either full-time or part-time, towards a nationally recognised qualification. There will be no minimum or maximum length of time that a YT programme must last. The position with regard to benefits stays the same as under YTS (see chapter 5).

Glossary

The meanings of most legal terms are explained in the text, but here are a few others.

Action	A civil proceeding started by a writ or summons
Appeal	A request granted to a party to bring a case before a higher authority in an attempt to have the decision changed or reversed
Appellant	The party who makes the appeal
Arbitration	The settlement of a dispute by reference to an independent third party
Bail	The release of a person held in custody on a promise he will return to court
Bailee	Someone who holds goods for another in accordance with his instructions
Bankrupt	A person who becomes insolvent and cannot pay his way; the court can declare him bankrupt
Beneficiary	A person who is entitled to property which is held in trust for him/her; a person who receives a gift under a will
Bill	The draft of a proposed Act of Parliament
Charge	Where a criminal accusation is formally made by the police
Claimant	The person in a civil action who brings the case in order to seek a remedy
Codification	The bringing together into an Act of Parliament all the rules of case-law on one topic without altering the previous law
Committal for trial	An examination of the evidence against an accused by the magistrates to see whether the accused should stand trial in the Crown Court
Compensation	A payment of money to make amends for injury or loss
Contested cases	Cases which are defended, or which are fought and argued in court
Conveyance	A transfer of the ownership of land
Conviction	The finding of guilty by a criminal court of law

Creditor	A person to whom a debt is owed
Debtor	A person who owes money and is obliged to play
Default action	A civil claim for a sum of money
Defendant	The person who is sued in a civil case or charged with an offence in a criminal case
Delegated legislation	Legislation made directly by ministers and/or local authorities under powers given to them by Parliament
Discharge	A release from a contractual obligation; where a person accused of a crime is set free because of lack of evidence
Entitlement	A welfare benefit due to a person based on his circumstances
Equitable	Fair and just
Equity	A body of rules founded on fairness
Injunction	A court order compelling the defendant to stop doing the act of which a complaint has been made
Layman	A person not qualified in the law
Legislation	The enactment of laws
Liability	Being answerable for an obligation or penalty
Litigants	The parties involved in a court action
Litigation	A court action
Mitigation	Pleas put forward by the defendant in an attempt to lessen the sentence or award against him by a court
Penalty	A punishment for a criminal offence
Petition	A written application which pleads a remedy by a civil court, e.g. a divorce
Plaintiff	The person bringing an action in a civil case
Pleadings	The name given to all the preliminary documents involved in a court case such as the particulars of claim in a civil case
Probate	The certificate given to an executor named in the will giving that person authority to carry out the instructions in the will
Prosecution	The starting up of criminal proceedings in the courts
Residue	That which remains of a deceased person's estate after the payment of debts, funeral expenses and legacies
Respondent	The party who replies to an appeal made against him
Settlement	Where the parties in a civil dispute come to an agreement
Specific performance	A court order compelling the defendant who has breached a contract to carry out the terms of the contract where damages would be an inadequate remedy

Glossary

Subpoena	A court order commanding the attendance of a person to give evidence in a court
Surety	A person who makes himself responsible for an accused person's appearance in court, and pledges a sum of money if he fails
Statute	An Act of Parliament
Statutory	Under powers granted by an Act of Parliament
Summons	An order to appear before a specific court
Tortfeasor	A person who commits a tort, i.e. a civil wrong
Warrant	A document which is an order from a magistrate addressed to the police for the arrest of a particular person, or to make lawful an entry into private property
Writ	A document issued out of the High Court commanding the person to whom it is addressed to do or not to do something mentioned in the writ

Useful Addresses

Local information sources have been indicated in the text. This list is of national organisations from whom leaflets and information may be obtained.

General, Legal Services and Information

Government Bookshops – for HMSO publications
For personal callers, in Birmingham, Bristol, London
Manchester, Edinburgh and Belfast
For orders by post: PO Box 276,
London, SW8 5DT

National Association of Citizens Advice Bureaux,
Press and Pulications,
115–123 Pentonville Road,
London N1 9LZ

or your local branch.

The Legal Aid Board,
Newspaper House, 8–16 Great New Street,
London EC4A 3BN
(There are also a number of regional offices around the country)

The Lord Chancellor's Department,
Treveyan House,
30 Great Peter Street,
London SW1

Manchester Law Centre,
595 Stockport Road,
Manchester M13 0RX

Cobden Trust,
21 Tabard Street,
London SE1 4LA

Useful Addresses

Consumer

Direct Selling Association Ltd,
44 Russell Square,
London WC1B 4JP

Office of Fair Trading,
Field House,
Breams Building,
London EC4 1PR

OFT: Stores and Distribution,
184 Shepherds Bush Road,
London W6 7NP

National Consumer Council,
20 Grosvenor Gardens,
London SW1

Consumers' Association,
14 Buckingham Street,
London WC2N 6DS

British Standards Institute,
2 Park Street,
London W1

Consumer Affairs Division,
Department of Trade and Industry,
10–18 Victoria Street,
London SW1H 0NN

Employment

Careers and Occupational Information Centre,
Moorfoot,
Sheffield S1 4PQ

Department of Employment,
Publications Department,
Caxton House,
Tothill Street,
London SW1H 9NA

or 12 St James' Square
London SW1Y 4LL

Department of Trade,
Information Division,
Publicity and Publications Branch,
Millbank Tower,
Millbank,
London SW1P 4QU

Health and Safety Executive:

  For 6 copies or less: Enquiry Point,
                          Health and Safety Executive,
                          Baynards House,
                          1 Chepstow Place,
                          Westbourne Grove,
                          London W2 4TF

  For more than 6   HSE Enquiries,
  copies: St Hugh's House,
                          Stanley Precinct,
                          Bootle,
                          Merseyside L20 3QZ

National Federation of Self Employed and Small Businesses Ltd,
146 Lower Marsh Street,
London SE1 7AE

National Association of Shopkeepers in GB and N. Ireland,
Lynch House,
91 Mansfield Road,
Nottingham

Advisory, Conciliation and Arbitration Service (ACAS),
Page Street,
London SW1P 4ND
(There are various regional offices around the country)

Industrial Tribunals (Central Office),
93 Ebury Street,
London SW1W 8RE

Confederation of British Industries,
103 New Oxford Street,
London WC1

No job

Social Security Publications,
Curzon House,
20–24 Lonsdale Road,
London NW6 6RD

Housing

Shelter,
157 Waterloo Road,
London SE1 8UW

Building Societies Association,
3 Saville Row,
London W1Z 1AF

Family

National Youth Bureau,
17–23 Albion Street,
Leicester LE1 6GD

Children's Legal Centre,
20 Compton Terrace,
London N1 2UN

Family Rights Group,
6–9 Manor Gardens,
Holloway Road,
London N7 6LA

Rights of Women,
374 Grays Inn Road,
London WC1 8BB

Health Education Council,
78 New Oxford Street,
London WC1 1AH

Civil liberties

Commission for Racial Equality,
Elliot House,
10–12 Allington Street,
London SW1E 5EH

Equal Opportunities Commission,
Overseas House,
Quay Street,
Manchester M3 3HN

British Institute of Human Rights,
17 Russell Square,
London WC1B 5DR

National Council for Civil Liberties,
21 Tabard Street,
London SE1 4LA

Amnesty International,
British Section,
5 Roberts Place,
London EC1

Amnesty International,
International Secretariat,
1 Easton Street,
London WC1

Joint Council for the Welfare of Immigrants,
44 Theobalds Road,
London WC1X 8SP

Crime and punishment

Police and Complaints Authority,
10 Great George Street,
London SW1 3AE

Howard League for Penal Reform,
320/332 Kennington Park Road,
London SE11 4PP

Prison Reform Trust,
Nuffield Lodge,
Regents Park,
London NW1 4RS

National Association for Care and Resettlement of Offenders (NACRO),
169 Clapham Road,
London SW9 0PU

The Community Liaison Officer of your local police station is also worth approaching for material on policing the community

Suggested reading, teaching guides and educational aids

It is essential to check that your material is up-to-date.

General

Atiyah, P. S., *Law and Modern Society* (Oxford: OPUS, 1983).

Berlins, Marcel and Clare Dyer, *The Law Machine*, 3rd edn (London: Penguin Books, 1989).

Boucher, Eric and David Corns, *GCSE Law Casebook* (London: Blackstone Press Ltd, 1989).

County Court booklet, *Small Claims in the County Court*.

Curzon, L. B., *A Dictionary of Law* (Plymouth: MacDonald & Evans, 1983).

Eddey, K., *The English Legal System* (Andover: Sweet & Maxwell 1987).

Edmonds, Judith, *Rights, Responsibilities and the Law* (London: Nelson in association with ILEA and the Cobden Trust, 1983).

Padfield, Colin F., *Law Made Simple*, 6th edn, revised by F. E. Smith (London: Heinemann, 1982).

Pritchard, John *The Penguin Guide to the Law*, 2nd edn (London: Penguin Books, 1986).

Read, James and Malcolm Tapp, *Man and the Law* (London: Harrap, 1979).

Reader's Digest (ed.) *You and Your Rights – An A to Z Guide to the Law*, 7th edn (London: The Reader's Digest Association Ltd, 1984).

Smith and Keenan, *English Law*, 9th edn, updated by Dennis Keenan (London: Pitman 1989).

Understand the Law (educational packs on a variety of GCSE topics – *The Individual and Society, Implementing the Law, Using the Law*, and *Going to Work*). A Law in Education Project – a joint initiative of the School Curriculum Committee and Law Society. Details and sample material available from: Edward Arnold, Hodder & Stoughton, Special Order Dept., Mill Road, Dunton Green, Sevenoaks, Kent TN13 1YY.

It's Your Law – a series of eleven books published by Oyez Longman and written in conjunction with the Law Society on the topics of: the police, the motorist, accidents, the home, doctors, marriage, the courts, the rights of consumers, solicitors and company affairs.

The Voluntary Agencies Directory, issued yearly by the National Council of Voluntary Organisations (London: Bedford Square Press).

Consumer law

Borrie and Diamond, *The Consumer Society and the Law* (Harmondsworth: Pelican, repr. 1986).

Lawe R., and G. Woodroffe, *Consumer Law and Practice* (Andover: Sweet & Maxwell, 1985).

The Office of Fair Trading publish a considerable range of colourful leaflets and booklets for the consumer and trader.

OFT, *Fair Deal – A Guide to Shoppers' Rights and Family Budgeting* (London: HMSO, 1988).

Stanesby, Anne, *Consumer Rights Handbook* (London: Pluto Press, 1986).

Which? The Consumer Association monthly magazine and other publications provide an endless source of material for the student on consumer matters.

World of work

The Department of Employment provide a wide range of leaflet and booklet material on employment law and Industrial Tribunals.

Selwyn's Guide to Employment Law (London: Butterworths, 1988).

Waud, Christopher, *Guide to Employment Law 1989* Harmondsworth, Daily Mail Publication, 1989).

Housing

The Department of The Environment publish various booklets on *Assured Tenancies* and the rights of landlord and tenant. (Available from local authorities and CABx.)

OFT booklet, *Home Sweet Home – A Guide for First-Time Buyers* (London: HMSO, 1988).

Robertson, Kate and Gail Lowther, *Buying, Selling and Moving House, The Complete Planner* (London: Collins 1987).

Family law

Lee, Simon, *Law and Morals: Warnock, Gillick and Beyond* (Oxford: Oxford Paperbacks, 1986).

Rae, Maggie, *Children and the Law, Young People and Their Rights* (Harlow: Longman Self-help guides, 1986).

Civil liberties

Malone, Michael, *A Practical Guide to Discrimination Law* (London: Grant McIntyre Ltd, 1980).

Hewitt, Patricia, *The Abuse of Power: Civil Liberties in the United Kingdom* (Oxford: Martin Robertson, 1982).

Sherr, Avrom, *Freedom of Protest, Public Order and the Law* (Oxford: Basil Blackwell, 1989).
Seighart, Paul, *Human Rights in the United Kingdom* (London: Pinter Publishers, 1988).

Crime and punishment

Crime Law and Society (Clasp). Published by the Schools Council and the Home Office (1984) – a four-part resource with cassette on the topics of *A Night Out, Car Theft, Shoplifting, Burglary*.

Walker, Nigel *Crime and Criminology, A Critical Introduction* (Oxford: OPUS, 1987).

Video cassettes

Civil Trial (Tort of Negligence): Fox v. Rocktech Ltd. (Sheffield City Polytechnic).

Police and Criminal Evidence Act 1984 (CFL Vision).

Unfair Dismissal 1. Advice and Conciliation; 2. The Tribunal Hearing (Sheffield City Polytechnic).

A large catalogue of films and video tapes on a variety of topics which are available, either for purchase or hire, can be obtained from Concord Films Council Ltd, 201 Felixstowe Road, Ipswich IP3 9BJ.

Table of Cases

Andrews v. DPP (1939) AC 576	217
Beard v. London Central Omnibus Co. (1900) 2 QB 530	97
British Railways Board v. Herrington (1972) 1 All ER 749 HL	12
Carlill v. Carbolic Smoke Ball Co. (1893) 1 QB 256	43
Century Insurance Co. v. Northern Ireland Road Transport (1942) AC 509	97
Chatterton v. Secretary of State for India (1895) 2 QB 189	185
Donoghue v. Stevenson (1932) All ER Rep 1 H.L.	41
Fisher v. Bell (1961) 1 QB 394	36
Gillick v. West Norfolk Health Authority (1986) 3 All ER 402 HL	169
Haywood v. Cammell Laird Shipbuilders Ltd (1988) 2 All ER 257	76
Hyde v. Hyde (1866) LR 1 P&D) 130	160
Jackson v. Hopperton (1864) 16 CB(NS) 829	186
Lister v. M. Thom & Sons Ltd (1975) IRLR 47	74
MaCarthys Ltd v. Smith (1981) 1 CR 672, CA	76
Malone v. Commissioner of Police of the Metropolis (1979)	188
Marshall v. Southampton & South West Hampshire Area Health Authority (1986) 2 All ER 584, ECJ	77
Nash v. Inman (1908) 2 KB 1	35
Pename Ltd v. Paterson (1989)	75
Pepper v. Webb (1969) 2 All ER 216	74
Peters v. Fleming (1840) 9 LJ Ex 8	35
Pharmaceutical Society of Great Britain v. Boots Cash Chemist (Southern) Ltd (1953) 1 All ER 482	37
R v. Dudley and Stephens (1884) 14 QBD 273	226
R v. Skipp (1975) Crim. LR 46 CA	221
R v. Walkington (1979)	220
Roberts v. Gray (1913) All ER 870	82
Rylands v. Fletcher (1868) LR 3HL 330	13
Stanley v. Powell (1891) 1 QB 86	14
Strathclyde Regional Council v. Porcelli (1986) IRLR 134	77
Winstanley v. Bampton (1943)	186

Table of Statutes

Abortion Act 1987   163
Access to Personal Files Act 1987   189
Administration of Estates Act 1925   170
Administration of Justice (Miscellaneous Provisions) Act 1933   260
Administration of Justice Act 1969   264
British Nationality Act 1981   175
Broadcasting Act 1980   192
Children Act 1972   23
Children's and Young Persons' Act 1969   214
Children's and Young Persons' (Harmful Publications) Act 1955   192
Cinematograph Acts of 1909 and 1952   193
Companies Act 1985   10
Congenital Diseases (Civil Liability) Act 1976   164
Consumer Credit Act 1972   54–7, 189
Consumer Protection Act 1987   37, 39, 40, 50
Control of Substances Hazardous to Health Regulations 1989   95
Convention for the Protection of Human Rights and Fundamental Freedoms (1950)   269–70
County Courts Act 1846   251
Criminal Attempts Act 1981   222
Criminal Damage Act 1977   222
Criminal Law Act 1967   200
Criminal Law Procedure (Insanity) Act 1964   226
Data Protection Act 1984   182, 188, 205
Defamation Act 1952   14, 184, 185, 186
Domicile and Matrimonial Proceedings Act 1973   175
Education Reform Act 1988   209
Employment Act 1980   100
Employment Act 1988   68, 100
Employment Protection (Consolidation) Act 1978   68–74, 81, 83, 266
Equal Pay Act 1970   68, 76–7, 104, 266
Factories Act 1961   24, 95
Fair Trading Act 1973   54
Family Law Reform Act 1969   16
Family Reform Act 1987   166
Food Act 1984   39, 40, 50, 214
Habeas Corpus Acts 1679 and 1816   206

285

Health and Safety at Work Act 1974   68, 80, 91, 93–5, 214, 266
Homicide Act 1957   226
Housing Acts 1961, 1980 and 1985   128, 131, 133, 135, 140
Housing Act 1988   128, 131–2, 135, 136, 137
Housing and Building Control Act 1985   140
Housing (Homeless Persons) Act 1977   143–5
Immigration Act 1971   175
Immigration Act 1988   175, 176, 177
Interception of Communications Act 1985   182, 187–8
Industrial Training Act 1971   266
Inheritance (Provision for Family and Dependents) Act 1975   171
Judicature Acts 1873–5   246
Law Reform (Contributory Negligence) Act 1945   92–3
Libel Act 1843 (amended 1845)   186
Licensing Act 1988   222
Limitation Act 1980   248
Local Government Act 1972   193
Matrimonial Causes Act 1973   160
Matrimonial Family Proceedings Act 1984   168
Minors' Contracts Act 1987   35
Misrepresentation Act 1967   45, 46
Misuse of Drugs Act 1971   222–3
Occupiers Liability Acts 1957 and 1984   132, 140–1, 148, 151
Obscene Publications Acts 1959 and 1964   191, 192, 194–5
Offences Against the Persons Act 1861   163, 218
Offices, Shops and Railway Premises Act 1963   95
Official Secrets Acts 1911, 1920 and 1988   182, 187, 195, 259
Police and Criminal Evidence Act 1984   196–9, 200–2, 203–5, 207, 241, 259
Prevention of Terrorism (Temporary Provisions) Act 1989   195, 199
Protection from Eviction Act 1977   141–2, 150
Public Health Act 1936   140
Public Order Acts 1936 and 1986   11, 143, 201, 203, 206–8, 241
Race Relations Act 1976   68, 73, 76, 77–8, 105, 209, 266
Rehabilitation of Offenders Act 1974   203
Rent Acts 1957, 1966 and 1974   128, 133, 135, 137, 139
Road Traffic Act 1972   207, 217, 223–4
Sale of Goods Act 1893   32
Sale of Goods Act 1979   32, 34, 35–40, 45, 51, 52
Sex Discrimination Act 1975   68, 76, 77–8, 104, 209, 266
Sexual Offences Act 1956   218
Small Claims Act 1971   251
Suicide Act 1961   217
Supply of Goods and Services Act 1982   46, 47–8
Supply of Goods (Implied Terms) Act 1973   32, 57
Surrogacy Arrangements Act 1985   164

Table of Statutes

Theatres Act 1968   191, 194
Theft Acts 1968 and 1978   219–21
Torts (Interference with Goods) Act 1977   12
Trade Descriptions Act 1968   49–50, 214
Trade Union Act 1984   68, 98, 100
Trade Union and Labour Relations Act 1974   98, 99, 100
Unfair Contract Terms Act 1977   48–9, 51, 53–4
Universal Declaration of Human Rights 1948   270
Unsolicited Goods and Services Act 1971   43–4
Video Recordings Act 1984   191, 194
Wages Act 1986   71
Weights and Measures Act 1963   50

Index

accommodation 127–42
  agencies 130
Acts of Parliament 6–8
advice agencies 241–2
Advisory, Conciliation and Arbitration Service 267
aliens 177
apprenticeships 80–3
arrest, *also see* police powers
  arrestable offences 152, 203
  detention 201–2, 204–5
  evidence 202, 204–5
assault, crime of 218
  tort of 12
Attorney General 264

bail, magistrates' 264
  police 204
barristers 242–3, 250
battery, crime of 218
  tort of 12
benefits, *see* state benefits
betting and gaming licences 27

case-law, *see* judicial precedent
censorship 190–5
children, adoption 166–7
  rights 162–9
  unborn 163–4
Citizens Advice Bureau 110–17, 236, 241–2, 246
citizenship 29–30, 174–9
civil liberties 15, 180–211

Commission for Racial Equality 78
community charge 145, 146, 150–1
consumer law 31–60
  advertisements 42–3
  consumer credit 26, 54–7, 58
  consumer protection 39, 50
  contract, the 31–3
  credit notes 40
  debtors 58
  deposits 55, 56
  estimates 47, 59
  exclusion clauses 48, 51, 53–4
  false trading 48–50, 54
  faulty goods 36–42, 57
  implied terms 34, 37–40
  'invitation to treat' 36–7
  labelling goods 49–50
  mail order protection 42–4
  manufacturers' liability 39, 40–2
  minors 9, 26, 34–5
  misrepresentation 44, 46
  private sales 45–6
  quotations 47, 59
  receipts 33, 59
  repossession of goods 58
  sale goods 36–7
  seeking a solution 236
  standard form contracts 33, 48, 52

Index

supply of goods and services 44, 47–8
unsolicited goods 42–4
warranties 52
weights and measures 50
wise buying 59–60
consumer protection, *see* consumer law
contract, common law of 9–11, 31–3
 breach 11
 capacity 9–10
 deeds, or specialty 9
 duress 10
 exclusion clauses 48, 51, 53–4
 formation of 9, 33, 58–60, 66–9
 illegal contracts 10
 'invitation to treat' 36–7
 minors' liability 9, 26, 34–5, 82
 misrepresentation 10, 46
 mistake 10
 termination of 11, 73–5
 undue influence 10
conveyance, deed of 19, 128, 145–6, 148–9
coroner's court 265
corporations, capacity 10
counsel, *see* barristers
courts of law 246–64
 civil 248–56, 263–4
 criminal 256–64
 hierarchy 247
Criminal Injuries Compensation Board, the 231
criminal law 15, 213–31
 actus reus 213
 alcohol misuse 222
 assault 218–19
 attempt to commit a crime 222
 battery 218–19
 blackmail 220

burglary 220
children, *see* minors
conspiracy to commit a crime 222
corporations, liability of 214
criminal damage 222
drug misuse 222–3
elements of a crime 213–14
general defences 225–7
grevious bodily harm 218
handling stolen goods 220–1
homicide, unlawful 216–18
incitement to commit a crime 222
infanticide 217
manslaughter 217
mens rea 213–14
minors, liability of 214
murder 217
offences against the person non fatal 218–19
parties to a crime 215
rape 218–19
road traffic offences 217–18, 223–5
robbery 219–20
specific crimes 216–27
strict liability 214
suicide 217
theft 219
theft by deception 221
trade unions, liability of 101
victims of crime 230–1
criminal punishments 227–9
 theories 230
criminal trial, the 262–3
crossbows 25
Crown Court, the 259–63
Crown Prosecution Service, the 259

damages, 231, 234, 268
data protection 182, 188–9, 205–6
defamation 12, 181–7

delegated legislation 8
democracy 3
demonstrations and meetings 201, 203, 206–8
dictatorships 3
diplomatic immunity 177
Director of Public Prosecutions 256
discrimination, race 69, 73, 76, 209
  sex 76–8, 209
divorce, *see* family law
domicile 175

EEC nationals 177
education, grants 114–15
  state benefits 115–16
electoral register 178–9
Employment Appeal Tribunal 239, 268
employment law 23–5, 66–107
  apprenticeships 80–3
  contract 67–8
  dismissal 69, 73–5
  equal pay 76–7
  health and safety 80, 93–5
  holidays 71
  main terms and conditions 67, 69–71
  minors' liability 82
  notice entitlement 72
  termination of the contract 73–5
  trade unions 95–6, 98–101
  wages 78
enterprise agencies 86
environmental health 140, 151
Equal Opportunities Commission 78
Euro–MPs 179, 269
European Court of Human Rights 268–9
European Court of Justice 269–70

false imprisonment, tort 12
family law, marriage 158–61
  children 163–9
  divorce 161–3
  wills and succession 169–71
firearms, licences 26–7
freedom of association 208–9
freedom of movement 207
freedom of worship 209
general defences, to a crime 225–7
  torts 13–14
Green Form Scheme 244, 245, 250

habeas corpus, writ of 201, 202, 206
health and safety at work 80, 93–5
High Court of Justice 254–6
  Judges 256, 259–60
  Masters 256
hire-purchase (credit) agreements, *see* consumer law
home insurance 146, 151
home ownership 145–51
  conveyance, the 145, 149
  mortgages 145–6, 148–9
  surveyors' reports 147, 149–50
homelessness 142, 143–5
House of Lords 263–4
housing 127–52, *see also* rented acommodation
housing benefit 116, 120, 134, 137, 237
human rights 180, 269–70

immigration 175–7
income support, *see* state benefits
income tax 79, 85
indentures 181
indictable offences 257, 260
industrial injuries 80, 86–93

Index

industrial tribunals 75, 80, 266–8
Irish citizens 179

judges 253, 256, 259, 260, 263–4
judicial precedent 5–6
juries 27, 260, 262, 265
Justicies of the Peace, *see* magistrates
juvenile court 254, 258
juvenile offenders 214, 229

landlords, *see* rented accommodation
law, aims of 4
  definition 4
  making of 5–9
  private 5
  public 5
law centres 246
Law Lords 263–4
Law Society 244, 246
lay visitors 206
legal aid
  assistance by way of representation 244–5
  civil courts, for 245, 250–1, 266
  criminal courts, for 245, 264–5
  legal advice and assistance scheme 244, 245, 250
legal services, *see* advice agencies
legal time limits 248
libel, *see* defamation
licences 26–7
  betting and gaming 27
  driving 26
  firearms 26–7
  intoxicating liquor 27
licensee of land 135
Lord Chancellor 250, 256, 264, 266
Lord Chief Justice 256, 263

Lord Justices of Appeal 256, 263

magistrates' courts 257–9
  civil jurisdiction 254
  clerk to magistrates 258
  domestic court 254
  duty solicitors 259
  juvenile court 254, 258
  magistrates 257–8
  probation officers 259
  stipendary magistrates 258
mail order protection 44
marriage, *see* family law
Master of the Rolls 256
maternity rights 90
medical care 20
Members of Parliament 179, 239, 240
  minors, age limits and liabilities 16–30
  civil actions by 26
  consumer contracts 9, 25–6, 34–5
  criminal liability 214
  employment 23–4, 82
mortgages, *see* home ownership

name, change of 22–3
nationality 174–7
  spouses 176–7
National Council for Civil Liberties (NCCL) 209
national insurance 78–9, 85, 110, 111, 117–20
National Joint Councils 83
negligence, tort of 13, 37, 39, 41–2, 91–3
  contributory 92–3
  independent contractors 97–8
  vicarious liability 95–7
nuisance, tort of 12, 148, 151–2

occupational superannuation   79
occupier's liability   132, 140–1, 148, 151
Office of Fair Trading   56, 60, 239–40
official secrets   181, 182, 187, 195
ombudsmen   239

passports   23, 75
pilot's licence   26
planning permission   151
pleadings   255
police–community liaison groups   241
police powers   195–206
   complaints against   242
poll tax, *see* community charge
possession of land   132, 143, 251
President of the Family Division   255, 256
Press Council, the   184, 189
probate   168–70, 251
probation, *see* criminal punishments
property, actions   251, 255
   freehold   146, 150
   leasehold   146, 150
   real   150
public order   207–8

recorders   253, 259
redundancy   25
remedies, out of court   236–46
   through the courts   246–65
Rent Assessment Committees   134, 136–7
rented accommodation   19–20, 129–42
   assured tenancies   131–3, 135
   contract, the   128
   council (secure) tenancies   131, 135–6

eviction   136, 139, 142
landlord's harassment of tenants   141
lodgers   133, 135
multi-occupations   137–8, 140
notice to quit   132, 133, 135, 136
rent books   131, 138, 139
rents   131, 134
repairs and improvements   138, 139–40
service tenancy   136
rule of law   3
Rylands v. Fletcher, tort of   13

savings   18
self-employment   84–6
Senate of the Inns of Court   250
sex, laws on   21
sickness entitlements, *see* state benefits
'signing on'   117–18
slander, *see* defamation
social fund, *see* state benefits
social security, *see* state benefits
societies   2–3
Solicitor-General   264
solicitors   242–4, 246
   fixed-fee interview   246
squatters   142–3
standard-form contracts
state benefits   18, 86–90, 109–14, 116–22
   appeals   238
   family credit   112
   income support   18, 110–12, 121
   sickness and disability   86–7, 89, 120
   social fund   121–2
   students and trainees   113–17, 123

Index

unemployment 111, 119–20
strict liability 13, 40, 214, 223
summary offences 257
surveyors, *see* home ownership

telephone tapping 182, 187–8
tenancies, *see* rented accommodation
tenant of land 134
terrorism, prevention 199
tort, law of 10–15
  children 11
  defamation 12, 181–7
  general defences 14–15
  negligence 13, 37, 39, 41–2, 91–3, 95–7
  nuisance 12, 148, 151–2
  Rylands v. Fletcher 13
  trespass to goods 12
  trespass to land 11–12, 133–4, 135, 142, 143, 207
  trespass to the persons 12–13, 218
Trade Associations 51, 54, 60, 236, 240
trade unions 95, 96, 98–101
traders, codes of practice 48, 54, 60
  consumer protection 48–59
Trading Standards Departments 39, 54, 236, 239–40

tree preservation orders 151
trespass, tort of 11–13, 133–4, 135, 142, 143, 207
tribunals 75, 266–8

unemployment benefits, *see* state benefits
UN Universal Declaration of Human Rights 270

value added tax (VAT) 85
vicarious liability, criminal 214
  tort of 95–7
Vice-Chancellor 255
victims of crime 230–1
visitors, to Britain 178
vote, right to 29, 175

Wages Councils 69, 71–2, 237
ward councillors 179, 239
wardship 167
water rates 151
welfare benefits, *see* state benefits
wills 169–72
witness, being a 28
work experience 109, 113–14, 123
work permits 178
working conditions 95

Youth Training Scheme (YTS) 83–4, 113–14